CONTENTS

The use of the word *frontier* to characterize areas of the country with low density of population has led to misunderstanding in studies of the development of the United States. Rather, the nature of an area's economy is a closer measure of the region's status than is the number of people living within it. As long as the pioneer settler had to meet his economic needs through his own ingenuity and resources, he was living in the frontier stage of economy; as soon as merchants, bankers, lawyers, and other functionaries moved into the area to serve these needs, the frontier stage gave way to established communities. The transition from frontier settlement to established community usually required a number of years and the combined efforts of the farming, mercantile, and professional segments of the area. Viewed in this light, the merchant, who usually arrived before the professional men, was, with the settler-farmer, an integral part of frontier life and an important force in converting the primitive economy to the more urban patterns.

Some may object to my use of the word *Mid-America* in my title and thus adding to the plethora of titles already created to designate certain regions of the American West. The term is not new, however, as the Catholic Historical Society of Chicago adopted it as the title for a quarterly magazine in 1929. Furthermore, it is useful; in dealing with the area of American history that I shall discuss, *Mid-America* serves two purposes: that of conveying the time element in a rapidly changing scene and the other of disregarding modern state boundaries as a means of designating trade areas. In general, I use *Mid-America* to refer to the territory now included in Iowa, Illinois, and Missouri. Transportation and historical factors made this territory a loosely unified region in the period between 1820 and the Civil War. By 1820 white population was sufficient in certain places along the waterways in those three states to attract merchants and their stores. Saint Louis, at the junction of the Missouri with the Mississippi River and near the mouth of the Ohio, was the center from which merchants, both itinerant and established, expanded their activities into the surrounding country. Three decades later, the railroads were breaking down the old lines of trade, mercantile organization had become more specialized, and Chicago, another decade later, was disputing the leadership of Saint Louis. Therefore, a title defining time and territory to be discussed in this study serves to indicate the scope of the study itself.

The business life of Mid-America seems to have been typical of most of the Mississippi Valley in the same stage of development. I refer to this broader area whenever the available basic mercantile records justify such inclusion. I do not claim knowledge of all the cross currents and local peculiarities that undoubtedly operated in the regions bordering Mid-America, but I hope, by introducing these peripheral influences, to illuminate the role of the frontier merchant as he carried on his business operations in his community.

Improvements in this revised and enlarged edition of my original study of pioneer merchandising owe more to the craftsmanship of Margery Mulkern McKinney, Senior Editor of the University of Missouri Press, than to me. In addition to bringing the style of an early piece of writing to a maturer form, she has woven material from articles that I originally published elsewhere into the fabric of my monograph so skillfully that it seems to have belonged there always. To her and to all those concerned with the University of Missouri Press I express my appreciation for making my study available again in improved form after being out of print so many years.

My own contribution to this edition has been limited primarily to modernizing bibliographical citations by noting changes in names of depositories and in the location of materials that I cited in 1939. Such changes have simply been added to my original citations, on the grounds that I thereby can continue to credit collectors and sponsors whose names have inevitably but unfortunately become less closely associated with citations of historical materials they helped preserve. Moreover, this procedure may demonstrate for younger scholars that nomenclature of historical depositories—and even their existence—may undergo significant change within three decades. My views of history and of historical standards have also changed during the thirty years, so I have had to decide to produce either a totally new manuscript or to restrict myself to very limited involvement, such as reading proof on this new edition. Since I chose the less ambitious of the two alternatives, the main body of this Preface constitutes basically the Preface of the 1939 edition.

I wish to acknowledge the courtesy of the editors of the following journals for permitting inclusion here of parts of articles published by them: *Agricultural History, The Journal of Southern History, The Kansas Historical Quarterly, The Louisiana Historical Quarterly, Mississippi Valley Historical Review,* and *Missouri Historical Review.* Professor Jonas Viles and Professor Russell S. Bauder of the University of Missouri contributed valuable suggestions for the preparation of my study. The editors of the *University of Missouri Studies,* especially Professor H. M. Belden, gave much assistance in preparing the manuscript for the press. Most of all, I am indebted to Professor Elmer Ellis, who directed this study in its original form; then and since, his encouragement and assistance have been invaluable. Last, I wish to express my appreciation to my wife, Louise Webb Atherton, for her help in preparing the manuscript.

L. E. A.
Columbia, Missouri
May, 1971

CHAPTER I

THE FRONTIER
MERCHANT

In the late 1830s John Beauchamp Jones was engaged in merchandising at Arrow Rock, Missouri, a village on the Missouri River some two hundred miles above Saint Louis.[1] For Jones, merchandising was but a means to accumulate sufficient wealth to sustain a literary career, which he pursued under the pen name Luke Shortfield. The urge to write accentuated Jones's appreciation of all details that would enliven any theme he might undertake and made him sharply aware of the significant part merchants were playing in the transformation of Western society. In the preface to his book *The Western Merchant*, he stressed the services performed by the mercantile class:

> *The merchants of the West, and particularly of the Far West,*
> *constitute a distinct class of society. This class is not only*
> *important from its numbers, but powerful and influential from*
> *its intelligence, enterprise, and wealth. . . . He [the merchant] is*
> *a general locum tenens, the agent of everybody! And familiar*
> *with every transaction in his neighborhood. He is a counselor*
> *without license, and yet invariably consulted, not only in matters of*
> *business, but in domestic affairs. Parents ask his opinion before*
> *giving their consent to their daughters' marriages; and he is always*
> *invited to the weddings. He furnishes the nuptial garments for*
> *both bride and groom, and his taste is both consulted and adopted.*

1. William Barclay Napton, *Past and Present of Saline County Missouri,* 314. Armistead Churchill Gordon's biography of Jones in the *Dictionary of American Biography* omits all mention of his mercantile career. Napton's identification of Jones as a pioneer merchant adds great value to Jones's writing on Western merchandising by establishing the fact that the author was actually engaged in the mercantile trade. His writing was marred by his continual striving for effect, which helps to explain his neglect by historians, who have tended to ignore his too florid account of pioneer life. Jones must needs dress up his scenes and characters; consequently, his descriptions seem to be mere costume pieces. In reality, he came very close to a precise report of the frontier life of his time.

*Every item of news, not only local, but from a distance,—as he
is frequently the postmaster, and the only subscriber to the
newspaper—has general dissemination from his establishment, as
from a common center; and thither all resort, at least once a
week, both for goods and for intelligence.*[2]

The records of the time fully support this estimate, but Jones's
ebullient language suggests overstatement. Regarded as a eulogy of
the Western merchant, his description has received little notice, and
students of Western history have neglected the leads he provided.
Despite the availability of this rich resource of contemporary observations, "Luke Shortfield's" colorful account of the role of the merchant in the transformation of Western society from primitive to
urbane has attracted less attention than it deserves.

On the other hand, historians of the West have firmly established
the influence Mid-America exercised in the making of America. They
have plotted the successive waves of migration and have given a
generalized picture of the type of individuals constituting each wave.
The work has been done so thoroughly that every American can
visualize the life and dress of the various groups that conquered the
West. The American Indian, the explorer, the hunter and trapper,
the pioneer mother—all these, and more, have achieved reality
through the research of the historian. However, with the absorption
of the frontier into the communities that advanced on it from the
Midwest and the Pacific Coast in the eighties, interest concentrated
on the last of the popular frontier characters, the American cowboy,
and he has continued as a focus of attention and representative of
what is now considered a romantic phase of American history.

Only when one considers the highest type of civilization these frontier classes could erect does the full significance of Jones's emphasis
on the mercantile class become apparent. If the story of the frontier
is to be told solely in terms of occupations like those of the cowboy
and the farmer, the process of transforming the raw settlements into
modern specialized communities will remain incompletely understood. At one period or another all America was in the frontier stage.
How the transition to specialized economies occurred has not been
studied sufficiently, and the story of this transition should prove as
valuable as the descriptions of other developments in explaining
American life. When told, it will be in terms of the merchant class
and professional groups—lawyer, doctor, and teacher—in addition to
those of the trapper, soldier, and settler.

2. John Beauchamp Jones (pen name, Luke Shortfield), *The Western
Merchant* . . . , Preface.

Jones's estimate of the services of the mercantile group grew out of his experiences in Missouri in the late thirties. James Hall held the same view as the result of his own observations in Ohio in the forties, which convinced him that the prosperity of the West was due in large part to the mercantile class. Hall felt that merchants' contributions had been neglected—worse, criticized—by those who swayed the political power of the country, and he suggested that, in order to improve their reputation, merchants concentrate less on money-making. They should, he wrote, place more emphasis on education and culture to lessen prejudice against the power their wealth brought to bear on community affairs. In his discussion of their problems he recognized fully the influence of their wealth, social standing, and leadership in community charities and kindred enterprises.[3]

In a description of the West as it was in 1817 E. P. Fordham expressed similar views. He pictured Western society as composed of four classes: the hunters who lived by the rifle; the first settlers who also hunted, but devoted most of their time to farming; the true farmers and the enterprising men from Kentucky and the Atlantic states who founded towns and instituted the means for trade, speculated in land, and laid the basis for the fabric of society; and a fourth class of old settlers, who were really the third class in its maturity.[4] This classification recognized both the complexity of Western society and the modifying influence of the business and professional men.

Fordham's list also placed the different groups in the approximate order of their arrival on the frontier. Hunters, farmers, and land speculators naturally preceded the business classes, since a market for their services was necessary to attract these later groups. Of these the merchants were the most numerous and usually the first to arrive. A new town attracted professional men, but a store—the source of supplies—was the most important element of Western towns. Real estate promoters, eager to start a new town, realized the necessity of attracting merchants and frequently offered town lots free to prospective buyers who would agree to erect store buildings. The promoters' advertisement in 1825 of the new Missouri River town of Rocheport listed the general advantages of the location and closed with the statement:

And as it is the desire of the proprietors rather to promote improvements than to realize cash from the amount of sales,

3. James Hall, *The West: Its Commerce and Navigation*, 20-25.
4. Elias Pym Fordham, *Extracts from letters . . .* , Letter dated Shawanoe Town, Illinois Territory, November 15, 1817. Manuscript book in Edward E. Ayer Collection, Newberry Library, Chicago. This material, edited by F. A. Ogg, has been published under the title, *Personal Narrative of Travels*, Cleveland, 1906.

*no lots will be sold except subject to certain improvements
to be made within 18 months from purchase, say at least a log
house 18 by 20 feet, on each lot. To merchants or mechanics,
who wish to become settlers & make extensive improvements,
donations of Lots will be made.[5]*

If two or three merchants could be attracted by such inducements, the nucleus of a town was assured, and the promoters could then hope to draw teachers, doctors, and lawyers to the new location. In many cases merchants took the lead in establishing towns, motivated by the desire either to follow frontier trade west or to profit from the sale of town lots. An example of these motivations is the enterprise of the Lammes, merchants who arrived in Missouri in the early twenties and who sought to create a new town in what is now Livingston County, Missouri.[6]

New towns soon attracted doctors, but it is difficult to differentiate between their merchandising activities and professional practice. Frequently, a doctor operated a drugstore, which, in a curious combination of merchandise, generally sold paint and glass as well as drugs— the natural sideline to the practice of medicine. An advertisement by Doctors Crews and Benson of the town of Fayette, Missouri, in 1830 announced that they were conducting a wholesale and retail drugstore, with a large stock of drugs, paints, surgical instruments, and patent medicines.[7] Such men should be classified as merchants as well as professional men in the early stages of transition to a specialized community life.

Lawyers preferred to settle at the capitals of territories and states and in county-seat towns. They arrived as early as the merchant in those instances when the seat of government for a new district was to be located where no village already existed. Usually, however, government offices were situated in already well established towns. Consequently, the history of the business and professional groups in the West should begin with study of the mercantile class and the rise of towns and then branch from those focal points to consideration of the other groups and the urbanization of the area.

In analyzing Western merchandising it should be borne in mind that frontier conditions demanded a type of enterprise more varied than that in the East. Buying and selling were only part of the mer-

5. Franklin *Missouri Intelligencer*, September 23, 1825.
6. L. T. Collier, "Livingston County Pioneer Settlers and Subsequent Events," *Missouri Historical Review*, 6 (1912), 205.
7. Columbia *Missouri Intelligencer and Boon's Lick Advertiser*, August 7, 1830. This paper was moved from Franklin, Missouri, to Fayette in 1826, and then to Columbia in 1830.

chant's activities. Ninian Edwards of Illinois owned and supervised five stores in Illinois and three in Missouri, practiced law, engaged in farming and in real estate speculation, operated saw- and gristmills, and served as governor of Illinois while it was in the territorial stage and as governor and United States senator after Illinois entered the Union as a state.[8] Varied interests were the general way of life rather than the exception for these men, and in this respect merchants conformed to the patterns of the West. After his arrival in a settlement, however, the merchant's activities relieved other residents of their communities of certain functions—the farmers' need to market produce, for one instance—thereby advancing specialization by one effective step. The Western merchants speeded up the progress toward a modern economy by continuing as enterpreneurs in varied areas when they entered a pioneer community.

As a citizen of the small western village, which he helped to create, the merchant's first, and most obvious, service was the retailing of manufactured goods and groceries. In this capacity he provided expansion from the self-sufficient stage in which the community lived when he first appeared. His varied stock of drygoods, hardware, groceries, and drugs liberated the resident on the developing frontier from the necessity of being a jack of all trades and producer of all needs. He brought to the West the products of the more specialized communities of the East and Europe and, with these, the challenge to the West to lift itself to a higher degree of economic organization.

If the merchant had been satisfied to stop with this service, more time would have elapsed before the West reached economic maturity than was the case. Money was scarce; but the most bountiful supply of goods was worthless without some medium of exchange. In the absence of banks, a market for bartering of crops would have served the farmers' needs, but such did not exist. Faced with this situation, the merchant had no choice but to assume the double burden of banker and dealer in agricultural crops in addition to his primary functions as importer and seller of goods.

The simplest and most profitable banking operation was to care for the funds of farmers who feared to keep their money at home. In the forties, one merchant in Davenport, Iowa, regularly received money on deposit from his customers, and he continued this service until a bank opened its doors in that town. Customers withdrew their money from the merchant's coffers as needed or used their deposits for the purchase of goods, and the merchant profited both

8. Ninian W. Edwards, *History of Illinois, from 1778 to 1833, and Life and Times of Ninian Edwards. By his son, Ninian W. Edwards*, 241-43. See also Ninian W. Edwards Papers.

from the additional sales and from the use of the money as operating capital.[9] This happy state was not general, however. As a rule the merchant supplied the capital for business operations, and rare indeed was the farmer who had money credit at a store.

The merchant's chief contribution to his community in the way of capital resulted from whatever credit standing he had in the wholesale centers where he traded. He could secure credit without great difficulty from wholesale houses, the usual terms being six months' credit, payable in twelve, with interest ranging from 6 to 10 per cent after the first six months.[10] In turn, a large percentage of the sales to customers was on a credit basis. Thus, the typical Western merchant operated, throughout the period from 1820 to 1850, on one to two years' supply of credit from the East, and, through credit sales, Western farmers shared in the benefits. The procedure was undoubtedly expensive to merchant and farmer, for the prices of goods bought on credit were much higher than those for cash; but the West was developing, and Westerners could afford to pay high prices for what they bought.

The merchant, deeply involved in the community's future, soon realized the need for banks. Many bought their goods directly in the East, a practice that required annual remittances of large sums of money. A storekeeper in a village without banking facilities sent paper money through the mails to the larger Western cities in order to purchase bills of exchange with which to make remittances in the East. Such a procedure was dangerous, since the uncertainty of the mails made the transfer of money extremely hazardous. Even more serious a problem was the transfer of specie. This often was moved to the larger cities in the wagons of freighters who hauled goods for merchants, or it was concealed in shipments of produce, with the knowledge of the consignee. Such devices demonstrated the value of banks to the mercantile class, and many of them ultimately became bankers to fill an acute need.

The mercantile barter system helped to ease the money situation somewhat. Farmers exchanged their crops for groceries and drygoods and thereby evaded the need for currency. Furs, meat, wheat, beeswax, flax, hemp, honey, whiskey, ginseng—anything of value—could be exchanged for goods at the neighborhood store. Through barter, the storekeeper could dispose of his wares to a population that lacked ready cash with which to buy. All over the West this pattern of bartering goods for produce existed, the merchant serving as a middleman between producer and manufacturer or wholesaler. He con-

9. J. M. D. Burrows, *Fifty Years in Iowa* . . . , 29.
10. Jones, *The Western Merchant*, 119-21.

signed the farm crops he took in exchange for goods and shipped them to commission merchants in the larger Western cities and in New Orleans, and with the proceeds from the sale settled his bills to the eastward. The produce trade with midwestern merchants burgeoned, and competition among commission houses for a share of the business caused them to adopt a policy of advancing money on goods deposited for sale, a practice that added appreciably to the small supply of money available in the West.

Some merchants avoided the added expense of dealing through commission merchants by accompanying their shipments of produce to the larger markets, where they could, at the same time, buy finished goods to stock their stores. But merchants of the region who traveled to the centers of trade with the produce they had taken in barter for goods ran many risks. Not only did they chance encountering a glutted market but also they exposed themselves and their produce to accidents. For storekeepers, the necessarily long trips were unwise and expensive in addition to their immediate cost, for the journeys absented them from their local businesses for indefinite periods of time.[11]

The same risks and expenses for the farmer who tried to market his produce in the larger centers are evident in the piteous and indignant letter of a Missouri farmer to the editor of his county paper in 1821, a letter obviously inspired by the refusal of merchants in Franklin, Missouri, to take depreciated paper or farm crops in payment for goods.[12] He berated the Franklin merchants for advising farmers to take their crops to New Orleans and exchange them there for sound money with which to purchase goods. His father had wisely warned him against the dangers of running off to New Orleans with produce and leaving his farm to the whims of fortune and weather in the interval. The letter pointed out that, even if four farmers should pool their resources and get their pork ready by the middle of December, they could not get the meat on board ship for New Orleans before the first of April. And apparently the dangers of navigating the Missouri and Mississippi rivers were as nothing compared to the bewildering and fearful experiences awaiting rural people in New Orleans: bells ringing day and night; rumors of fever, plague, smallpox, and death; thousands of farmers from Kentucky, Virginia, Pennsylvania, Ohio, Illinois, Indiana, Tennessee, Mississippi, Arkansas, and Missouri lining the levee with produce, and no one to buy.

11. Lewis E. Atherton, "John McDonogh and the Mississippi River Trade," *The Louisiana Historical Quarterly*, 26 (1943), 4.

12. Letter, signed "a farmer," to editor of the Franklin *Missouri Intelligencer*, September 25, 1821.

Then, at long last, a merchant—possibly from Franklin, in New Orleans to purchase groceries—might come along and buy the load for less than the expenses of the trip down river. The four farmers might, on their return home, find their farms "gone to wreck" and only half a crop under way. The writer was undoubtedly indulging in exaggeration, but such a trip was, in fact, no light undertaking for an untraveled farmer.

Many merchants operated farms of their own. Better read and more widely traveled than the average farmer in their region, they were interested and informed in scientific farming and took the lead in fostering it. Solon Robinson, whom U. B. Phillips has termed the most important agricultural writer in the North in the pre-Civil War period, operated a store in Indiana from 1836 to 1850. His store earned for him a small but satisfactory living during the period, but his chief interest was, even then, in scientific agriculture. His Day Book for the period is a well-kept accounting of daily mercantile transactions, but interspersed between records of drygoods and grocery transactions are records of his agricultural experiments.[13] Ultimately, his interests in writing and in the science of agriculture caused him to leave merchandising and move to New York City, where he continued his work for advancement in agriculture.[14] It is of interest here that, for fourteen years, a Midwestern merchant-agriculturist dispensed his advanced views on agriculture across his store's counters along with the drygoods and groceries in his stock.

Ninian Edwards of Illinois, merchant, cultivated a choice collection of fruit trees, grape vines, and shrubbery on his farm and was much interested in improving the breed of livestock in the state.[15] Aull, Glasgow, and Compton, all astute Missouri merchants, persuaded farmers in the territory bordering Grand River to start raising and grading tobacco, and in 1845 the crop in that vicinity was worth $400,000.[16] Jared Warner of Wisconsin made various entries concerning experiments with fruit trees and grains in his Day Book for the years 1836 to 1849.[17] Through such activities the merchant aided in increasing the value of the annual yield in the West—a service of great significance, in view of the fact that the balance of trade was always in favor of the East.

13. Solon Robinson, Account Book 1840-53.
14. Solon I. Robinson, *Solon Robinson, Pioneer and Agriculturist, Selected Writings*, Herbert A. Kellar, ed., Vol. I, Introduction.
15. Edwards, *History of Illinois*, 241-43.
16. Editorial reprinted from the Glasgow *Pilot* in the Jefferson City *Jefferson Inquirer*, May 29, 1845.
17. Jared Warner, Day Book 1836-49.

Furthermore, the mercantile class played a prominent part in developing manufacturing. James Wier at Lexington, Kentucky, owned and operated a rope walk and yearly sent large quantities of bagging and rope to Charleston and New Orleans in the South and to New York City. Through this enterprise he was able to establish credits in Eastern cities with which to meet his wholesale bills. Thus, in 1811 Wier drew on a New York City firm for $3,000, payment to be made within 120 days. Before the draft came due he had sent his creditors a shipment of hemp, tobacco, and yarn.[18]

The Lamme family of merchants operated stores at Liberty, Franklin, Columbia, and Independence, Missouri, in the twenties,[19] but they were interested also in manufacturing. In 1821 William Lamme and a partner opened a tobacco factory at Franklin. An advertisement announced that they were prepared to fill any order, and they invited Missouri and Illinois merchants and those holding government contracts on the Missouri and Mississippi rivers to call and examine their products. All tobacco produced by the firm was branded, a device that supported their money-back guarantee.[20] The same family opened a steam-powered flour mill near Columbia in 1833.[21] These ventures proved more successful than their paper mill at Columbia, which was in operation for only a short time after its establishment in 1834;[22] a limited market apparently caused the failure of the enterprise.

The Aull mercantile firm owned a rope walk at Liberty, Missouri. Operations began in the autumn of 1829, and Aull shipped between 60,000 and 70,000 pounds of bale rope to New Orleans in the first year. The shipments increased in quantity in succeeding years, and New Orleans continued to be the chief market.[23] In enterprises of this type the merchant achieved his most advanced position in the pre-Civil War period. He bartered goods from the Atlantic seaboard to the Western farmer for his leading crop; he then processed the farm crop, thereby reducing its bulk and increasing its value before paying freight charges to ship it to the wholesale markets. Some of the commodities went to markets in the South, thus fulfilling the West's function in the three-cornered trade pattern of that period.

18. Entry of September 1, 1811, in James Wier, Letter Book 1805–16.
19. Fayette *Missouri Intelligencer*, December 25, 1829.
20. Franklin *Missouri Intelligencer*, November 20, 1821.
21. Columbia *Missouri Intelligencer*, November 23, 1833.
22. Columbia *Missouri Intelligencer*, December 27, 1834.
23. Letter of James Aull to Tracy and Wahrendorff at St. Louis, Missouri, dated Lexington, Missouri, September 4, 1829, and to Breedlove at New Orleans, September 4, 1830, James Aull, Letter Book B, James and Robert Aull Manuscript Collection.

The process built credit in New Orleans, and these credits, transferred to the Eastern cities, met the wholesale bills the merchants contracted during the winter months for goods to be shipped when navigation opened in the spring.

While the mercantile group will be judged primarily on the basis of their material contributions to Western life, they also performed certain services of a social nature, services generally credited wholly to the professional groups. Western stores constituted a social center for the farming classes, and the storekeeper came in contact with individual farmers much more frequently than did the lawyer, doctor, or preacher. Sometimes a merchant resented the fact that his store had become a loafing place for the country people, and he advertised his resentment in the papers, as did a Saint Louis merchant in 1825:

> *Mr. Printer—I am a storekeeper, and am excessively annoyed*
> *by a set of troublesome animals, called Loungers, who are in the*
> *daily habit of calling at my store, and there sitting hour after*
> *hour, poking their noses into my business, looking into my*
> *books whenever they happen to lie exposed to their view, making*
> *impertinent inquiries about business which does not concern*
> *them, and ever and anon giving me a polite hint that a little grog*
> *would be acceptable.*
>
> *Do, Mr. Printer, give this an insertion; some of them may see*
> *it, and take the hint. If it should not, however, answer the*
> *purpose, I shall certainly be under the necessity of disposing of*
> *my goods the best way I may, shutting up my shop, mounting*
> *a Vide Poche Cart, and crying "Marche donc", take myself off to*
> *some more favored country where I shall not be bored to*
> *death by loungers.* Yrs. T. Will Yardstick.[24]

Not all loungers were so meddlesome, but they might be none the less irritating. Around 1820, in Arrow Rock, Missouri, a dignified old gentleman who enjoyed all the amenities of an ample fireplace at home spent considerable time loafing in one of the stores. Accustomed to a large target for his tobacco juice when at his own hearth, his aim was notably bad when shooting at the stove in the store that he favored with his presence. As a result, the clerk spent much time cleaning the area around the stove after each visit of "the Colonel." Finally, in desperation, the clerk arranged for a colleague in a neighboring establishment to put in an appearance when the colonel was present, for the express purpose of spitting in the general direction of the stove. The friend arrived on schedule and performed with admirably faulty marksmanship; the clerk then gave him a sound "cuss-

24. St. Louis *Missouri Republican*, September 12, 1825.

ing" in front of the colonel for his carelessness and told him loudly and vehemently to use the spittoon or get out in the street. The colonel, however, failed to take notice, and, unperturbed, continued his devastating work.[25] Many merchants, however, kept a barrel of whiskey in the back room for regular customers, with a tin cup hospitably tied at the side.[26] Clearly, the advantages of maintaining a center for socializing outweighed the disadvantages.

Because of his education, business connections, and need to travel over the country, the merchant was called upon to perform a variety of services for customers and friends during the course of the day's business. James Aull at Lexington, Missouri, must have written twenty-five letters a year to order periodicals for his customers, the *Missouri Republican, Saturday Evening Post, Quarterly Review, Nashville Banner,* and *Nashville Whig* being among the favorites in his locality. Subscribers disliked sending money through the mail, drafts and bills of exchange were far too expensive and time-consuming for such small transactions, and it was easier to bother the merchant; let him write the letter and do the worrying about getting the money to the paper. On the merchant's part such favors constituted good business, and, indeed, he was better equipped to transact such matters than anyone else in his community. For example, Aull made remittances for newspaper subscriptions through his agents, Tracy and Wahrendorff at Saint Louis, and thereby eliminated the necessity of sending money through the mail. Sawmill and gristmill owners generally asked Aull to write their letters when they ordered equipment; his wide business connections assured them of getting the best service available. In another area of commerce, if county residents were engaging in a risky business, such as building and launching a flatboat, they asked Aull to arrange for insurance.

A local resident who met with difficulties or disaster while traveling in another state usually appealed to his home-town merchant for help. Such was the reaction of James Moore of Lafayette County, Missouri, who had gone to Natchez, Mississippi, on a horse-trading expedition. As a precaution against robbery, he had mailed a check for $400 to Aull at Lexington before setting out on the return journey. His fears were justified, as his pocketbook, containing some money and the duplicate of the check, was stolen from him, a loss he discovered when he reached the mouth of the Ohio River. Subsequent events demonstrated his wisdom in choosing a merchant to care for the check. The check had been drawn on the Bank of the United States in Philadelphia. After the robbery it was possible that

25. Thomas C. Rainey, *Along the Old Trail* . . ., 49-50.
26. Burrows, *Fifty Years in Iowa*, 26.

both the original and duplicate copy might be presented for payment, and any quarrel over the rightful ownership would result in a long delay before collection could be made. To prevent such a delay, Aull wrote to Philadelphia and asked that payment be stopped on the duplicate if it should be presented; at the same time he sent the original to a Philadelphia firm with which he did business. This company, known as a responsible firm, cashed the check without any difficulty, and Moore received his money. Only a member of the mercantile class could have handled the situation with such dispatch, since success depended on established connections in Eastern cities.

Home-abiding men, too, when faced with problems beyond the scope of their knowledge, came to the merchant for a solution. A poor, illiterate citizen of Lafayette County chopped and ricked a large supply of wood near the river bank in 1831. The steamer *L. B. Yellowstone* took on a supply of wood for its engines without inquiring about the ownership of the rick, which was some distance from any house. The woodchopper appealed to James Aull for help, and Aull wrote to Tracy and Wahrendorff, who collected for the wood when the steamboat arrived there.[27]

Merchants also facilitated travel for those who visited in the West. Students of history are familiar with Francis Parkman's description in *The Oregon Trail* of Westport, now a part of Kansas City, Missouri, and the services he obtained at that place. J. Patterson, English traveler in the West in the thirties, was exceedingly grateful to John O'Fallon of Saint Louis for aid and courtesies extended to him. He had been entertained in O'Fallon's home, and his journey east was made easier by letters of introduction furnished by the Saint Louis merchant.[28]

Less distinguished men did not hesitate to call on Western merchants with letters of introduction, in the hope of obtaining employment in the new country. Some applicants advertised for positions through the columns of local newspapers, but fully as many sought work through personal letters. Typical of these is a letter from Peter Cartwright to O'Fallon in 1827.

> To Col. John O'Fallon at St. Louis and all others it may concern—*This is to certify that I have been long and intimately acquainted with Mr. Carlton R. Galton, and after transacting a great deal of Business with him and being intimately acquainted with his manner of life, and mode of conducting business: I*

27. Lewis E. Atherton, "James and Robert Aull—A Frontier Missouri Mercantile Firm," *Missouri Historical Review*, 30 (1935), 3-27.
28. Letter of J. Patterson to John O'Fallon at St. Louis, Missouri, dated New York City, October 2, 1830, John O'Fallon Papers.

feel no hesitancy in recommending him as a gentleman of sound,
Moral, Honest principles and well qualified to transact business
in the line which he has been accustomed to, i.e. merchandising.
This is the character he has Borne in Kentucky and Springfield,
Illinois, from early life—much more might be said of Mr. Galton
by way of commendation but it is unnecessary as a small
acquaintance with him will satisfy any candid man—any faviour
[sic] bestowed, or, attention paid to him will be greatfully [sic]
acknowledged by me. . . .[29]

The frequency of such letters in mercantile records attests their efficacy in aiding men to obtain employment.

Nor were such services always performed in the hopes of ultimate economic gain. The comments of one merchant show that the proprietors of frontier stores sometimes sensed the effect of a drab and lonesome existence on the women in their localities and viewed with sympathy their quiet enjoyment of a visit to their stores:

I have often seen a hard-worked country lady come into a store
and inquire for all the handsomest goods in the stock, and admire
them, comment on them, take out great strips of pretty patterns,
and with her knotted fingers fold them into pleats and drape
them over her plain skirt, her face illumined with pleasure at
the splendor of such material could she wear it. It was really
pathetic and deserving of sympathy. The love of what is beautiful
was as intense in her soul as in that of her more fortunate sister
who could afford to wear it. Bright, harmonious colors, and fine
fabrics, over which she would draw her tired hands caressingly,
soothed and gratified her. Who could grudge her such a privilege?[30]

Storekeepers of this type helped to mitigate the bleakness of frontier existence for those who settled before community life was fully developed.

When all these services by the mercantile class are summed up— the building of towns, wholesaling and retailing, banking, the development of a market for farm crops, the promotion of agriculture, and the start of manufacturing—they attain great significance. They were the services necessary for the West to pass from a self-sufficient economy to interdependent economic specialization. Without them an advanced economic order was impossible; with them the West rapidly emerged from the pioneer stage. It is because of their leader-

29. Letter of Peter Cartwright to John O'Fallon at St. Louis, July 4, 1827, John O'Fallon Papers.
30. Rainey, *Along the Old Trail*, 64-65.

ship in this transition period that the mercantile class deserves a prominent and honorable place in the story of the frontier.

ORIGINS AND TRAINING OF THE MERCANTILE CLASS

In general, the merchant class followed the lines of migration of other Western settlers.[31] Most Kentucky merchants in the period from 1820 to the Civil War were either born within the state or had come directly from Virginia. A few claimed New Jersey, Pennsylvania, or New York as birthplace, but like other classes in the Blue Grass State, the majority were of Old Dominion stock. Many Missouri merchants were born in Kentucky; a statistical study of the origin of twenty-five Missouri merchants indicates that one third came from Kentucky. Here again the lines conformed to migration movements for other classes, since Missouri drew heavily on Kentucky and Virginia for her population in the early years of statehood. Even in that period, however, the middle Atlantic seaboard and New England states were well represented in the mercantile population, a representation that increased in the years immediately preceding the Civil War.

Before 1840, Illinois had a large representation of merchants from the southern states. As central and northern Illinois became settled, and as Chicago rose to commercial prominence in the fifties, an increasing number of the mercantile group came from states farther to the north. In the newer sections of the state there was a marked tendency for young men to come directly from the seaboard to work as clerks in the mercantile establishments already in operation. Considering the pre-Civil War period as a whole, almost a third of the fifty Illinois merchants whose careers were studied claimed New York State as their original homes. Other middle seaboard and New England states were also well represented in the group, but only 20 per cent of the group came from Kentucky, Tennessee, and Virginia.

31. The following sections, unless otherwise indicated, are based on a statistical study of 140 merchants in Iowa, Missouri, Kentucky, Illinois, and Wisconsin. Biographical encyclopedias for the various states yielded the information, and the subjects were chosen with no intent to focus the study on particular types of merchants. The study has been frankly a sampling, and the biographical sketches are known to be not altogether reliable. The material undoubtedly places undue stress on the careers of the more successful merchants and those especially prominent in other activities of their respective states. Nor is a sampling technique as responsive to changes in population trends over short periods of time as desired. The general conclusions drawn from the study, however, harmonize quite closely with the information obtainable from the papers left by merchants and the periodical material of the time. The latter sources have been used as checks on the statistical study.

The settlement of Iowa did not get under way until the thirties, a period in which many Northern merchants were moving West. New England and Pennsylvania were the points of origin for many, but no one state supplied a preponderance of the merchants who were entering the new territory. The later period of settlement and the development of economical means of transportation along the northern route account for the greater number of Northern merchants in Iowa and northern Illinois. The patterns of migration and ease of transportation became more striking as influences in the settlement of regions still farther to the north, like Wisconsin. There, over one-third of the merchants in the study claimed one state, New York, as the place of birth.

Because the merchant engaged in so many enterprises other than merchandising, it is not at all remarkable that he followed the general lines of migration. Frequently as much a farmer as a merchant, it was natural for him to migrate with other farmers. Some general exceptions must be made, however. The merchant class comprised middle seaboard and New England immigrants to a greater extent than did the population as a whole. Eastern firms frequently sent young men west to open stores, and after the construction of the Erie Canal it was not unusual for a young man with a background as a clerk to drift westward gradually from New York State and to engage in storekeeping in Illinois, Iowa, or Wisconsin. It is interesting to note that the Jewish merchant did not play a large part in this earlier phase of merchandising in the West.

As a whole, the merchants were well informed and were somewhat skilled in the necessary business techniques—a tribute to their intelligence and industry when one considers that most of them had little formal education. Not over 15 per cent of the men whose careers were examined in the study attended school beyond the age of fifteen. Indeed, many were clerking in stores at that age and had not advanced beyond the simplest studies before leaving school. College graduates made up less than 1 per cent of the men who chose merchandising as a career; yet, one rarely picks up a letter book or ledger of the period, even of a merchant in the smaller communities, without being impressed by the excellence of the penmanship and English. Here are none of the terse and formal letters of modern business. Certain words had a wide circulation among the class, such as "the needful" for money; but each man had his own individualistic style and vocabulary. Some confined their letters exclusively to business, others did not hesitate to comment on broader topics; in all there are indications of breadth of interest and a wide range of reading.

The communities' recognition of these superior skills is evident in the accounts of such events as celebration of the Fourth of July, which in pre-Civil War days was honored with appropriate ceremonies.[32] Frequently, the festivities opened with a parade to some central location, where the leading lawyer of the village delivered a patriotic address. Then followed the reading of the Declaration of Independence by some less gifted individual who was honored in the community for some reason, such as being a veteran of the Revolutionary War. After this ceremonial recognition of the day, the group gathered at some tavern to attend a banquet and offer toasts to the great men of the nation. Although these banquets were open to all who could afford to pay, the attendants were principally the business and professional people of the locality. The merchants played a leading part by making the arrangements and acting as marshals of the customary parade. For that matter, during the more convivial portion of the evening, after the banquet, they held their own with lawyers and preachers in the matter of toasts.[33]

These toasts, as reported in the local papers the following week, are reminders of the interests and scope of the reading of the mercantile group. On the Fourth of July, 1834, William Cornelius, a merchant of Columbia, Missouri, toasted the founder of our country: "George Washington: In purity, dignity, glory, he stands alone. Let no future Plutarch dare the iniquity of finding a parallel to his character." The next year Cornelius urged support of common education with the toast, "The Cause of Common School education—is one with which the perpetuity of our free institutions and happiness is associated. It claims the support of all." Another merchant followed with a toast to agriculture as the bulwark of our country, and a third eulogized Henry Clay.[34] In the Territory of Arkansas the merchants seem to have confined the subjects of their toasts to historical themes. At the celebration at Arkansas in that territory on July 4, 1825, Mr. Ennall's toast was, "The memory of the gallant Decature [sic], the brightest ornament of our infant navy," and Mr. Muir followed with, "The President of the United States, Washington, and Lafayette."[35] Space limits the quotations from these Independence Day toasts, but an investigation of the numerous examples in contemporary newspapers will show the mercantile class

32. A good illustration of the arrangements and conduct of an old-fashioned Fourth is contained in the *DuBuque* (Wisconsin Territory) *Visitor* for June 22 and 29, and July 6, 1836.

33. Frances L. McCurdy, *Stump, Bar, and Pulpit: Speechmaking on the Missouri Frontier*, 59-67.

34. Columbia *Missouri Intelligencer*, July 12, 1834, and July 11, 1835.

35. *Arkansas* (Arkansas Territory) *Gazette*, July 5, 1826.

of the time to have possessed an acquaintance with the classics, an interest in American history and politics, and an understanding of national issues. Lacking formal education, where did they acquire their information?

For one thing, their occupation was conducive to study. As frontier conditions retarded specialization in one line of merchandise, they encouraged the stocking of a wide variety of goods. Practically all stores offered books for sale, and these ran the gamut of literature. Parson Weems's story of George Washington and the cherry tree, *Pilgrim's Progress*, the Bible, and numerous other books of a religious and moral nature were displayed for sale on the shelves of many stores. The great literary names of England—Shakespeare, Scott, and Milton—appeared alongside the staple fare, and Fielding and Smollett added a salty flavor. Histories of every age, the classics of Greece and Rome, and law and medical books gave weight to the usual collection. One merchant in a small Missouri town in 1829 advertised the works of Josephus, Byron, Shakespeare, Cervantes, Scott, Fielding, Herodotus, Hume, Smollett, Milton, Defoe, Homer, Bunyan, and many others.[36]

Furthermore, conditions of trade before the fifties provided the merchant with long periods of little activity. Severe cold weather held customers to their own hearths, and, if a storekeeper had any intellectual interest at all, sheer boredom drove him to reading. Jones, in his highly imaginative treatise on merchandising in the thirties, pictured himself as spending a lonely winter in a Western store while his brother went east to purchase goods for the spring season. An occasional chess game with a disgraced army lieutenant helped to while away the time between the infrequent calls of customers, but with the time heavy on his hands he read every book in the establishment. Such reading was conducive to thought, for speed was not necessary when one was trying to get through a long winter day in the most pleasant manner possible.[37]

In many isolated communities merchants were the only people available to serve as postmasters. These official appointments increased their incomes and gave them opportunity to read all periodical material and newspapers that came through their offices. Through his position as clerk in such a store, J. L. Marshall never missed reading an issue of the *St. Louis Republican* over a period of several years, although he did not subscribe to the paper.[38] Under such conditions the merchant could educate himself easily, and no

36. Fayette *Missouri Intelligencer*, July 3, 1829.
37. Jones, *The Western Merchant*, 117-18.
38. Letter of J. L. Marshall to the *St. Louis Republican*, June 29, 1908.

enthusiast ever set up a more ideal stimulus for learning. More closely in contact with the people than either the lawyer or the preacher, the storekeeper could dispense the news and display his learning across the counter to his heart's content. Radio, television, and telephone were still unknown. What an ideal opportunity for a man to shine in the community!

Colleges did not establish schools of business before the Civil War, but if merchants wished to study business methods the means were available. James P. Holcombe published a work on the legal relation between debtor and creditor in each state in the Union and in Canada; John S. Jenkins brought out a book of legal forms for use by businessmen, including examples of properly drawn notes, different types of bills of exchange, and information on the legal obligations of auctioneers and of the members of a partnership. B. F. Foster published a number of books treating of every subject that was useful to a businessman, from the general principles of economics to double-entry bookkeeping, and he also conducted a school in New York City to train young men for positions as clerks in mercantile establishments.[39]

Travel added greatly to the education of the Western merchant. Until well into the forties many of the owners of larger stores found it advisable to go east once a year to purchase goods. The trip easily consumed six weeks of the merchant's time—even more, if he accompanied his goods on the return journey. Philadelphia was the chief wholesale center, but it was superseded by New York in the forties and fifties. Boston and Baltimore also drew a number of the Western storekeepers. The trip could not be called pleasant, yet it served to broaden the horizon of the mercantile class and to make them men of the world to a much greater extent than any other group in the West. They alone were conversant with the business life and pleasures of both the frontier and the largest cities of the time.

J. B. Jones described in detail one of these trips to the East in the thirties. Because his story agrees with mercantile letter books in regard to the general nature of the trip and also supplies details that merchants seldom bothered to record, it is worthy of notice here. In company with several other merchants he rode horseback to Saint Louis; from Saint Louis the party traveled by steamboat down the Mississippi to its juncture with the Ohio, whence they continued the journey up that river by the same means. Since Jones was traveling

39. B. F. Foster, *The Merchants Manual* . . . , and *A Practical Summary of the Law and Usage of Bills of Exchange and Promissory Notes* . . . ; John S. Jenkins, *The New Clerk's Assistant* . . . ; James P. Holcombe, *The Merchant's Book of Reference*.

in the company of men engaged in the same occupation, the time on board passed rapidly.

They spent their nights at the card table, with brag, euchre, backgammon, whist, and checkers for entertainment. Conversation occupied the group during the day; one merchant acted as chairman of the informal meeting, while the others, occupying seats in a half circle on deck, their feet propped on the railing, smoked good cigars to add to the comfort of the occasion and conversed. Their conversation ranged from business matters to the best form of government— a subject that called forth many references to ancient history and authority. Every problem that confronted the Western merchant had a hearing at this impromptu conference. The relative value of wholesale markets, the methods employed by Eastern merchants to draw trade, and social intercourse between Eastern and Western men received attention.

In regard to the social attitudes, there was a marked difference of opinion: some thought that the Eastern merchants were snobbish; others defended them from the charge. To feed the debate, the following incident was related: On one occasion a group of Western merchants had gone to a play in Philadelphia, and, finding all the seats taken, had entered the box of a local merchant from whom they had purchased goods. That person, arriving later in the evening with a group of ladies, unceremoniously ejected his unbidden guests, much to his financial injury in the West. The leaders in Jones's discussion group defended the Philadelphian in his action, with the argument that the Eastern wholesalers treated Western merchants as well as the Westerners' individual manners permitted. After all, a merchant who traveled east and attended the theater without changing from his workday garb did not deserve the same consideration as one who dressed suitably for the occasion. How could a man, dressed in fine cloth and clean linen and accompanied by ladies, be courteous to intruders who were garbed in coarse boots, huge blanket coats, and foxy caps, wore long unkempt beards, and mouthed great chews of tobacco that constantly needed attention?[40]

The days spent in New York, Baltimore, and Philadelphia were busy, yet there was much to be seen and done in the evenings, if the drummers could be avoided. In New York City, Niblo's Garden was displaying on January 12, 1835, an enormous biblical painting that had just arrived from London. At a neighboring hotel a Chinese lady, Afong Moy, was demonstrating the effect of the Chinese custom of binding the feet of ladies of quality in infancy. A full-grown woman with feet only four inches long! Museums were advertising

40. Jones, *The Western Merchant*, 170-75.

displays of rare animals, mechanical marvels, and fancy glass-working as means of drawing crowds. At the Park Theatre it was possible to see two operas—*Love in a Village* and *John of Paris*—and a farce, *The Spoiled Child,* for prices ranging from twenty-five cents for a seat in the gallery to one dollar for a box seat.

The emphasis on the pleasures of the city had many defenses. After all, the merchant engaged intensively in business dealings during the day and by evening was ready to be amused. Tired businessman that he was, he could be excused if he attended the Bowery, where Mademoiselle Celeste was playing her last night in the "celebrated traditionary drama," *The Wept of Wish-Ton-Wish,* to be followed by the farce *I'll Be Your Second,* and the melodrama *The French Spy, or the Wild Arab of the Desert.*[41] Seated in a seventy-five-cent box, the merchant could enjoy the additional thrill of viewing the ladies of doubtful character scattered throughout the audience.[42] Had he visited Philadelphia as early as September, 1836, he could have seen Mademoiselle Celeste in the same plays that he witnessed in New York in 1835. By that time, however, she had added two numbers to her repertoire, a new grand opera dance called "La Preciosa" and a specialty entitled "The Wild Arab Dance."[43]

At the end of two or three weeks the merchant was on his way home again, to a life where Indian, hunter, and pioneer farmer made up the bulk of the population. For the next ten months he would be in a world foreign to that which he was leaving. Stimulated by two contrasting environments, the merchant developed a somewhat cosmopolitan point of view and a store of information that excited admiration and envy among his customers, and won for him a position of leadership in the community.

THE MERCHANT IN POLITICS

As a leading citizen in the community the merchant naturally was interested in politics. Of the 140 investigated, 35 men, or 25 per cent of the total, held political offices of one kind or another. Politics in the West aroused much vehement discussion then, and the storekeeper's participation could be strongly partisan. Some, indeed, were primarily politicians who carried on their merchandising as a sideline, as did Ninian Edwards of Illinois. With clerks available for as little as $150 a year and silent partnerships widely practiced, a man

41. New York *The Evening Post,* January 12, 1835.
42. New York *The Evening Post,* October 12, 1830.
43. Philadelphia *Public Ledger,* September 12, 1836.

could supervise a business and engage actively in politics at the same time. Mention has been made of the large number of postmasterships held by merchants. More important offices also fell to them frequently. Edwards became governor of Illinois, and C. F. Jackson held the same position in Missouri. M. H. Pettit of Wisconsin served in the state legislature and was later elected lieutenant governor. Biographical encyclopedias undoubtedly mention only the most successful and outstanding merchant-politicians; the names of a host of lesser officials have been lost. A marked aptitude for politics on the part of some leading merchants is a good indication that others also were involved in civic matters, though on less notable levels.

Of the 85 merchants whose politics could be determined, 70 per cent belonged to the Whig party, and these figures are substantiated by newspaper and personal records.[44] After the downfall of the Whigs in the fifties the majority of the merchants joined the new Republican coalition. Henry Clay was the subject of toasts by merchants in their Fourth of July celebrations in the thirties and forties more frequently than any other public character. The population of the upper Mississippi Valley as a whole was not nearly so much in favor of the Whig party as these figures show the merchant class to have been. What then were the reasons for the dominance of that party among the merchants?

For one, they were in agreement with Henry Clay on banking policies. A continuing problem for the Western merchant was the fluctuating values of state bank notes. Kentucky paper might be accepted at one discount in Illinois, at another in Missouri, and at still another in the East. Throughout the country this situation retarded trade. Even in so simple a transaction as hiring a wagon to haul goods from Philadelphia to Pittsburgh the problem could vex the merchant. Dr. John Hamm of Zanesville, Ohio, visited Philadelphia in 1819 to purchase a supply of drugs. On leaving for home he gave his agents $35 to pay the wagoner's bill to Pittsburgh. The money was state currency, and, because it was at a discount in Philadelphia, the wagoner refused to accept it. Temple and Smith, Hamm's agents, gave the driver money that was circulating at par and charged Hamm's account with $1.75, the discount on the $35 he had left to pay the bill.[45] Such incidents were everyday occurrences and sometimes involved much larger sums of money. Under such circumstances it is not surprising that almost three-fourths of the

44. John V. Mering, *The Whig Party in Missouri*, 56-70.
45. Letter of Temple and Smith at Philadelphia to Dr. John Hamm at Zanesville, Ohio, dated Philadelphia, 1819, Temple and Smith Letter Book, 1819–22.

merchants embraced the national banking program of the Whig party.

Still another plank in the Whig platform appealed to storekeepers. Buying their goods in the seaboard cities and transporting them 1,000 miles westward over primitive roads and on dangerous rivers, paying freight rates that equaled one-fourth the cost of the goods, occasionally suffering the loss of a year's supply of merchandise, swept away in one disaster—such experiences as these made the storekeepers in the West believers in a program of internal improvements. Waterways were the principal routes for transportation of merchandise until Civil War times, and a small expenditure of money for improvement of navigation of the rivers frequently resulted in great savings to commerce. Snags alone occasioned property damage of $1,362,500 on the Ohio and Mississippi rivers in the years 1822–1827. The government's snag boats began operating in the latter year, and the losses in the next five years were reduced to $381,000—clear evidence of the value of improved waterways.[46] Insurance premiums ranged from 10 to 18 per cent during the thirties, so, understandably, the merchant supported the Whig party's program of internal improvements on a nation-wide scale, in the hope of reducing risks and the consequent high cost of insurance.

The tariff views of the Whig party probably made no direct appeal to the mercantile class. Wholesalers in the seaboard cities wished for the competition of European importers under the auction system to be curbed by legislation; otherwise, tariffs received little support from the group. But money from the tariff was to be used for internal improvements, so merchants in all sections, for this secondary result, favored the program. After all, the merchant's primary aim was to sell as cheaply as his neighboring competitor, and the tariff would not directly affect the competition but would, indirectly, reduce his cost of operation.

On the other hand, the political outlooks of Democratic administrations frequently irritated commercial interests, especially during Jackson's Presidency. The Jacksonians were not the gentlest of opponents, and it was hard for a Whig merchant to see his favorite projects defeated and at the same time to endure the vociferous attacks of the Jackson men. Shortly after the inauguration of Jackson in 1829, Charles Keemle started the *St. Louis Beacon* as a Democratic paper. The leading newspaper at that time was the *Republican*, devoted to the opposition. Keemle did not hesitate to attack it in the approved Jackson manner, always employing a cudgel even though a lighter weapon might suffice. One of his earliest and most faithful

46. Hall, *The West*, 61-62.

advertisers was the commission firm of Hill and M'Gunnegle, a company with connections along the Ohio River and in New Orleans. Since they held large quantities of goods on consignment, they frequently placed several advertisements in one issue of Keemle's paper. In the summer of 1830, however, G. K. M'Gunnegle ordered his subscription to the *Beacon* stopped because his Whig attitudes balked at the strong pro-Jackson material Keemle was serving him. Shortly afterward, Hill and M'Gunnegle ceased advertising in the paper, and a few other merchants followed suit. Keemle charged that he was being abused by "federalist" tactics, a hardship, he asserted, the "republican press" had always been compelled to endure. "Many of these withdrawing characters are merchants and tradesmen, who live by buying and selling; and, it is not for the undersigned [Keemle] to say how far they intend to exclude Republican customers from their stores and shops, by ceasing to advertise in the only Republican newspaper in the place; . . . of mixing politics and trade."[47] In a ringing statement of defiance to the enemies of his paper he threatened the merchants with loss of trade; he asserted that four-fifths of the people and nearly all farmers were "Jackson Republicans." The controversy brought 200 new subscriptions to his paper, and, as most of the merchants continued to advertise with him, the "persecution" resulted in a financial gain. In the end, those who had withdrawn their advertising returned, including Hill and M'Gunnegle.

Nor was Missouri the only state where merchants complained against the Jackson regime. On December 1, 1834, a merchant who resided near the Atlantic seaboard expressed his dislike for the Administration in a letter to a Baltimore wholesaler.

> As respects money, I do say *as far as my little experience and business in this world's concerns have extended, there has not been a time in which there was so much cry for money, and about the scarcity of it, as at the present. But we must try to weather out the storm and hope that a more propicious* [sic] *time is awaiting us, and is perhaps not far distant, when a sufficient change shall be made in the administration of our political system, as to cause a return of general prosperity.*[48]

47. *St. Louis Beacon*, September 9, 1830. Democratic newspapers at this period often referred to themselves and to members of the Democratic party as upholding "republican" principles, in the sense that they favored representative government. Of course, the modern Republican party did not originate before the middle of the 1850s.

48. Letter of Jacob Weaver to Garrett and Company at Baltimore, dated December 1, 1834, Mechanicsburg, state omitted, in Garrett Family Papers 1820–80.

The letter demonstrates that Eastern and Western merchants alike were irritated by the Jackson regime, and they favored the Whig party, which was the party that maintained the tradition of respectability, in the eyes of the propertied classes. When the Civil War broke out, the mercantile class constituted a strong link in Union sentiment, even in the border state of Missouri. Indeed, their records well serve to represent the close ties that developed between East and West during the twenty years that preceded the struggle. Most of their business connections were to the East; Western merchants thought in terms of goods flowing east and west rather than north and south—in terms of Philadelphia, Boston, Baltimore, and New York rather than in terms of the southern cities. Their problem of transportation was a national problem. In view of these factors they naturally sided with the Union against the Confederacy when the test came.

THE MERCHANT IN COMMUNITY LIFE

Unanimity of opinion among the merchants was far greater in politics than in religion. Moses U. Payne, who operated a store in Columbia, Missouri, for a number of years in the pioneer period, was an ardent Methodist preacher, gave generously to the construction of the first church in Columbia, and contributed to the Methodist colleges in the area. Land speculation provided him with a substantial fortune, but prosperity did not lessen his religious ardor.[49] On the other hand, Jared Warner, a Wisconsin merchant, was the exact opposite of Payne. Payne was a committed churchman, Warner an agnostic. As a young man, while he drove a peddler's cart about the countryside with a modest stock of merchandise to be sold in small quantities from house to house in Ohio and Illinois, he passed the long hours by reflecting on and relishing passages of poetry. Warner often copied an appealing selection in his business records, Wordsworth and Shakespeare being among his favorites, and he interspersed his thoughts on immortality and kindred subjects among his daily accounts. He read and admired Paine and Voltaire. No wonder, then, that he should be the founder of the first freethinkers' organization in the state of Wisconsin, a society he established at a meeting in his home July 4, 1852.[50]

While Payne and Warner represent the extremes of religious attitudes of the time, the great majority of merchants held less definite

49. "Biography of Moses U. Payne," in *Encyclopedia of the History of Missouri* . . . , Howard L. Conard, ed.
50. Jared Warner Manuscript Collection.

views. A few of the 140 men investigated were noted for their piety, a few were classified as nonbelievers or liberals; some of their biographies did not mention church membership, but most were members of a Protestant church. The statistical study indicates a preference for the Presbyterian church, but the tendency is so slight that the choice of a second group for study would probably show another denomination in the lead. Newspapers of the time, however, frequently mentioned mercantile support of religious enterprises. Thus, when the first Presbyterian Church was erected in Dubuque, Iowa, in 1836, two of the three men chosen to act as trustees and supervise the construction were leading merchants of the town.[51] But as a class, merchants displayed no variation in this aspect of life from the average citizen. Apparently, the daily concerns of a merchant had little influence on his religious inclinations.

Between 1820 and the Civil War, the ideas of the Age of Reform swept through America. Slavery, harsh penal laws, denial of rights to women, to mention only a few targets, came under attack by organized groups. As such movements age they attract the more moderate classes, but in the beginning they are usually supported by those who can afford fanatical allegiance to an almost hopeless cause. The merchants were, in general, well-fed property-owning citizens, a type to which weak causes seldom make strong appeal. Consequently, it is not surprising that the records dealing with merchandising are silent in regard to most of the reform movements of the period. Whatever services merchants rendered to the community, they cannot be credited with leading the fight for social reform in America.

In regard to some of the reform movements, however, one finds an occasional expression of opinion, or a common action, that indicates how the merchant viewed a particular issue. For example, the prohibition movement did not prevent the average storekeeper from serving whiskey to his customers. In the twenties and thirties grocers carried liquor as a part of their stock. Although a few merchants, like J. M. D. Burrows, sold only "dry" groceries, storekeepers as a whole offered little support to the antiliquor crusaders.

A few reform movements did receive support from the propertied classes, among which the merchants may be numbered. Public schools were toasted at civic dinners by some merchants as early as the middle thirties because the value of the public schools in helping to curb the excesses of democracy made their support a respectable move. Approval of colonization and other moderate schemes for settling the slavery problem also paraded under the banner of respectability, and merchants indicated some interest in them. Of course, in

51. *DuBuque* (Wisconsin Territory) *Visitor*, July 13, 1836.

the area this study discusses, slavery was not a flourishing institution, and there was little reason for merchants to rise to its defense. A few storekeepers in Missouri, like the Lammes at Franklin, owned slaves, but abolition would have worked no heavy hardship on them. Therefore, while eschewing all radical schemes, some merchants supported plans for ultimate emancipation, as did a number of Saint Louis merchants who belonged to the African Colonization Society.

James Aull of Lexington, Missouri, on the Missouri River, expressed moderate views on slavery. In 1834 and 1835 he advanced money to buyers for the New Orleans slave market, and he arranged for these men to remit his advances directly from New Orleans to his agents and creditors, Siter, Price and Company, at Philadelphia. The latter were Quakers, with a decided dislike for slavery. In a forceful but friendly letter to Aull they explained that conscientious scruples would not permit "any dealing in human flesh" on their part and that they preferred not to receive money involved in slave trading. Although they declined any participation in the trade, their position was moderate; they held no brief, either, for colonizationists and abolitionists.[52] In his reply to the letter Aull explained that he was personally opposed to the slave trade and that only a desire to oblige friends had led him to advance the money. He pointed out that many slaveholders in Missouri would be glad to be rid of the institution of slavery and that he thought such an outcome might be expected within a few years. But, he added, he had not talked to a man who would be willing to let the Negroes remain in the state after they were freed. To do so would result in the worst population imaginable.[53] In the states farther to the north some merchants supported the idea of no further extension of slavery in the territories; a merchant, Dexter Knowlton of Freeport, Illinois, was the Free-soil nominee for governor in 1852. Obviously, storekeepers expressed the prevailing sentiment of their community but did not assume leadership in creating a new attitude to a social change.

They did, however take a leading part in community activities. For example, on Saturday, July 27, 1836, citizens of Dubuque held public meetings to develop plans for a new hotel and to arouse interest in a canal project. In these meetings the offices of chairman and

52. Letter of Siter, Price and Company to James and R. Aull at Lexington, Missouri, dated Philadelphia, May 12, 1835, James Aull, Day Book 1833–35, Aull Collection.
53. Letter of James Aull to Siter, Price and Company at Philadelphia, dated Lexington, Missouri, June 15, 1835, Day Book 1833–35, Aull Collection.

secretary were held by merchants.[54] Chambers of commerce of course were headed by merchants, as in Saint Louis in 1836.[55] In the same city in 1826 the citizens of the Middle Ward organized a volunteer fire company, with a merchant as secretary; two other merchants, working with a lawyer, drew up the constitution and by-laws. Mrs. Paul, Mrs. Wahrendorff, and Mrs. Tracy, wives of leading merchants, served in 1824 as officers of the Female Charitable Society, an organization for relieving the distress of the poor.[56] Recognized as rich men, marked as leading citizens, and aware that support of community undertakings was a business asset, the merchant class bore the responsibility of such enterprises in towns all over the Middle West.

In spite of their prominence in community life, considerable evidence indicates that merchants did not regard their occupation as distinguished. For example, if a man engaged in merchandising and a number of other pursuits at the same time, he was likely to preserve all his records but those that related to trade. The case of Ninian Edwards has already been cited. John O'Fallon of Saint Louis started as a merchant, but as his interests widened he kept a record of his philanthropies and correspondence with noted individuals and let the preservation of his business records lapse.[57] Solon Robinson wrote voluminously on the subject of agriculture, but his Account Book seems to be the only record remaining of his twenty years as a merchant. Wynant Van Zandt, New York City merchant, dropped all reference to trade as soon as he ceased active participation, but kept careful record of his public honors.[58] Eastern and Western merchants alike held these attitudes. Further evidence of the merchant's derogation of his role is the fact that few advised younger men to follow business as a career. John O'Fallon prospered as a merchant, but he advised his younger brother to choose a different occupation, with the argument that times had changed.

Few merchants recorded their business careers at any length. John Beauchamp Jones dressed his experiences in romantic garb and published them in the work already cited. The book reached an audience large enough to cause him to expand and republish it five years later, in 1854, under the title *The Life and Adventures of a Country Merchant*, but Jones was more interested in the work as literature than

54. *DuBuque* (Wisconsin Territory) *Visitor*, July 27, 1836.
55. Membership list given in the *St. Louis City Directory for 1836–37*, Charles Keemle, ed.
56. J. Thomas Scharf, *History of St. Louis City and County*, 720, 1752.
57. John O'Fallon Papers.
58. Wynant Van Zandt Papers.

as a faithful record of business life. J. M. D. Burrows' book was written in the closing years of his life. He had made and lost two fortunes in Davenport, Iowa, and economic necessity compelled him to bring out the book, in the hope of some financial remuneration. In 1833 John C. McCoy opened the first store in the settlement that is now Kansas City, Missouri. He, too, penned a record of his experiences as an early merchant, stimulated no doubt by the rapid growth of Kansas City during his lifetime.[59] Otherwise, the mercantile group in the West seems to have remained silent about their experiences, while men in other areas of public life recorded biographical material.

The tendency for storekeepers to shift to other occupations in later life is further evidence of the low esteem in which they held merchandising. In part, their moving into other enterprises can be explained by increasing specialization in the West, but the shift from merchandising to banking and other commercial enterprises along the eastern seaboard in the same period indicates a preference for such occupations. Of the 140 merchants studied, 14 per cent shifted to banking in later life. Politics was their first preference, then banking; of the others, many retired from merchandising at an early age and did not enter another occupation.

ORIGIN AND EXTENT OF MERCANTILE WEALTH IN THE WEST

Frequent reference has been made to the wealth of the mercantile class, and, as money was scarce in the West, the question naturally arises as to the origin of the money used in the commerce of the area. The United States census estimates do not give complete data on trade before 1840, but the returns for that year show a large amount invested in merchandising in the West. In Illinois a little less than $5 million was invested in retail stores, which placed her second to Missouri, where the investment aggregated a little better than $8 million. As compared with $35 million in Pennsylvania and $42 million in New York, these were small sums, but the differences in population account in part for the disparity. In Iowa Territory the investment was around $500,000, but again, the paucity of population explains in part the comparatively small investment.

If one considers the average amount of capital per store, the West compared favorably with the East. In Arkansas the figures were $6,003; in Missouri the average was $7,370. These figures are greater

59. The McCoy diary was in the possession of his descendants at the time this study was made and was unavailable for research purposes.

than those for Pennsylvania, where the average amount employed was only $5,485. New York and Massachusetts fell far behind, with an average investment of around $3,500, a figure that compared favorably only with the regions of low average investment in the West, like Iowa Territory. Clearly, the average Western store employed more capital than the average Eastern store.

Furthermore, the average number of people served by each store was much larger in the West than in the East. Pennsylvania averaged one store for 260 people, by far the largest ratio in any of the seaboard states; the average for the group as a whole was around 200. In Missouri and Illinois the ratio was 340 inhabitants to each store, and in Arkansas the average was 370.[60] These figures indicate, then, that the Western stores, on an average, served more customers and employed more capital than did comparable merchandising units in the East. The smaller average size in the East was probably due to specialization. There, at least in the larger cities, the general store was no longer an economic necessity. If the merchant lacked capital, inclination, or training to handle a general stock of goods, he could confine himself to clothing, groceries, or shoes. In the West in 1840, specialized stores were not common outside of a few towns like Saint Louis. Consequently, the average merchant carried a general stock of goods, which demanded a relatively larger investment.

Few of the Western merchants inherited their capital. Less than 10 per cent of the 140 men whose biographies were examined had inherited sufficient money to be of appreciable help in their business, and less than 1 per cent were able to begin business solely on such capital. So unusual was he in this respect that Elisha S. Wadsworth of Chicago deserves special mention. His father was a Connecticut businessman who permitted his son to choose an occupation. Elisha entered merchandising, selected Chicago as a location, and opened a store there on money furnished by his father. Few parallel cases could be found in the West, especially before 1850. But in one respect Wadsworth's career was typical of Western merchants. He engaged promising young men as clerks, and four of these later became prominent merchants in their own right, the typical way in which individuals entered the field.

Of the merchants investigated, 46 per cent began as clerks in the stores of other men. Lloyd Selby clerked for fourteen years in Pennsylvania before he began business in Iowa. John Culbertson started clerking at fifteen years of age and saved sufficient capital to start in business for himself. If we add those who combined farming and

60. *Compendium of the Enumeration of the Inhabitants and Statistics of the United States—6th Census*, 1841.

merchandising to the 46 per cent who started as clerks, it is possible to describe the beginnings of the careers of 70 per cent of the store-keepers. Jacob Eldridge started farm work at thirteen years of age at a salary of $6 a month. At seventeen he was able to purchase a team, and for two years he engaged in transporting merchandise. At nineteen he sold his team and started clerking in a store. He bought the stock at the end of the first year and continued the business until he moved to Davenport, Iowa, in 1845. His story was repeated in many instances in Mid-America, as men branched out for themselves after clerking in an already established store.

This pattern provided the West with tradesmen who were thoroughly conversant with the business problems of the region. Of course, some merchants lacked such preliminary experience; 15 per cent entered merchandising directly from agriculture; another 5 per cent taught school to earn enough capital to get started. Some hotel keepers, skilled artisans, and day laborers became merchants, although never in large numbers. Whatever his origin, the merchant was generally a man who began with nothing and accumulated his own capital.

Some men started in business simply by practicing frugality to an extreme degree. The young man who lived in a frontier community had little temptation to spend his money, and frequently he had saved most of his earnings at the end of the year. If his employer did not object, he might invest his savings in merchandise, to good advantage. Jones pictured himself as a clerk in his brother's store, where, in his spare time, he was allowed to deal in furs, an enterprise that netted over $350 in one year.[61] Through operating a sideline and saving his earnings, a man could expect to accumulate sufficient capital to enter business for himself in a few years.

In many cases, if a young clerk displayed sufficient energy and ability, he received an offer of a partnership in an established firm. J. M. D. Burrows described such an incident in his own career.[62] He had been in business only two years when a hotel keeper introduced him to R. M. Prettyman, "a capable and worthy young man," who wanted to clerk in a store. Burrows needed a clerk but did not feel that he could afford to employ one. Prettyman agreed to work for no pay for a time, but at the end of a month he had proved so valuable that Burrows put him on a salary. In less than two years a merchant in a neighboring town offered Prettyman a half interest in a new store to be opened in a nearby village. Rather than lose Prettyman's services, Burrows made him a partner in his firm.

61. Jones, *The Western Merchant*, 86-87.
62. Burrows, *Fifty Years in Iowa*, 34-35, 67-68.

Running through Jones's book is the story of the brother, Joseph, who started out as a clerk in Missouri in the twenties. Because he displayed aptitude his employer started him in business in a new locality farther up the Missouri River and paid him half the profits in return for his labor. At the end of six months these profits aggregated $1,200, and in another six months Joseph was able to buy out his employer. On the recommendation of the employer, Joseph was able to secure $7,000 worth of goods in Philadelphia on credit; thus, in a short while he became an established merchant.[63] Nor are these examples of unusual enterprise and good fortune; the biographical encyclopedias are full of stories of successes that rival those of Horatio Alger.

Profits and rewards were high, if the merchant could evade certain pitfalls. Gottfried Duden, commenting on Western merchandising in the twenties, explained that the attraction of the soil prevented destructive competition among storekeepers. There were too many uses for capital in the West for it to stagnate in an enterprise that was unprofitable. According to his estimate, saddles that cost $5 in the seaboard cities brought $12 to $14 in Saint Louis, and even more in the smaller towns.[64] With such prices for his goods, it was possible for a merchant to acquire in a very short time sufficient money for the conduct of a good business.

One other illustration is necessary to balance the picture, however. William Darby was clerking for a firm in Kentucky in 1822. His income was at the top level of wages paid to clerks, and his employers trusted him to make the trips to New Orleans to purchase goods for the firm. According to the pattern described in previous examples, he should have been a prosperous merchant within a few years, but he did not succeed. In 1829 he wrote a piteous letter to John F. Darby, his distinguished and successful brother who was living in Saint Louis. In his letter he explained that he had been working on a snag boat on the Mississippi River for two months at a rate of $15 a month. His wages were stolen from him the day they were paid, and he was left stranded in Paris, Kentucky. His wife and three small children were still in Salem, Kentucky, but had no protection— ". . . for God's sake help me." In 1832 he was in Tennessee, the owner of ten acres of land and teacher of a small school, but there was no money to be made in his situation. If his brother would send him groceries to the value of $400, he could make some money, as the stagecoach passed his place and there were no competitors for

63. Jones, *The Western Merchant*, 46.

64. Gottfried Duden, "Gottfried Duden's 'Report,' 1824–27," trans. by William G. Bek, *Missouri Historical Review*, 13 (1919), 251-79.

the travelers' business. The letter must have been heeded, for William's luck changed. In 1835 he wrote to his brother that he could now command about $600 of the money advanced to him for goods. As fast as it came in, he was investing his money in bacon and flour —bacon purchased at 6¢ a pound readily retailed at 10¢. He was making more money than ever before, and there was no danger that John would lose any of the money he had advanced. The letter ended with a promise to be in Saint Louis when the money was due.[65] Here the record closed. Perhaps he arrived in Saint Louis at the appointed time bearing the money. Whether or not he did, his career demonstrates that merchandising was not an assured and comfortable route to immediate wealth for all who chose to follow it: a merchant's career was, in reality, fraught with rough detours and many hazards.

65. Letters of William M. Darby to John F. Darby at St. Louis, dated May 16, 1822, December 19, 1829, July 25, 1832, and June 25, 1835, John F. Darby Papers.

CHAPTER II
THE WESTERN STORE

The slow settlement of Mid-America prior to the War of 1812 retarded the development of merchandising in the first two decades of the nineteenth century. Permanent trading establishments were unprofitable, except in the few regions where white men had settled in numbers. The more thinly populated areas were served by Yankee traders who penetrated the West as far as the Missouri and the upper Mississippi rivers, bringing on flatboats merchandise that they auctioned and peddled to inhabitants from their transient stores.[1] This type of trading continued on a modest scale even after the area became more heavily populated. Travelers on the Ohio River as late as 1833 commented on the presence of flatboats at most of the villages along the stream. These offered corn, pork, bacon, flour, whiskey, cattle, and fowls for sale and generally carried an assortment of notions bought in the large river towns like Cincinnati as well. Brooms, cabinet furniture, cider, plows, and cordage constituted part of the stock of one boat observed by a traveler. The floating stores remained in one place until the stock was sold out, if the trade proved brisk; but if sales were slow, they moved to another location farther down stream. After cargoes were sold, the merchants disposed of their flatboats and returned home by steamer.[2]

Advertisements in a Jackson, Missouri, paper in the early twenties indicate that some traders varied the itinerant practice by transporting an assortment of goods directly to certain villages, with the intention of remaining only long enough to dispose of the stock on hand. For example, John Guest advertised a supply of goods he had brought to Jackson from New Orleans and was selling at Judge Bullett's house.[3] Guest advertised for only a short while, which may

1. Victor S. Clark, *History of Manufactures in the United States 1607–1860*, 343.

2. Emory R. Johnson and others, *History of Domestic and Foreign Commerce of the United States*, I, 242.

3. Jackson (Missouri) *Independent Patriot*, June 8, 1822.

indicate that he sold only the one shipment; it is very likely that some of the advertisements of the type represented single ventures by merchants who did not intend to settle in the community. With increasing settlement, however, traders found it profitable to locate in one place, where the larger population provided a market that justified the decision. By 1820 many places in Mid-America had reached this stage, and the permanently located merchant had become by far the most common type.

Some men started as peddlers and through enterprise and thrift were able to open stores. Jared Warner, who became a successful merchant and dealer in produce and lumber in Wisconsin, peddled goods in his early business career. Perhaps his migratory existence caused a quotation from *The Lady of the Lake* to hold a special appeal for him; at least he took the trouble to copy it in the Day Book he carried on a trip in 1834:

> *Like the dew of the mountain*
> *Like the foam on the river*
> *Like the bubble of the fountain*
> *Thou art gone, and forever.*[4]

Warner's outfit consisted of merchandise bought in Pittsburgh at a cost of $324.71, a horse at $45, a wagon at $6, and harness at $14— a total outlay of $389.71. Approximately half of his goods were bought on credit. On June 23 he started westward with his merchandise and a cash reserve of $2.15, which had increased to $260 by September 3 at Terre Haute, Indiana, four days before he started home. Warner traveled from 6 to 20 miles a day on the trip west, passing through Ohio, Indiana, and Illinois. His outward journey covered a distance of 620 miles, and was made in a little over two months' time. On September 7 he started back toward his home at Canfield, Ohio, and reached there shortly before the end of the month. The route traveled homeward was shorter than the one followed on the outward journey, and Warner made fewer stops to trade along the way. He replenished his stock by small purchases in Richmond and Indianapolis, but it is likely that his merchandise had been sold down to the point where it was useless to try to continue regular sales. The Day Book does not give complete figures on the trip, so it is impossible to learn how much he profited from his three months of trading. By 1836, however, he was operating a store at Canfield, Ohio, and his later journeys were confined to occasional trips up and down

4. Jared Warner, Book E 1st Peddling Trip, June 12, 1834.

the Ohio River for the purpose of buying and selling produce and merchandise.[5]

The careers of the great naturalist John James Audubon and his partner Ferdinand Rozier offer other interesting sidelights on the relation of the migratory merchant to the settled mercantile trade. These men operated a store at Louisville, Kentucky, for a number of years early in the nineteenth century, but financial difficulties caused them to move to Henderson, Kentucky, where their finances worsened. Consequently, they decided to try to sell their remaining stock of goods in the French settlements on the Mississippi River. The trip consumed two months' time, as cordelling a heavily laden flatboat was an arduous task, especially when ice clogged the river. At Sainte Genevieve the villagers' supplies were low, and the partners' goods brought excellent prices. Audubon sold out to Rozier, who decided that the town was an excellent place to settle and establish a business.[6] While the Audubon-Rozier trip was not a peddling expedition in the true sense, it does indicate the freedom with which merchants moved to other settlements when they found the old location unprofitable.

After merchandising took on a more settled aspect, merchants paid little attention to peddlers, although an occasional advertisement did attempt to win their wholesale business. Kerr and Guild at Jackson, Missouri, in 1826, ran a two-column announcement of goods recently purchased in the East, which they were offering at very low prices at wholesale and retail. The advertisement invited peddlers in the southern part of the state to call and examine the stock.[7] Jackson was located some distance below Saint Louis and peddlers were likely to consider the trip to Saint Louis for goods too long and expensive. Since their stocks of goods were necessarily small, they probably purchased new supplies at the nearest store of any size, so Kerr and Guild's advertisement undoubtedly attracted some business.

Increasing migration to Mid-America favored the established merchant because the advantages of a larger stock of goods, barter, credit, and a better acquaintance with the people of the local community enabled him to win customers away from the peddler as soon as the local market would support a permanent store. Consequently, after 1820, the story of Western merchandising revolved around the permanent merchant, making the records of his store far more important than those of the diminishing number of peddlers who continued the losing fight for a share of Western trade.

5. Jared Warner, Day Book 1836–49.
6. Constance Rourke, *Audubon*, 37-85.
7. Jackson *Independent Patriot*, April 1, 1826.

THE PHYSICAL PLANT OF THE FRONTIER STORE

Store buildings of course varied according to the location. The largest and most expensive stores in Mid-America were in Saint Louis and Chicago. Around 1835 a merchant who arrived in Saint Louis with the intention of entering business chose a location best suited to the type of store he was to operate. If his capital was too small for the wholesale trade, the river front was a poor location. Front Street in that section was open on the river side. From the street to the river bank, the sloping ground was paved with cobblestones and brick, and throughout the day the rumble of carts and the clop of horses' hooves accompanied the bustle of business inside the stores. Importing, wholesaling, and commission firms dominated Front Street, where proximity to the wharf enabled them to move goods back and forth from the river to their four-story limestone warehouses, which faced away from the wharf and gave an imposing appearance to the river section. The wholesale drygoods firms extended into the next block, just beyond Front Street and the river wharf. Still farther on were the stores of the retailers, men who engaged only in the local trade[8] but who lived in hope of some day emulating their more successful business associates along the river.

By the fifties Saint Louis could boast of some imposing business structures. Nicholson's store claimed to be the "largest retail and jobbing family grocery" in the United States. It occupied a pretentious building of Renaissance style, four stories high and three rooms wide, with engaged columns adding to the impressiveness of the façade. The name *Nicholson* was spelled out in large letters at the top of the fourth story and again at the level just above the ground floor. In between these displays of the firm's name the company advertised its wares by a sign, "Tea, Coffee, Sugar, Wine and Liquor Warehouse."[9] Few stores, even in Saint Louis, rivaled Nicholson's size or architectural triumphs. In 1820 Asa Wheeler rented a store at the corner of First and Main streets for $40 a month. The premises were the property of Auguste Chouteau and consisted of a grocery with two rooms at the back, a bakehouse with two ovens, a yard, and a cellar. All this in the best business location available! In 1823 Chouteau gave James Lansdell and Joseph Branson an even better bargain by renting them a house and lot fronting on Market Square for $10 a month. At the time, the men were using the house as a cabinetmaker's shop and grocery store, but the new contract stipulated that they should build a log cabin to house the cabinetmaking

---

8. *Gazetteer of the State of Missouri,* Alphonso Wetmore, compiler, 193.
9. J. N. Taylor and M. O. Crooks, *Sketch Book of St. Louis,* 321-22.

business. The structure was to become Chouteau's property at the end of four years.[10]

In the smaller towns and frontier outposts, store buildings were less imposing and, consequently, even less costly. Jared Warner, who progressed from peddling to becoming a merchant at Millville, Wisconsin, owned considerable property in addition to his store. His real estate assessment for 1850 listed his own dwelling at $270, two other houses, which he rented, at $155 and $170, and his store building at $170.[11] The assessment indicated that a good dwelling was valued at a third more than a store building and that houses occupied by renters in small towns were worth fully as much. The reasoning behind these evaluations becomes apparent when one examines the structure of such a store building in detail.

J. B. Jones described a frontier store building in his book on Western merchandising, a picture drawn from his own observations while keeping a store at Arrow Rock, Missouri. The framework was of hewed logs, laid lengthwise, the chinks between the logs filled with clay and lime. The structure itself consisted of two rooms, each about 20 feet square—one to be used for a salesroom, the other for storing goods. Door and window in the salesroom were equipped with locks and bolts as a precaution against robbers. Located in a clearing of trees, where rattlesnakes and deer could be observed occasionally, the building appeared little different from the scattering of log-cabin homes in the neighborhood. Interior walls were whitewashed, except in the salesroom, where shelves ranged along all four sides. A counter of boards, 30 inches wide and 12 feet long, extended from the window to the partition wall between the two rooms, dividing the salesroom into two triangular sections, the larger of which could be entered by the front door. The smaller section opened into the storeroom, an arrangement that permitted easy access to supplies not on the shelves and provided an area in which the clerk could sell goods without hindrance from customers. A large shoebox or hatbox served as a desk, and money was kept in a drawer under the counter, with a small hole cut through the top of the counter for convenience and safety when business was heavy.[12]

Some stores were even smaller and less well equipped than the one described by Jones; the first store in Davenport, Iowa, was a single-

10. Contracts of Auguste Chouteau with Asa Wheeler, December 1, 1820, and James Lansdell and Joseph Branson, August 15, 1823, Col. Auguste Chouteau Papers.

11. Jared Warner, Day Book 1849–54, entry on last page.

12. John Beauchamp Jones [Luke Shortfield], *The Western Merchant*, 41-42, 45, 52.

room, shingled log cabin, 16 by 20 feet in size.[13] As competition increased in the original location, the merchant might send a younger member of the firm farther out on the frontier to open a smaller store and thus gain the benefits of an exclusive market. Such stores were even smaller and cruder than those in the villages along the rivers and highways; Jones described one in a log hut that had originally been used as a henhouse by a settler.[14]

Sometimes the merchant went beyond the line of settlement, as did the sutlers who supplied troops at frontier outposts. John C. Symmes, sutler at Cantonment Davis on the upper Missouri River in 1815, had to construct his own buildings after reaching the fort. The vessel on which he made the trip served as a store until quarters were completed. The buildings cost $270—a reasonable sum, since they were to house a $9,000 stock of goods and serve as living quarters for Symmes as well. Four cabins, consisting of countinghouse, storeroom, store, and kitchen, made up the group. They were located near the river bank, with the countinghouse and store joined and facing downstream.[15] It is clear, from contemporary records, that, outside of the larger places, store buildings were inexpensive; for $200 or $300 the merchant could erect a structure large enough to house a $10,000 stock of goods, and that item of business expense was settled for the next few years.

Merchants provided their stores with locks and bars, a precaution that frontier settlers as a whole found unnecessary. Business establishments attracted thieves, as attested by an advertisement in an Arkansas paper in 1836 headed "Stop the Thieves," which illustrates the difficulties merchants experienced in safeguarding their stores. Robbers had broken in the door of a store near Fort Smith by using a fence rail and had made off with a considerable amount of merchandise and $800 or $900 in cash. Since notes and other valuable papers also were part of their prize, the advertisement warned the public against trading in any of these financial papers. The thieves were tracked 15 miles into the Cherokee Nation Territory, but there the trail vanished. All resources to find and arrest the thieves having failed, the merchant was now offering $100 for the apprehension of the guilty parties and an additional $50 for the recovery of his property.[16]

13. *Davenport* (Iowa) *Democrat and Leader*, June 29, 1936. A replica of this store, which was opened in 1836 by Captain John Litch, has been constructed in a Davenport park.

14. Jones, *The Western Merchant*, 123-25.

15. Letter of John C. Symmes to his wife at St. Louis, dated Cantonment Davis, December 17, 1815, John C. Symmes Papers.

16. *Arkansas* (Arkansas Territory) *Gazette*, July 12, 1836.

It was a great day in the life of a Western community when a steamboat docked and began to unload the boxes and barrels of goods for the new store. People flocked from miles around to observe the process,[17] prompted only in part by backwoods curiosity. As indicated earlier, a store was a community resource, not only as a supplier of goods but as a trader in produce; as such, its presence in the settlement enabled farmers to concentrate on the most profitable line of activity. The store ended the farmers' days of economic self-sufficiency, for these early merchants attempted to purvey everything needed by the community.

Among the groceries package goods were as yet very few, and the bulk consisted of tea, coffee, sugar, flour, and liquor. James Aull of Lexington, Missouri, occasionally ordered 20 barrels of rye whiskey at one time, to supply the demand at his four establishments. He also sold peach brandy and Jamaica rum, but whiskey was the common liquor all over the West. Frequently purchased for as little as 25¢ a gallon, it retailed at prices that yielded satisfactory profit to the merchant yet entailed only a small outlay by the customer. J. M. D. Burrows, writing in the eighties, was proud that he had never sold liquor in his store at Davenport. Burrows frowned on the habit of some farmers who came to town on Saturdays to spend the day drinking. Some of his potential customers refused to trade with him because he did not sell liquor, but his business prospered none the less.[18] On the other hand, the merchants of Davenport who dealt in whiskey prospered quite as much as Burrows. The custom was almost universal and seldom involved a penalty, social or financial, for the mercantile class. A contemporary travel journal comments disapprovingly of the low character of the groceries in Saint Louis and rural Missouri. According to this account, the word *grocery* meant a gathering place for rowdy drinkers.[19]

Coffee purchased by the merchant was usually green, and the roasting was left to the customer's taste. Only two or three grades were available, a limitation that permitted the merchant to keep his supply in a small space in the storeroom, probably in little kegs. The same was true of tea; a few standard names like Imperial and Young Hyson dominated the field. Standard names did not guarantee uniform quality, however, as Young Hyson tea might, for example, vary from very good to very bad. Open barrels of brown sugar stood conveniently near the counter, since it sold more readily than the ex-

17. Jones, *The Western Merchant*, 42.
18. J. M. D. Burrows, *Fifty Years in Iowa*, 26.
19. Frederick Gustorf, *The Uncorrupted Heart: Journal and Letters of Frederick Julius Gustorf 1800–1845*, 81-83.

pensive white variety. A supply of soap, spices, flour, and salt completed the grocery stock of the average Western store, but not the inventory. Hardware and leather goods shared floor space with the groceries. Axes, log chains, kettles, pots, pans, kegs of nails, and other similar articles in wide variety, being durable in nature, could be piled in some unoccupied space or suspended from the rafters on cords. Shoes, saddles, and harness added to the bewildering variety of goods on display.

Dishes, drugs, books, and drygoods occupied the shelves around the sides of the building. In the matter of dishes, Queensware was considered standard. Although it was originally imported from abroad, potteries began to manufacture the ware in the United States before the Civil War, and the name had probably ceased to have more than a general significance. Patent medicines, physics, and sedatives were the principal items in the drug supply. E. D. Sappington's store at Jonesboro, Missouri, stocked licorice balls, pill boxes, oil of sassafras, calomel, camphor, Godfrey's Cordial, Bateman's Drops, laudanum, paregoric, rhubarb, asafetida, turpentine, sweet oil, and opium, all purchased in Philadelphia.[20] If one adds Epsom salts to this list, it is representative of the drugs available in the general store of the time.

The drygoods and clothing stock was so varied that one can do no better than list the goods offered for sale in the newspaper advertisements. John Collier and Company at Saint Charles, Missouri, advertised the following items in 1820: "Superfine and common Cloths, superfine and common Cassimers, Callicoes, Ginghams, Irish Linen, Brown Holland, India, Book, Mull, Jaconet, Cambrick, Leno and Figurd Muslin, Nankeens, Senshaws, and Sasanets, Shawls and Handkerchiefs, Plain and Figured Canton Crapes, Hosiery and Gloves—Straw Bonnets, Seersuccer and Cotton Cassimers, Bombazetta & Diapers—Vestings, Ribbons, Steam Loom Shirtings, Russia Sheeting, Plaids and Stripes, Sheeting, Shirting & Bed Ticking, Shoes and Boots, Morocco Hats and Skins. . . ."[21] The list is impressively long and varied.

Most of the drygoods consisted of coarse and serviceable cloth, but fashion played its part even in the rougher areas of the West. In 1830, on his buying trip to Philadelphia, James Aull purchased artificial wreaths, pink crepe, lutestring cravats, green gauze veils, and black silk gloves. Leghorn bonnets for women and palm leaf hats for men were also on the list. The wholesale bill for "rack, dressing,

---

20. List of goods purchased April 2, 1835, Governor M. M. Marmaduke Manuscript Collection.
21. St. Charles (Missouri) *The Missourian,* June 24, 1820.

side, and Spanish combs" came to $69.85.[22] Leghorn bonnets were especially fashionable at one time. Big Shoal Creek Meeting House in Clay County, Missouri, a church of the Primitive Baptists, became so noted for its display of these hats and new dresses on the second Sunday in May each year that the occasion was dubbed "The Bonnet Show."[23]

As living conditions on the frontier eased, the stores offered articles for amusement. James Aull bought a music box, chessmen, violin strings, and jew's-harps on the trip in 1830. No wonder, then, that the store attracted customers, for, along with the many necessities, it offered something desired by each member of the family—liquor for the men, fine cloth for the women, a bit of peppermint candy or a lump of brown sugar for the children, and games and musical instruments for everyone's leisure hours. How much the enterprising merchant mitigated the harshness of frontier life can only be imagined.

THE STORE IN OPERATION

Stores opened at dawn, and it was not unusual for a clerk still to be selling goods by the feeble glow of candles at ten o'clock at night. Farmers who lived nearby arrived in the forenoon to dispose of produce and do their trading. Those at a distance reached the store later in the day, and some did not arrive until bedtime. As they were anxious to be on their way again early the following morning, it was necessary to care for their produce and put up their bills of goods before the store closed for the night.[24] In addition to the habitual loafers who crowded the store, the merchant held long visits with his regular customers that were occasions for working out the details of profitable trades. A trip to town was often an all-day affair, no matter how close to the store one lived, since the store offered the richest opportunities for social as well as business intercourse. Although they might lack money or credit to purchase goods, some came anyhow to participate in the political arguments and exchange of gossip around the stove. Women were as frequent visitors as men. Gottfried Duden warned his German readers not to come West with the expectation of making a living by peddling goods, as people postponed filling their needs so they could buy at the stores where they could also obtain free gossip: "Most of the girls and women would

22. James Aull, Invoice Book D, covering the period February 18, 1830, to June 20, 1832. List of purchases, firms, and amounts bought in 1830. James and Robert Aull Manuscript Collection.

23. D. C. Allen, "The Bonnet Show at Big Shoal Creek Meeting House, Clay County, Missouri."

24. Burrows, *Fifty Years in Iowa*, 73.

very reluctantly forego the opportunity occasionally to ride to the stores of the cities, or even to the country stores, where there is usually a concourse of strangers."[25]

The patronage of younger women made merchandising more palatable for the clerk who was working and saving to get ahead. J. B. Jones obviously enjoyed waiting on the real counterparts of his fictional "Maria." From the minute "Luke," the young clerk, assisted her down from her horse in front of the store until she departed for her home, she was the object of his closest attention. Maria was a timid lass, all the more embarrassed because an attractive young man was waiting on her. She wanted to purchase stockings, but her modesty permitted her only to look in the direction of the small paper boxes. Luke, fully attentive, asked if she desired anything off the shelf. At her reply, "Hose," it was Luke's turn to be embarrassed, and he reached for garden hoes, suspended from the ceiling, instead of the desired article. But Maria's mother was equal to the occasion; she told her daughter forthrightly not to be embarrassed but to call for stockings right out. After all, she reasoned, Maria ordered flannel without being disturbed, and every storekeeper knew it would be used for petticoats. The logic was sound but scarcely operative in lessening the embarrassment of Luke and Maria. But not all the girls were as demure as she, and Luke recovered his aplomb very quickly. While cutting drygoods for Maria, Luke had been requested by her father to include a thumb in the measurement, and Luke gallantly offered a whole hand. Such readiness of wit and good nature were assets in merchandising, but "Polly," who had none of Maria's timidity, proclaimed her willingness to accept Luke's hand. In typical Western fashion, she carried the joke to the point where poor Luke was much discomfited every time Polly appeared.[26]

Men customers constituted more problems and of a less agreeable nature to the merchant. Barter and higgling were universally practiced in the West. The one-price system did not come into general use until after the Civil War. "Mr. Middleton," Maria's father, had an established reputation as an expert higgler. In developing his story of the opening day in a Western store, Jones had Luke quote gingham to Mr. Middleton at 6¢ below the regular price in order to make a good impression and to check that gentleman's bargaining proclivities. Maria and the mother recognized the excellent offer, but Mr. Middleton would not be denied his pleasures. Beaten before he had

25. Gottfried Duden, "Gottfried Duden's 'Report,' 1824-27," trans. by William G. Bek, *Missouri Historical Review*, 13 (1919), 251-79.

26. Jones, *The Western Merchant*, 57-58, 62-65.

started, he still refused to surrender and insisted on arguing the matter of price with the clerk.[27]

Such debates were less disturbing to the routine of the business day than the occasional appearance of some individual who was looking for trouble. Jones included such an incident in his account of Luke's first day of business. Two characters of unsavory reputation entered and inquired the price of brown domestic cloth; a bolt of the cloth was on the counter at the time. The clerk priced it at 20¢, meaning per yard, but his customers insisted that he had sold them the whole bolt for 20¢. One clerk went for the constable, who could not be found. The argument continued until a third clerk, goaded to violence, began to hit one of his tormentors over the head with a yardstick. Enraged, the bully prepared to wreak vengeance by laying about him with an axe, but the clerk knocked him down with a two-pound iron weight.[28] Once a merchant demonstrated his ability to handle such problems, he could expect to carry on his business peaceably.

The average business day was much less exciting, however, and, because it was, the records for reconstructing it are less numerous. All stores kept "Blotters" or "Day Books" for immediate entry of sales, and these matter-of-fact records give the fullest picture available of the run of business.

Stores that faced little competition and were situated in out-of-the-way places were able to demand high prices. The advantages of being the sole merchant in an area emerge from study of a representative day's business for such a firm, F. Frisel and Company, at Jackson, Missouri Territory, in 1818. Nine customers visited the store on March 25 of that year, and all paid high prices for what they bought. The Widow Wright was the first customer; she purchased 6 pounds of coffee for $3, 2 handkerchiefs for $1, a comb for 12½¢, a set of plates for $1.25, 1 damaged sugar bowl for 25¢, ¼ pound of Hyson tea for 75¢, 1 shawl for $2.50, 6 yards of gingham for $3, and 2 thimbles for 25¢. Her bill totaled $13.125, but her expenditures placed in her possession the supplies most likely to enable her to win another husband. One could hardly blame her if she contemplated such action after her purchases, for the coffee and tea prices meant a return of 200 per cent to the store, if Frisel and Company had bought their supplies at the current wholesale prices. In this case, a widow's status had availed her little in the way of tempering the wind to the shorn lamb. The other prices were not unusually high, as compared with those in other sections of the West. Ezekiel Murray, who made

27. Jones, *The Western Merchant*, 56.
28. Jones, *The Western Merchant*, 60-61.

his purchases after Mrs. Wright had completed hers, limited himself to a pair of trace chains for $2.50. The next customer was even more rewarding than the Widow Wright, however. He bought 4 pounds of coffee, for which he paid at the rate of $1.12½ a pound, more than double the price paid by the widow and a sum in no way justified by wholesale prices and transportation costs. The customer was not daunted by the price, it seems, as he also bought a dozen buckles for 75¢, 6 skeins of silk for 75¢, 3 yards of plush for $9, 5½ yards of cloth for $4.81¼, and 1 straw hat for $3—a total of $22.81¼. This purchase was the last of the large bills for the day. The next customer limited his buying to a pair of shoes for $1.50. Following this came a purchase of shoes for $2, and two skeins of silk for 25¢. Ribbon made up the sole items in the bills of two customers, one being for 50¢ and the other for 33¢. In view of the sliding scale for coffee, it would be interesting to know if the ribbons for these two customers were of identical quality. Another customer bought a handkerchief for 25¢, and the last customer of the day bought a half pound of eightpenny nails for 28¢. The day's business totaled $43.54¾, excluding a few entries certifying collection for goods sold on credit at earlier dates.[29]

Records of daily sales are voluminous, but further illustration would add nothing to the explanation of merchants' practice, in so far as typical transactions are concerned. The sales of this firm illustrate the records of most other stores in a number of ways. For one thing, they show that purchases were not limited solely to the necessities of life, which was true in a general way but far from the extent often thought. People did buy ribbon and combs and plush cloth all over the West as soon as the stores made them available. A number of early arrivals on the frontier could afford to buy some luxury goods, even though such items might be limited to a pair of silk gloves or a silk handkerchief; one cannot turn many pages in a merchant's day book without realizing that such goods were in steady demand. Again, these accounts illustrate the general nature of the stock of goods carried by Western stores. In one day this firm sold drygoods ranging from gingham to plush and ribbons, besides groceries, hardware, shoes, and glassware—a typical day's custom as revealed by the entries in most day books. Furthermore, purchases as a rule varied as widely in amount as did the nine sales made by Frisel and Company. People who lived at a distance from the store might buy goods worth $50, while the next item, bought by a local resident, shows in the record as a 10¢ purchase. The total of sales for the day, reaching a little over $40, is also typical of the amount of business transacted by the Western store in the early period. This would

29. F. Frisel and Company Journal from March 9 to October 29, 1818.

make the weekly sales amount to $200 or $300, a figure that agrees with the estimates of merchants that business ran from $100 to $300 a week. Jones estimated average sales at $10,000 to $12,000 a year.[30] James Aull bought from $35,000 to $45,000 worth of goods a year in Philadelphia for his four stores in Missouri, and he supplemented this investment by many purchases by letter during the next twelve months.[31] At times Joseph Hertzog visualized Christian Wilt doing a $100,000-a-year business in Saint Louis, but letters of a more realistic mood set the total at from $180 to $200 a week.[32]

Some qualifications need to be made in accepting Frisel and Company's sales as typical, however. The general retail price of coffee certainly was far below the price charged by this one store. Coffee retailed for 25¢ a pound in the unidentified town Saint Helena in 1832 and at the same figure in Jonesboro, Missouri, in 1835. Similar prices prevailed in Iowa and Wisconsin. Sugar was even cheaper, frequently selling for as little as 12¢ a pound. Tea would not have sold elsewhere at the exorbitant price of $3 a pound.[33] The other prices were more in keeping with the scale charged in the West at the time, although one finds wide variations in the charges for drygoods, the result of differences in quality and nomenclature. Although the tendency to charge one customer double the rate at which an article was sold to another seems to bear out Jones's assertion that prices were quoted according to the customer's likelihood to pay, an investigation of some other day books reveals little of this practice in the sale of staples. Perry Wilson and Company, an Iowa firm, sold sugar at prices ranging from 15¢ to 18¢ in the twelve-month period ending November 7, 1837. Furthermore, the 3-cent variation was not a matter of day-to-day change, but developed over a period of time and without reference to individual customers.[34] The practice of varying prices according to individual customers applied usually to cash and credit customers; cash customers frequently benefited by a lower price. In assessing the profits of the merchant on the frontier, still one other qualification needs to be kept in mind: sales did not run at a uniform volume. Good weather and good roads meant increased purchases, and bad weather practically halted business. Thus, Frisel and Company did not transact sales amounting to $40 or $50 every day. Solon Robinson's day book contains only two entries for Satur-

30. Jones, *The Western Merchant*, 47.
31. James Aull, Invoice Book D, Aull Collection.
32. Joseph Hertzog, Letters.
33. Figures compiled from various day books listed in the bibliography.
34. Perry Wilson and Company, Day Book, November 4, 1836, to August 25, 1838.

day, February 29, 1840: John Cochran bought a half plug of tobacco at 25¢, and H. S. Pelton one gallon of molasses at $1.[35] Either Leap-Year Day was no occasion for celebration in 1840, or the roads were in wretched condition.

35. Solon I. Robinson, Account Book 1840–53.

CHAPTER III
WHOLESALE MARKETS

Canada and New Orleans were the sources of the first white immigration into Mid-America during the Spanish and French regimes. After the establishment of New Orleans in the first quarter of the eighteenth century most of the supplies for the settlers came from that city. Dorrance, in his study of the French at Sainte Genevieve, Missouri, has pointed out the social and economic as well as political influence of New Orleans in the upriver settlements. Raw products floated down the Mississippi River on flatboats, to be traded by factors for European goods; the return products came upstream on keelboats, cordelled against the current, to the French towns.[1]

With the acquisition of the region by the United States and the resultant influx of white settlers into southern Illinois and Missouri after the War of 1812, the trading pattern changed. Canada and New Orleans gave way to the cities of the Atlantic seaboard as the chief sources of supply, and Mid-America developed a system of merchandising that was to remain much the same in its general outlines, so far as wholesaling was concerned, for the next thirty years.[2]

This new American period, however, repeated the pattern of the old in the sense that retailers were still separated by great distances from the wholesale centers on which they had to rely. Naturally, full-fledged wholesale towns could not develop until the retail trade was well established. As a consequence, the early merchants in Mid-America relied on the seaboard houses for their supplies; when, later, wholesale centers developed nearer home, they had to compete against established houses in the older cities. For these reasons the story of the wholesale trade for Mid-America involves treatment of the geography and commercial life of the entire eastern half of the United States.

1. Ward A. Dorrance, *The Survival of French in the Old District of Sainte Genevieve,* University of Missouri Studies, 10:2 (1935), 17.
2. For the rapid transformation that had occurred by 1820, see Solon J. Buck, *Illinois in 1818,* 147.

Around 1828 Philadelphia held first place among the seaboard cities in supplying Mid-America, with Baltimore a close second. In the same period Saint Louis was the leading wholesale center in Mid-America, a position gained by her relatively early development as a supply and factoring center for the fur trade, which followed the Missouri River into the Northwest, and further strengthened by her excellent connections by river with many of the smaller towns that were developing in the surrounding territory. Saint Louis could scarcely compare with Philadelphia and Baltimore, however, in the sense of being a real wholesale center, although her progress in that field was rapid during the following thirty years. New Orleans, too, by virtue of her advantages as trade center for grocery supplies, obtained a share of the wholesale orders of Western merchants in this early period.

New York had not seriously challenged Philadelphia's supremacy as yet, but by 1830 advantages of communication and growing industrialization indicated that she would soon supplant Philadelphia. Consequently, the story of wholesaling in Mid-America must take account of the growing importance of New York. By 1850 her merchants had gained a stronger position than Philadelphians in northern Illinois and Iowa, and they had begun to compete successfully for the trade in Missouri and southern Illinois. Conditions in the West had changed by 1850, too. Saint Louis was still the most important local supply center for Missouri and southern Illinois, but Chicago was disputing her ascendancy in Iowa and northern Illinois. The rise of Chicago had been phenomenal and presaged her still greater influence after the development of the railroad. On the basis of railroad transportation she later surpassed Saint Louis, but the railroad era also marked the end of pioneer merchandising. Therefore, the story of the mercantile rivalry between Saint Louis and Chicago in the railroad age lies beyond the scope of this study. Only New Orleans continued to hold unaltered her position as a leading grocery wholesale center from 1820 to 1850.

In addition to the great marketing centers, the growing cities along the Ohio River played an important part in the trade patterns of the area throughout the thirty-year period. Pittsburgh, Cincinnati, and Louisville were representative of the cities that obtained a share in the wholesale trade of Mid-America because of their location on the line of communication between the East and the West. Each enjoyed other special advantages as well, but the group as a whole prospered most because of location. Local Western merchants patronized these widely separated markets on the basis of their individual advantages, and all must be considered in the story of wholesaling.

In choosing a market in that early period a merchant, like his modern successor, patronized those cities where transportation costs, prices, and the services obtainable from wholesale houses were best. But outside of this similarity in the general factors determining the choice of a market it is difficult to find much comparison with modern wholesaling. If a present-day merchant were placed in charge of the retail business of a pioneer store, he would find his experience with modern stores decidedly helpful, but in replenishing his stock he would encounter many unfamiliar and frustrating circumstances. Accustomed to modern transportation methods, he would be at a loss to understand the differences in freight rates between various cities. He would learn that in many cases it was cheaper to buy in a market a thousand miles away than in one closer. Because of the cheapness of water transportation it was often possible for a city that was located on a river to dominate the trade of stores throughout the river's basin, while nearer wholesale centers that lacked water connections were unable to obtain any of the business.

Equally strange would be the need to buy the bulk of a year's supply at one time and the necessity to absent himself from home and business for six weeks or two months on trips to purchase goods. Because of the distance traveled by Western merchants, Jones compared them to the traders of antiquity, traveling to and from Baghdad, Babylon, and Nineveh.[3] From whatever angle it is approached, the story of Western wholesaling reveals a situation that modern conditions have completely altered—a transformation that also marked the end of the pioneer stage in Western merchandising.

THE RELATION OF EAST AND WEST

A striking factor in the records of Western merchants is their obvious reliance on Eastern firms for goods. So widespread and so nearly complete was this dependence that the wholesale business of Eastern cities seems to have been maintained primarily by Western commercial orders. This impression is false, for storekeepers in other eastern states and in the southern portion of the United States were also good customers of seaboard merchants, even in those periods when the West relied most heavily on them for goods. On the other hand, some students familiar with records of many of the larger Eastern firms maintain in all seriousness that Philadelphia and Baltimore were primarily Southern rather than Western in the twenties and thirties, in terms of trade connections. Such a view is almost as erroneous as to label their orientation exclusively Western; actually,

3. John Beauchamp Jones [Luke Shortfield], *The Western Merchant*, Preface.

these cities dominated both the Southern and the Western markets, though, admittedly, they devoted more attention to the South.

Many Eastern firms confined themselves almost wholly to trade in the South, continuing connections that in some cases extended back to colonial times. And for some unaccountable reasons the business records of such firms have been preserved in far greater numbers than the papers of commercial houses that traded with the West. As illustration are the records of Levi Coit, a New York commission merchant from 1796 to 1816, who handled cotton sales to England and the Continent and accepted goods on consignment for sale in the United States.[4] All his business connections were in the South, doubtless because of his interest in the cotton trade. Robert Garrett and Company of Baltimore was a wholesale grocery and commission firm, and orders for the year 1836, which was representative of their business, came almost wholly from the state of Virginia.[5] The Philadelphia firm of Hildeburn and Woolworth sold jewelry in Ohio and Kentucky. The company carried on a good business with merchants in the latter state by way of Pittsburgh, but made no extra effort to overcome unusual transportation problems involved on that route. Consequently, two Lexington, Kentucky, firms failed to receive a supply of jewelry in the winter of 1817–1818, since their orders failed to reach Pittsburgh before the river froze over for the winter.[6] On the other hand, the firm kept two salesmen traveling constantly in Virginia, both Carolinas, Maryland, and Georgia. These men carried a supply of jewelry for direct sale to retailers, took orders for the firm, and collected notes that were due. Mr. Hildeburn, one of the partners, sometimes went on the road himself with as much as $15,000 worth of goods. Obviously, this firm devoted more attention to Southern markets, sales in the West being too small to require maintaining a sales force there. Furthermore, it is probably more than mere coincidence that advertisements in Eastern papers addressed to Southern and Western trade frequently listed the word *Southern* before *Western*. This order in the lists obviously related to the markets' standing, so far as value was concerned.

Many other firms followed Hildeburn and Woolworth's practice of concentrating on the Southern and seaboard markets while devoting some—but less—attention to Western trade. When Temple and Smith, Philadelphia druggists, moved to a new location in 1819, they

4. Levi Coit, Letter Books, 1804–16.
5. Orders for 1836, in Corerspondence and Business Documents of the Garrett Family 1820–1880.
6. Letter from Hildeburn and Woolworth to Asa Blanchard at Lexington, Kentucky, dated Philalephia, December 26, 1817, Hildeburn and Woolworth Letter Book 1815–18.

notified their out-of-town customers of the change of address. It is difficult to identify many of the stores listed for notification of this change because their addresses are lacking, but those which can be identified were located in Alabama, Georgia, Virginia, Ohio, Pennsylvania, Kentucky, and Illinois.[7] Lippincott and Company, a wholesale drygoods and grocery firm in the same city, carried on the bulk of their business with merchants in Pennsylvania, Delaware, New Jersey, and Ohio, but occasionally they sent goods to firms located in Maryland, Virginia, and Illinois.[8] Obviously, such companies looked for only a minor share of their business in the West.

On the other hand, there is ample proof that the Western market was important to some Eastern wholesalers. Letters of the Philadelphia firm of Siter, Price and Company appear in the records of many Western stores, for examples, Jackson and Prewitt, E. D. Sappington and Company, James Aull, and the Lammes of Missouri. The American Fur Company relied on Siter, Price and Company for the conduct of much of their business in Philadelphia, as evidenced in Grace Lee Nute's catalogue of the papers of the fur company, which lists over eight hundred letters; in his treatment of Western merchandising, Jones used the notation "S. P. and Company" in listing the firms patronized by Western men. Although the papers of this company do not seem to have been preserved in the collection of any historical society, it was evidently a large firm that cultivated extensive interests in the West.

Eastern newspapers provide further proof of the substantial value of Western trade. One issue of the *Public Ledger* in Philadelphia in 1836 is representative of the interest in the West as displayed by merchants of that city: Two transportation companies advertised the merits of their systems for transporting merchandise to Pittsburgh, the chief city from which shipments were dispatched for the Mississippi Valley; J. and M. Saunders addressed their advertisement on straw bonnets directly to "southern and western merchants"; several dealers in gentlemen's silk hats invited "country merchants" to investigate their goods while in the city; the editorial section called attention to the fact that four lines of stages were operating daily between Philadelphia and Pittsburgh, with travel so heavy that passage had to be booked one or two weeks in advance. The editorial went on to state that March marked the time for the influx of Southern and Western merchants, for which the wholesalers of Philadelphia had prepared by the importation of great quantities of

7. Temple and Smith, Letter Book March 5, 1818, to November, 1828.
8. Directory 1845, Lippincott and Company Manuscript Collection.

goods.[9] Such references show that Western trade connections were considered of prime importance in the Quaker city.

New York newspapers reveal the same interest in Western markets. In the *Evening Post* in January, 1835, Adam W. Spies offered a list of hardware articles on accommodating terms to country merchants. Doremus, Sydan and Nixon informed the public that their large warehouses contained a fine stock of drygoods for Southern and Western trade, perhaps the best assortment ever offered.[10] Western merchants with silent partners in the East, like Christian Wilt at Saint Louis, naturally depended on the seaboard for goods, but the prevalence of advertisements designed to appeal to the West shows that the practice of making purchases on the seaboard was general among merchants from the frontier.

Substantiating evidence of Eastern commercial connections with the West are the related advertisements in Western newspapers, such as those which carried the caption, "Just received and opening from Philadelphia and New York . . ."; nor is the evidence confined solely to mercantile records and newspapers. Army officers, stationed at posts in the West and compelled to rely on merchants in their area for money, found that drafts on Eastern cities were ideal for transferring funds. The merchant willingly accepted such drafts, since they could be transmitted east to pay for merchandise purchased there. Thus, Lt. Edgar Birdfall, stationed at Fort Leavenworth in 1828, explained to the Quartermaster General that he was dependent on two merchants at Liberty, Missouri, for funds. As all merchants in that area bought their goods in Philadelphia, the privilege of giving drafts on the quartermaster at that city would effectually solve the money problem at Fort Leavenworth.[11]

The Eastern merchant could well afford to seek markets in the West, even though in the early years trade to the West was not as extensive as trade to the South. Although economically undeveloped, the back country was so vast in extent and total population that the annual value of merchandise shipped west reached an appreciable figure. As early as 1817, 13,000 wagons rolled into Pittsburgh from Philadelphia and Baltimore with goods for the West.[12] Contemporary writers estimated the value of goods purchased in the East and brought down the Ohio River at between $16 million and $17 mil-

9. Philadelphia *Public Ledger*, March 25, 1836.

10. New York *The Evening Post*, January 12, 1835.

11. Letter of Lt. Edgar Birdfall to the Quartermaster General at Washington, dated Fort Leavenworth, August 19, 1828, Post Records of Fort Leavenworth.

12. Emory R. Johnson and others, *History of Domestic and Foreign Commerce of the United States*, 215-16.

lion a year.[13] Nor did this figure include the value of the merchandise that came up the Mississippi River by way of New Orleans. The Census of 1840 listed a total investment of $17,969,734 in retail stores in the territory occupied by Illinois, Missouri, Arkansas, Wisconsin, Kentucky, and Michigan. This evaluation excludes the capital invested in commission houses and omits states like Ohio and Indiana that received at least part of their goods by way of the Ohio River. The figure includes buildings and fixtures as well as the stocks of goods, but, as pointed out before, buildings and fixtures bore no such heavy relation to total capital invested in merchandising as they do today. These figures therefore harmonize very well and describe an annual market of around $15 million in the West as early as 1840. The total capital investment in retail merchandising in Missouri, Illinois, and Iowa in 1840, according to census figures, was over $12 million, indicating that Mid-America constituted a sizable part of the Western market by that date. Such a figure was especially attractive to Eastern wholesalers in a period when the national market was still small.

Fortunately for the Eastern group, the Western storekeeper believed that he would profit by purchasing his goods directly in the East, a belief shared by his customers. Although Saint Louis was the most successful Western competitor of the East in the early years, merchants of the area complained bitterly against the high prices demanded by Saint Louis firms. Jones felt that prices were 15 to 20 per cent higher in Saint Louis than in Philadelphia and that, because of more favorable prices, customers would patronize a merchant who bought on the seaboard in preference to one who bought in Saint Louis.[14] His estimate of the higher charges in Saint Louis included full allowance for the additional expenses for transportation and insurance from the East. His conclusions might be doubted if other testimony did not support him, as his book was published in Philadelphia and he later made his home in the East, but there is ample testimony to corroborate his statements. James Aull at Lexington, Missouri, bought many small orders from Tracy and Wahrendorff at Saint Louis and had close personal relations with them. In a small order for tinware in 1830, however, he explained that he had bought such articles farther east for the last three years; the higher prices

13. H. S. Tanner, *The American Traveller; or Guide through the United States*, set the figure at $17,885,000, in 1818 (p. 118). The figure was placed at $16 million or better in James Hall's *The West: Its Commerce and Navigation*, 145.

14. Jones, *The Western Merchant*, 130-31.

demanded in Saint Louis prevented his switching his orders to his friends there.[15]

The editor of the *Missouri Intelligencer* at Franklin, Missouri, in an editorial on April 8, 1823, explained that the current issue was printed on paper purchased from a Saint Louis merchant at $6 a ream—clearly, from the tone of the editorial, a higher price than he was accustomed to pay. He cited this price as an example of how the merchants at Saint Louis had "notoriously beaten" the printers of the state on paper prices. Consequently, the editor had made a permanent arrangement with an Eastern manufacturer for a supply of paper, far superior in quality and at least a third cheaper.

The increases in prices were cumulative: "A Citizen of Pike County" in 1822 wrote a letter to the same editor, complaining of his treatment by merchants in Franklin. He had made the trip to Franklin from a "remote part of the state," with a view to purchasing merchandise. But everything sold for double and sometimes three times the price asked to the eastward, and, in spite of such prices, the merchants would not take state paper money unless the unhappy customer was willing to sacrifice half its face value. "If this is the way I am to be imposed upon by your country shavers they may keep their goods and I will keep my money."[16] Merchants in small towns accused Saint Louis merchants of being Shylocks, and they in turn were characterized in similar vein by their customers. Although the targets for criticism varied, discontented buyers agreed that prices were lower to the eastward, even taking into account the additional costs of transporting the goods west.

The depth of customers' resentment is well illustrated by the advertisements that appeared in newspapers in Illinois. Saint Louis firms advertised widely in the papers in that area, as evidenced by one issue of *The Galenian*, which contained advertisements of Vairin and Reel, Runis and Cornwell, Holton, Brooks, Sproule and Buchanan, Henry Shaw, and Bull, Caseday and Taylor—all Saint Louis firms.[17] This patronage came in part from the hope of increased retail sales, but the firms were interested primarily in attracting wholesale business.

On the other hand, there were notices by men like John Hogan, who was engaged in business at Edwardsville, Illinois, and who ran large advertisements in the local paper. He emphasized the fact that

15. Letter of James Aull to Tracy and Wahrendorff at Saint Louis, dated Lexington, Missouri, June 21, 1830, Letter Book B, James and Robert Aull Manuscript Collection.

16. Franklin *Missouri Intelligencer*, March 6, 1822.

17. Galena (Illinois) *The Galenian*, May 16, 1832.

his goods were freshly purchased in Philadelphia and comprised a large and well-selected stock, personally chosen by the proprietor.[18] Hogan wanted his customers to know that he bought in the East, thus playing up to the popular idea that Saint Louis wholesalers could not compete with Eastern firms. Still a third type of advertisement appeared in the press in that region, illustrated by the notice of C. B. Fletcher's store. This advertisement occupied a whole cclumn in the paper and minutely listed the goods "just received." The origin of the goods was not an element of the notice, however.[19] Here was a firm that probably made its wholesale purchases in Saint Louis. The large advertisement and the continued policy of advertising mark it as a reasonably successful store. Nevertheless, it was unwilling to reveal the origin of its goods, thereby hoping, one suspects, to escape criticism by its customers for not buying in the East. The patterns of these advertisements appear in the files of newspapers throughout southern Illinois: the merchants who bought on the seaboard emphasized the source of their goods as a selling point in their announcements; those who bought their stocks nearer home avoided mention of that fact.

Even Saint Louis merchants doubted the cheapness of their own wholesale market. Early in his business career, John O'Fallon traded up the Missouri River, but family connections and a later business establishment in the town place him primarily as a citizen of Saint Louis. In a letter in 1819 he expressed the conviction that he could save "some thousands of dollars" by buying directly in New York and Philadelphia. Another year he expected to be able to buy his supplies personally in the East and in New Orleans. In the meantime he was seeking some way of obtaining $20,000 worth of goods from the East for the current season.[20]

Most merchants who bought in the East went directly to the markets and personally selected their goods. It was of course impossible to buy in one trip all the goods needed for twelve months, but such supplies as failed to last the year out or were needed to meet unexpected demands could be obtained by letter. Two letters of James Wier, a merchant of Lexington, Kentucky, illustrate this practice and also indicate why a merchant considered it so necessary to select personally his major stock. In July of 1817 Wier sent a small order for shoes to an Eastern firm, explaining that it was impossible for him to make the trip just at that time. His previous order for

18. Edwardsville *Illinois Advocate*, June 5, 1832.
19. Vandalia *Illinois Intelligencer*, April 6, 1826.
20. John O'Fallon to Dennis Fitzhugh at Louisville, Kentucky, dated St. Louis, July 11, 1819, John O'Fallon Papers.

shoes had been acceptable in every way, except those made of kid, which were to have been black instead of just colored. Still, he was well pleased, as indicated by his request to include anything in the "fashion of shoes" that appeared to be in demand in the Kentucky market. Such action would prevent any competing merchant who had found it possible to go east from returning with some new style that might capture the local trade. The letter indicated Wier's full confidence in the judgment of his wholesaler.

Again, in July of 1818 Wier found it necessary to place some small orders by mail, but within three months he was ready to do battle over the unjust deal, as he saw it, that he had received. In remitting $500 to the wholesaler Wier remarked that the sum did not represent his returns on the goods for which he was paying. They had proved unsuitable for the market, were not what he had ordered, and had cost 25 per cent more than other articles in the same line for sale in Lexington, Kentucky. Other merchants had advised him to return the goods, and he considered himself "very silly" for not having followed their advice, for the loss on one box alone was between $300 and $400. Under such conditions the wholesaler need not be surprised if he received no more remittances until Wier could come in person to the East.[21]

Such an experience naturally made a merchant wary of ordering by mail, especially if the order was for his major supply of goods for the next twelve months. If his stock failed to meet the requirements of the local market, the misfortune might ruin him, for a mistake on a wholesale order of $10,000 seriously endangered stores that were operating on limited capital. These considerations were reinforced by others. Goods had to be shipped a great distance, most of the route being unimproved and dangerous. Carelessness at Pittsburgh in the selection of a boat might raise the freight rate so high as to wipe out any prospect of profit from the sale of the goods. Insurance might be neglected or inadequate, and the whole cargo lost in transit down the Ohio. While the presence of the owner could not automatically eliminate such dangers, the greater care exercised in handling the goods when he accompanied them served to lessen the possibility of accidents.

The drawbacks to making the trip were many, however. A merchant could not hope to go east, buy a supply of goods, and accompany them home in less than six weeks—and six weeks was the minimum time required, even after the river improvements had been

21. Letter of James Wier to Conrad and Kelly at Philadelphia, dated Lexington, Kentucky, July 22, 1817, and letter to J. Adams Knox at Philadelphia, dated September 4, 1818, James Wier, Letter Book 1816–24.

made and canals built. As late as 1837 the arrival of goods at Saint Louis in two weeks' time from Baltimore was considered an event worthy of mention in the newspapers. A mercantile firm there had received ten packages that had been freighted from Baltimore to Wheeling in eight days; the remainder of the journey consumed only six more. The editor of the paper pointed out that the Baltimore and Wheeling Transportation Company was maintaining eight-day service between those two cities, and he suggested that a merchant now could reasonably expect to receive goods in two weeks' time. But he admitted that neglect and delay on the direct route in former years had caused some to prefer the circuitous all-water route by way of New Orleans.[22]

As goods could be brought from Wheeling to Saint Louis by water, two weeks' service to Saint Louis was much better time than merchants off the water routes could expect; but Saint Louis merchants learned that bad road conditions between Baltimore and Wheeling or other difficulties often lengthened the time of delivery far beyond the two-week period. Furthermore, the trip east consumed two weeks and the purchase of supplies another two weeks. With the best of luck, the trip required six weeks' absence from business at home. A few miscalculations or some bad luck could easily extend the time to two or three months. Added to the cost of time lost from business at home was the expense involved in making the journey. For instance, the direct trip from Saint Louis to Philadelphia, including all expenses, was estimated by Hall at $55. To go by steamboat and packet by way of New Orleans was even more expensive in money as well as time, since the fare was around $65.[23] The transportation expenses of $100 and better for the round trip were only part of the total cost, which necessarily included hotel bills, clothing, clerk hire, and unforeseen contingencies. The whole expense for buying in the East could easily reach $300 or $400.

As has been indicated, it was not absolutely necessary to visit the seaboard personally in order to obtain supplies from that section. Merchants frequently relied on acquaintances in a nearby town to make their purchases. E. D. Sappington and Company of Jonesboro, Missouri, bought supplies in Philadelphia and frequently filled orders for other merchants. Sappington seems to have purchased goods for some of his friends without charging them for the service. A memorandum of stock obtained in March of 1835 included the initials of a number of firms and the amounts bought for them, with

22. Editorial from the St. Louis *Republican*, quoted in *DuBuque* (Wisconsin Territory) *Visitor*, July 27, 1837.
23. Hall, *The West*, 363-65.

no indication of any additional charges. Thus, for "R&E" he filled an order for $1,307.69 at Siter, Price and Company's store in Philadelphia. Others were charged a 20 per cent advance on Philadelphia goods and an additional 5 per cent if they did not pay Sappington cash on delivery. The firm of Ringo and Allison commissioned him to buy $3,320.49 worth of merchandise for them and paid him $664.09, or 20 per cent, for buying and shipping the goods.[24] Ringo and Allison paid cash and avoided the extra charge. Even those transactions for which Sappington exacted no charges brought advantages to him. As he was able to buy on six months' time, without interest, in the Philadelphia markets, direct cash payments for goods brought west for other firms actually permitted him the use of their capital for six months without cost. Purchasing for other companies cost him no additional labor, and by increasing the total amount of his purchases, he was probably able to obtain his own merchandise at a reduction and to enhance his status with the wholesale houses in Philadelphia. While it is probable that the charge of 20 per cent covered little more than the cost of transportation and insurance, Sappington clearly derived profit from his enhanced financial position.

By 1845 companies were devoting much time to the purchase of goods for merchants who preferred not to undertake the journey to the seaboard. Henshaw and Shaw, wholesale grocers in Chicago, advertised such a service. They were willing to enter into contracts with responsible grocers in that city to execute orders for groceries and spirits in the East. These would be delivered in Chicago at actual cost, plus the freight rate and a commission of 5 per cent. The company pointed out that it would not be competing with retail grocers in the Chicago market, as its business was confined exclusively to wholesaling. Since it purchased directly from importers and employed competent judges to do the buying, it claimed to be able to deliver goods to Chicago retailers at less than such firms could buy them in the East.[25]

All these factors played a part in the merchant's decision for or against a personal trip east. He considered the seaboard cities to be the best market for goods, and he knew the advantages of personally selecting his stock. On the other hand, the journey required expenditures of time and money that cut heavily into any saving he might make by purchasing in the East. These considerations were especially cogent if the quantity of goods was small. The interaction of such considerations caused some to go and others to remain at home.

24. Memorandum of purchases by E. D. Sappington and Company in 1835, Governor M. M. Marmaduke Manuscript Collection.
25. Chicago *Daily Journal*, April 12, 1845.

References to purchases in the seaboard cities in the advertisements of the period indicate that, despite the cost in time, money, and possible mismanagement of their business at home, at least a third of the Western storekeepers decided to travel to the markets. An estimate based on the business records of stores where the origin of goods can be determined would be even higher—three-fourths of the Western merchants that left such papers bought their goods personally in the East. Such estimates must be viewed with reservations, however, for only the larger firms advertised generally and left business papers as a record for later times, and these were the merchants that were most likely to buy in the East.

THE EASTERN MARKETS

The widespread conviction on the part of merchant and customer alike that the Eastern wholesale markets were the best places to buy goods resulted from a number of advantages of the seaboard cities. Fundamentally, these centers were the source of supply for the wholesale houses in the West. Consequently, when a Western merchant bought goods from a local wholesaler, he paid a middleman's profit, for the goods had originally been purchased on the seaboard. If he personally went east he could eliminate the middleman and his charges. Most of the Eastern firms had direct connections with business houses in England and on the Continent, which put them in a favored position for purchasing foreign goods. Hildeburn and Woolworth, for example, sent one of the members of the firm to England annually to purchase jewelry. By 1825 Brown Brothers and Company had stores in Baltimore, Philadelphia, and New York, with a branch located in Liverpool to supply merchandise to their American outlets.[26] Americans preferred English goods, and because the seaboard cities had the best facilities for obtaining them, the Eastern firms were at a decided advantage in satisfying this preference.

Foreign firms frequently did not wait for American merchants to establish connections with them but chose to dispose of their goods by means of auctions in seaboard cities. Because the practice prevented Eastern merchants from securing complete control of the import trade and brought certain negative influences to bear on the stability of prices, the auctions were widely opposed by American businessmen. Nevertheless, auctions continued to flourish, and advertisements of sales to be made by that means can be found in Eastern

26. Victor H. Paltists, "Business Records of Brown Brothers and Company, New York—1825–1880," *Bulletin of the New York Public Library*, 40 (1936), 495-99.

newspapers as late as the Civil War. Every Eastern city had a large group of auctioneers, and these men were well known in European circles. Some foreign houses, if the aggregate of their business justified the expense, maintained agents in the American cities. Goods to be sold at auction would be consigned to the agent or directly to an auctioneer, and the auctioneer then advertised the goods in the daily papers. Gill, Ford and Company's announcement is typical. They advertised 250 packages of fresh, imported British drygoods for sale at their auction rooms at ten o'clock on Friday morning, January 1, 1830; six months' credit would be allowed on purchases. The advertisement enumerated the type and quality of goods in the consignment, explained that sample packages would be open for examination the day preceding the sale, and stated that a catalogue of the goods was available for prospective purchasers.[27] Some advertisements specified cash terms and others occasionally allowed twelve months' time for payment; ninety days to six months were the usual terms, however. Not all auctions gave the customer an opportunity to examine the goods, and frequently no catalogue was issued for the convenience of buyers.

Auctions were not limited to Eastern cities but operated throughout the country. One issue of a Saint Louis paper in 1820 contained announcements of four local auction and commission firms. For example, Owen McKenna advertised auctions on Tuesday, Thursday, and Saturday for merchandise, real estate, and furniture, with McKenna's agreement to advance money on goods deposited for immediate sale.[28] But auction firms located in inland cities had no opportunity to make original sales of foreign merchandise; their business was limited almost entirely to produce from the farms and consignments from American manufacturers. Occasionally the stock of some bankrupt merchant would be sold at auction, and good bargains were then available. In general, however, Western auctions never attained the popularity of those held in the East.

Bills were introduced in Congress as early as 1820 to eliminate auctions, a move supported by Eastern wholesalers. When Congress failed to grant their demands, the merchants turned to the practice of criticizing auctions to their prospective customers. They argued that auctioneers never allowed completion of a sale for a low bid. The auctioneer, always in control of the sale, prevented goods' going for an unfavorable price by allowing members of the auction firm to bid in the offering when the price bid was low. Storekeepers also insisted to their wavering customers that only inferior goods were

27. Philadelphia *Poulson's American Daily Advertiser*, January 1, 1830.
28. St. Louis *Missouri Gazette and Public Advertiser*, July 5, 1820.

offered at auction and that the purchaser, therefore, made no real saving. This latter argument found its way into current usage in Mid-America, as illustrated in the argument of Jones against the goods of a new competitor. He charged that his rival had bought "tender goods," or seconds, at auction in Saint Louis. Such arguments had a deterring effect on customers who had been tempted by savings at auctions, according to Jones.[29]

The private papers of Eastern merchants clearly show why they feared the competition of auctions. In 1813 Joseph Hertzog was able to buy flints at auction $3 under the wholesale price anywhere in the East.[30] Hildeburn and Woolworth of Philadelphia became much disturbed in 1816 over the sale at auction of watches manufactured by the firm from which they customarily bought their stock in England. The watches were sold for cash at $5 less than the wholesale price Hildeburn and Woolworth had paid. Even though they maintained drummers in the Southern states, such prices were beyond competition. They complained to the English firm that sale at auction cheapened the watches in the eyes of the public. If the manufacturers would be lenient with credit and limit the sale of watches to their firm only, they were sure their Western and Southern connections would provide a profitable market.[31] Here, apparently, was the crux of the matter. Auction prices could not be equaled by established Eastern houses. The only solution, then, was to put such sales in the worst possible light.

The efforts to eliminate auctions were fruitless, for the same situation prevailed twenty years later. In 1837 Lewis and Company at Philadelphia had drygoods on consignment from a New York City firm for private sale. In a letter in September of that year they advised letting the goods go at auction. To have taken such a step a month earlier would have been wise, as thousands of pieces had sold at auction in the interval. The letter offered no hope of obtaining the price wanted by the New York firm and explained that auctions were too well supplied for private sales to move goods.[32]

Such statements of course represent the strongest case for auctions. In spite of their advantages, however, the fact remains that Eastern merchants continued in business in competition with them. Indeed,

29. Jones, *The Western Merchant*, 131.

30. Letter of Joseph Hertzog to Andrew Wilt at Pittsburgh, dated Philadelphia, June 12, 1813, Joseph Hertzog, Letters.

31. Letter of Hildeburn and Woolworth to an unnamed English firm, dated Philadelphia, August 6, 1816, Hildeburn and Woolworth Letter Book 1815–18.

32. Letter of Lewis and Company to Elisha Riggs at New York City, dated Philadelphia, September 14, 1837, Riggs Family Papers.

auctions served as one of the chief sources of supply for Eastern wholesale houses. For instance, Hamilton and Hood, Philadelphia wholesale grocers, bought tea at auction from ships arriving direct from China and sold it to other firms along the seaboard. Through this means they purchased tea for Dinsmore Kyle and Company at Baltimore in 1825, who probably sold it to Western merchants.[33]

Competition from auction sales held down the prices asked by established seaboard wholesalers. The Western merchants, whose visits to the East were limited to two weeks, could hardly hope to purchase all their goods at auction, but some were able to buy stock in this manner, as advertisements in Western papers claimed. So, whether they bought from the Eastern wholesaler or at auction, they were purchasing on a market that was highly competitive. It was also a market in close contact with English and continental factories, an advantage Western wholesalers did not enjoy.

A liberal credit policy was another factor that persuaded merchants to buy their stocks in the East. Western merchants who had been able to build a good business on credit that an Eastern wholesaler had extended to them continued buying in the East because of past courtesies, even after Western markets had developed to the point where they could offer similar arrangements. Better prices could be negotiated if the merchant had money to pay cash, of course; in both East and West, a cash transaction reduced prices as much as 25 per cent. Joseph Hertzog at Philadelphia preached this idea to his partner at Saint Louis. Joseph was "quite disgusted" with buying goods on credit, for one could never make more than 50 per cent profit on items purchased in that manner. He advised his partner to develop the reputation of offering goods cheaply for cash and not to hesitate to "lay it on in proportion" when the customer needed credit. Hertzog himself sold wholesale orders on credit at the same price he obtained at retail—otherwise, he wrote, bad debts and expenses would have ruined him. On cash sales, however, he reduced prices as low as any of his competitors.[34] Much of Hertzog's preaching on a theme universally accepted as true came from the hope of spurring his young Western partner to making remittances rapidly enough to keep the Saint Louis store supplied with goods bought for cash. But exhortations were not sufficient. In this case, as in most others, the firm was able to purchase some supplies for cash, but most of the goods

33. Letter of Hamilton and Hood to Dinsmore Kyle and Company at Baltimore, dated Philadelphia, March 30, 1825, Hamilton and Hood, Letter Book, 1824–39.

34. Letters of Joseph Hertzog to Christian Wilt at St. Louis, dated Philadelphia, September 12, 1811, and April, 1812, Joseph Hertzog, Letters.

were bought on credit. Any wholesale center that refused credit to its customers lost its business in a short time.

The usual arrangement was six months' credit, with the bill payable in twelve. No interest was charged for the first six months, but 6 per cent was collected if the account ran into the second six months of grace. Before credit bureaus developed, it was impossible to keep an accurate rating on merchants who lived 1,000 miles from the seaboard. Men who were traveling east for the first time generally carried letters of recommendation from other merchants who were known to the wholesale houses—the chief way of determining a customer's reliability. For example, Hicks, Jenkins and Company of New York City were well acquainted with James Wier of Lexington, Kentucky, having dealt with him satisfactorily for some time. Robert Worth, a merchant who lived in Wier's locality, called on them for goods and asked credit on the usual terms. In answer to their inquiry about Worth, Wier characterized him as "a steady, honest, upright man." He possessed some property, and his father was a wealthy farmer. Wier believed Worth would do his best to fulfill any engagements entered into in the East.[35] Such a recommendation was generally sufficient for the purchase of a large stock of goods in the early days. According to Jones, a man's reputation for honesty and his familiarity with the conduct of Western business were sufficient to obtain credit in the East.

In the thirties, however, credit rating bureaus began to develop. Shortly after 1837 a Mr. Church established a bureau in New York City to serve wholesalers who desired information on out-of-town customers. About 1840 the first mercantile reference book was issued. Others soon followed, and for years the competition was keen.[36] A more detailed report of credit investigations appears on pages 147-49.

Papers of Western merchants bear testimony to the wide practice of buying on credit. E. D. Sappington and his various partners usually sought credit terms. Early in the history of the company S. and J. Tarns of Philadelphia credited them for a large bill of glassware, as did Montelius and Fuller of the same city for a drygoods order totaling $1,200. The arrangement was a note signed by the partners, payable in six months. Their orders in Philadelphia in 1835 exceeded $3,500, on credit for six months without interest and on interest-bearing notes for the next six months. On some of their accounts they paid the interest in advance, knowing that the note would

35. Letter of James Wier to Hicks, Jenkins and Company at New York City, dated Lexington, Kentucky, February 1, 1816, James Wier, Letter Books.
36. Paul H. Nystrom, *Economics of Retailing*, I, 92.

necessarily run for the full twelve months. One such instance was their account with Everly and Rees at Philadelphia in 1832.[37]

In some cases Eastern houses bore down heavily on credit collections. Temple and Smith at Philadelphia gave 5 to 10 per cent discount for cash payments in an endeavor to foster that method of doing business. They also firmly adhered to the policy of not granting more than six months' credit. Letters asking for longer time and explaining why goods could not be sold within six months were politely but firmly answered with the statement that longer credit was not the policy of the company. In addition, the company threatened delinquent debtors with legal action. For instance, Dr. J. Congor of Shawneetown, Illinois, bought drugs in March of 1818 on six months' credit. A year later the bill was unpaid. Temple and Smith wrote Congor a short, direct notice to pay the bill if he desired to prevent legal action being taken.[38] In general, however, Eastern houses veered as far in the direction of liberality as possible.

Liberal credit terms were not the only means used to persuade merchants to become customers. Wholesalers in the seaboard cities also promoted the development of their business by careful attention to the wants of customers and through the extension of courtesies to merchants who traded with them. Temple and Smith, while strict on credit arrangements, well represent wholesalers who were eager to attract Western trade. They extended every courtesy in their power to customers who dealt with them, even permitting some to draw on the company to meet small bills to other houses in the city. When they learned of a new store in their trade area they immediately wrote to the owner to solicit his business. A few weeks before a customer was to travel eastward to buy supplies, he received a letter that asked for a renewal of his past patronage. A customer who had not given them an order for a year or so might receive in the mail a list of the firm's current prices.

During the period when Western merchants were in town, many firms kept a display of goods in the hotels the storekeepers patronized. "Drummers" or "borers" were stationed at these hotels by some companies to represent their respective firms and to urge merchants to examine the goods of their employers, a practice that some Western men disliked.[39] The custom of putting men on the road in the West can be traced to the assignment of drummers to the hotels

37. Memorandums of orders by E. D. Sappington and his partners, Marmaduke Collection.

38. Letter of Temple and Smith, to Dr. J. Congor at Shawneetown, Illinois, dated Philadelphia, March 20, 1819, Temple and Smith, Letter Book.

39. Jones, *The Western Merchant*, 168.

where Western merchants stopped. The next logical step was to send out salesmen, a practice that started before the period under consideration ended, although it did not become general until after the Civil War.[40]

One of the greatest advantages of purchasing in the East was the wider selection of goods. As early as 1820 many seaboard firms confined themselves to wholesaling in only a few lines. At the same time, Western stores sold their goods at both wholesale and retail and tried to carry goods of every kind—a policy that required investment of large amounts of capital. Should the merchant lack sufficient resources, he could limit the quantity and range of articles in his stock. Such a solution did not eliminate a company from the wholesale trade completely, however, even in the East. Weems and Rawlings carried on a wholesale and retail business in Philadelphia around 1820, and their day book shows sales ranging from $5 to $1,000.[41] An unidentified firm in Philadelphia in the same period sold goods all over the South and as far west as Ohio, many orders running from $400 to $700. For April 4, 1818, the company's day book records a Cincinnati house's order for $400 of goods; the next sale listed in the book was to "Beaula Mirely (fishwoman)," who bought 2 shawls at a total cost of $9.[42]

As might be judged, because of their earlier establishment and broader opportunities and experiences, the wholesale houses in the East were larger and more specialized than those in the West. Order books of Western merchants show that they drew upon this specialization in choosing supplies. Thus, when E. D. Sappington bought his goods in 1835, the orders were distributed among a number of houses—hats and caps from Marseilles and Martin; drygoods from Montelius and Fuller and from Dickson; drugs from Farr and Kunzep; groceries and spices from Robert Toland; fine goods from Hallowell and Ashbridge; and a general selection of drygoods from Siter, Price and Company.[43] James Aull of Lexington, Missouri, pursued the same policy in placing orders amounting to $20,000 in 1830: drygoods from J. and M. Brown, J. N. and L. Dickson, Siter, Price and Company, Davis, Sheppard and Jones, and Toland and Magoffin; fine goods from W. P. and T. N. Bryans, Charles Harkness, and Gill and Ferguson; luxury goods from Chapron and Nedelet; fine hats from Charles Toland and Company; fine combs from Smith and Poultney; combs and cards from Adam Everly and Son; books from Uriah

40. Nystrom, *Retailing*, I, 94.
41. James N. Weems and Benjamin Rawlings, Day Book 1818–22.
42. Day Book E 1817–18, of an unidentified Philadelphia firm.
43. Memorandum of purchases by E. D. Sappington, Marmaduke Collection.

Hunt; bow strings from William Camm; shoes from Joshua C. Oliver and Company; saddles from John Fairbairn; hats from Abner Elmes; medicine from Isaac Thompson; and tableware from L. and J. Tams.[44] Aull employed Siter, Price and Company to handle orders sent by mail and called on them for many favors during the course of the year. In spite of a close personal relationship with this company, he bought less than $3,000 worth of goods from them in 1830. Firms that specialized in definite lines could quote better prices, and good business sense compelled him to place his orders with those firms, despite his long and friendly association with Siter, Price and Company. The competition was even sharper for Western wholesalers, and it remained so until conditions in that region permitted specialization and concentration on the wholesaling of one line.

One of the most obvious tests of the comparative value of wholesale markets is price. The determination of actual prices that prevailed in separate markets and a fair comparison of these in the period under review is almost impossible, however. For one factor, weather conditions made the prices of goods fluctuate. Merchants at Saint Louis charged higher wholesale prices just before the ice broke up on the rivers than at any other period during the year, since the supply of goods had dwindled by that time. The following table is an illustration of that fact:

Wholesale Prices in St. Louis, Missouri, 1834[45]

Article	Price on January 9	Price on February 13
Coffee	16½ - 17	14 - 15
Sugar, New Orleans	9½ - 10	8½ - 9
Sugar, white	12 - 19	12 - 13
Cut nails	6½ - 7½	7½ - 8
Young Hyson tea	90 - 1.00	80 - 1.00

As the table indicates, all prices dropped in a period of just over a month, with the exception of cut nails, which advanced in price. Nails were usually purchased in Pittsburgh, and boats had not as yet arrived with a new supply to replenish the stock depleted by sales during the winter. The other articles came from New Orleans, and,

44. Memorandum of purchases by James Aull, Invoice Book D, Aull Collection.
45. Wholesale prices quoted in St. Louis *The Farmers' and Mechanics Advocate*, January 9 and February 13, 1834. The table is in cents per pound.

as the ice broke up early in the winter of 1834, boats had brought in the fresh supplies by February 13. Merchants who lived in Mid-America could buy supplies in Saint Louis as late as April and still get them home in time for the spring trade. If they went east, however, purchases had to be made earlier to allow time for transportation. To compare Saint Louis prices with Eastern prices in the period when merchants were going East for their stocks would give the advantage to the Eastern market. The only fair comparison should be made when the wholesale trade was at its height in each place, a period that is difficult to determine with any accuracy.

To add to the difficulty of comparing the markets equitably, the lists of wholesale prices published in the papers do not give a true picture of prices that actually prevailed in the market. As was pointed out in the discussion of auctions, prices quoted for goods on consignment or for sale by private houses did not define the market. Goods might be going at auction for 20 per cent less than the price asked at private sale. It would, therefore, be misleading to assume that, because calico was quoted at 30¢ in both New York and Saint Louis, one could buy as cheaply in one market as in the other. At one of the New York auctions calico might be purchased for a third less. Cash prices varied in separate markets, thereby adding to the problem of comparison. Furthermore, transportation costs probably played a greater part in the success or failure of a wholesale market than did the prices that prevailed there.

A list of the prices quoted in various markets at the same time offers some interesting data, however, as illustrated in the following table.

Wholesale Prices Current in Various Cities, December 23, 1837[46]

Article	St. Louis	Cincinnati	New York	New Orleans
Beeswax	18	18 - 20	20 - 22	22 - 23
Sperm candles	45 - 46	38	30 - 31	36 - 37
Mould candles	16	13 - 14	12 - 14	18 - 19
Coffee	14 - 16	13 - 14	9 - 15	9 - 12
Cotton yarns	34 - 35	29 - 35	18 - 26	- - - -
Juniata iron	150	140	100	100
Cut nails	9	8 - 9	6½ - 7	7 - 8
Brown sugar	8 - 9	7 - 8	7 - 8½	5 - 7
Havana sugar	16 - 17	- - - -	11 - 12	13
Imperial Gunpowder tea	80 - 90	68 - 85	55 - 100	70 - 73

46. St. Louis *Missouri Argus*, December 23, 1837. The table is in cents per pound, except for Juniata iron, which is based on dollars per ton.

This table demonstrates the difficulty of comparing prices with any accuracy, since the Cincinnati and Saint Louis prices shown are higher than they would be later in the year. It does give some significant information, however. For example, beeswax is the only article in which Saint Louis shows a price advantage—2¢ lower than in other markets; other prices were higher, since beeswax was a product of the Mississippi Valley and entered the market at Saint Louis. Its low price is indicative of the influence of freight rates on the prices of commodities. These charges generally totaled around one-fourth of the value of the goods if the supplies were brought all the way from the seaboard. Thus, as one looks at Cincinnati and Saint Louis prices, it should be borne in mind that they are high, in part, because they include freight charges. The low price on beeswax alone illustrates the fact that Mississippi Valley wholesale houses bought most of their goods at a distance, generally on the seaboard, and had no easy, direct contact with manufacturers. Naturally, the costs of bringing the goods so far inland increased prices. Other items worth noting on the table are prices on brown sugar and coffee at New Orleans. These explain why New Orleans controlled a large share of the wholesale grocery business in the Mississippi Valley. In other respects, New York prices held the advantage, especially on cotton yarn. Comparative quotations on other items in the drygoods line would reveal the same story, since close contact with European manufacturers benefited the Eastern wholesalers.

In sum, the Eastern markets held certain well-defined advantages over the Western. Closer contact with European firms permitted them to profit through European trade, except in the matter of auctions. Even in that respect, the conduct of sales provided broader opportunities for Eastern businessmen, since commission and auctioneering firms comprised a large segment of the commercial group along the seaboard. Cheap prices, liberal credit policies, close attention to the needs of customers, and large stocks of goods from which to make selections added to their supremacy. With such advantages to offer, it is easy to understand why they drew storekeepers to their markets from the farthest reaches of the frontier.

THE DIVISION OF TRADE AMONG EASTERN CITIES

Baltimore and Philadelphia shared the larger part of the trade with Mid-America around 1820, although, of the two, the latter city easily held first rank. The explanation for Philadelphia's and Baltimore's dominance is, in part, the pattern of migration toward the west. Kentucky and Tennessee, the first states to draw large migrations, were closer to Baltimore and Philadelphia than to New York, and trade for the region naturally went to the closest markets. Missouri was settled preponderantly by Kentuckians, and merchants retained their connections with wholesalers in Philadelphia. To some extent, the same influence operated in southern Illinois, the section most densely populated when that state entered the Union. Furthermore, southern Illinois and Missouri were closer to Philadelphia and Baltimore than to New York, and, in view of the freight rates, the reduction of mileage brought a more or less substantial reduction in costs. Thus, Mid-America was for a time outside the New York trade orbit. Philadelphia had an advantage, too, in that her industrial organization was equal, if not superior, to that of any other seaboard city of 1820, and she maintained her leadership for at least two more decades. By 1840, however, New York City was making such inroads on her markets that, for a time, it seemed that New York might secure a monopoly of Western trade.

A number of factors contributed to this shift in dominance of the Western markets. By 1840 the population of the upper Mississippi Valley had burgeoned, and that region had, from early days, been a market for goods from New York. Merchants in Michigan, Wisconsin, and northern Illinois had increased their purchases at a rapid rate in the twenty-year period, a growth that provided New York with a greatly expanded wholesale trade. One might argue that there was no shift, since Philadelphia held her markets; New York's growth resulted from the increase in population and trade in an established marketing area rather than from former customers of the Philadelphia merchants. Still, New York's market continued to grow at an alarming rate, so far as Philadelphia was concerned. According to Ritter, the change came in part from New York City's harbor being more open during the winter months. This circumstance caused several Philadelphia silk houses to move to New York City, as did the ribbon house of Bruggiere and Tessiere.[47] Another factor was the discovery of anthracite coal in Pennsylvania, which diverted investors' attention and money to the development of mining. Mining and manufacturing now competed with wholesaling for the use of Philadelphia's capital.

The greatest factor, by all odds, in the shift in dominance of markets was the opening of the Erie Canal. Its completion made possible the shipment of goods directly from the Eastern markets to the Great Lakes, whence rates were cheap to northern Illinois. Merchants located farther south in the Mississippi Valley could now bring goods from New York City to Pittsburgh, their chief shipping

47. Abraham Ritter, *Philadelphia and Her Merchants*, 23.

point, by means of canal—an all-water route except for eight miles over land. Freight rates immediately tumbled, some to as low as one-tenth of their cost before the canal was completed. Here was a new and effective factor in the competition for markets, and, while other cities along the seaboard had not been passive concerning the prospect of cheaper freight rates via the new route, they were not able to develop a system of communication with the interior quite equal to the Erie Canal.

The effect of such improvements in transportation is clear when one considers the difficulties of communication between Philadelphia and Pittsburgh in an earlier period. The shortest distance between those two cities was only 240 miles, but herculean efforts were required to move goods by land. Freight rates were so high that low-priced goods could not bear the transportation costs on that route and were sent by way of New Orleans. Elias Fordham paid $7.50 per 100 pounds to have his baggage transported from Philadelphia to Pittsburgh in 1817, the prevailing rate for some years to come. Sturdy Conestoga wagons made the trip in sixteen days, traveling from 12 to 20 miles a day. Fordham was impressed by the strength of the wagons and the feats of driving performed by the freighters. It was a marvel to him to see wagons "scrambling over the hills" where English vehicles would have been dashed to pieces. And even though he was paying a high price to have his luggage carried, the freighters did not hesitate to ask him to put a shoulder against the wagons on the down grade to keep them from upsetting.[48] Despite the dangers, risks, and difficulties, several million dollars' worth of goods passed over that route in the early period. Western merchants simply added the large carrying charges to the price of goods when they reached their destination.

Obviously, any seaboard city that could devise a route that would reduce the difficulties and thereby the freight rates to the regions beyond the Allegheny barrier stood an excellent chance of winning most of the Western trade. Baltimore began to cut into Philadelphia's supremacy as early as 1818, when the new National Road was opened from Cumberland to Wheeling, Virginia. From that time on, many merchants freighted their goods to Wheeling on the Ohio River and completed the journey by water. To retain its commerce Philadelphia started a series of canals as early as 1826 and finished the main line in 1834. When completed, the project was over 300 miles long. Canals constituted the system, except in the mountains where, on inclined planes several hundred feet high, the canal boats

48. Elias Pym Fordham, letter dated June 7, 1817, Bedford County, Pennsylvania, in Fordham, "Extracts from Letters," Edward E. Ayer Collection.

were drawn over the crest of the mountains by stationary engines, which furnished the motive power. The system was never as successful as the Erie Canal, which followed a route that presented no such topographical problems. Nonetheless, the ingenious series of canals and inclines was a decided asset in helping Philadelphia to protect her trade; the cost of freight from Philadelphia to Pittsburgh dropped to $1 and less per 100 pounds by 1835.

The interest with which Westerners watched the development of such enterprises is illustrated by the advertisement of a Pittsburgh commission firm in a Columbia, Missouri, paper in 1832. Part of the advertisement was given over to a list of charges made by the company for its services, but the balance of the notice was a full report on the building of the Pennsylvania canals. The advertisement stressed the reduction in costs and in time required to move goods.[49] Through such sources of information, citizens in small towns throughout the Mississippi Valley watched the progress of internal improvements with intense interest, realizing that whichever Eastern city won the race for Western markets the West would be sure to profit also.

Kentucky and Missouri merchants continued to favor Baltimore and Philadelphia over other cities until Civil War times. Their dominance was long-lived, for George Sibley, in a letter written at Fort Osage on the Missouri River in 1817, had remarked that most of the drygoods sold in Missouri Territory were purchased in the wholesale markets of Baltimore and Philadelphia.[50] Newspaper advertisements of that earlier date substantiate Sibley's statement. The pull of the New York market was beginning to affect buying patterns, however, and advertisements in the forties show that an increasing number of merchants were buying there. In spite of his bias in favor of Philadelphia, Jones's fictionalized account pictured Missouri merchants en route to the East as discussing the New York market among advantageous places to buy. Many of those who took part in Jones's discussion had never been to New York, so the chairman of the meeting, who had made some purchases there, was recognized as the authority. In his opinion, prices and methods of doing business were more nearly uniform in Philadelphia, and fewer "shyster" firms endangered the market. A merchant needed to spend more time in contacting good houses in New York City, but the speaker usually visited both cities and thereby obtained a broader variety of styles.[51]

49. Columbia *Missouri Intelligencer*, May 12, 1832.
50. Letter of G. Sibley to James G. Mask at Henderson, Kentucky, dated Ft. Osage, on the Missouri River, March 29, 1817, quoted in William Darby, *The emigrant's guide*, 302-5.
51. Jones, *The Western Merchant*, 163-64.

It would seem, from Jones's story, that Missouri merchants who had bought in Philadelphia for years were, by 1830, including New York in their itineraries, and some were breaking their associations with Philadelphia and dealing solely with New York houses. The tendency of merchants in southern Illinois to divide their wholesale business between Saint Louis and Philadelphia has already been noticed. Located in the same trade orbit as Missouri, they too felt the drawing power of New York City. Thus, in 1832, Mather, Lamb and Company, which operated stores at Chester, Kaskaskia, and Springfield, advertised goods purchased in New York City, Philadelphia, and Baltimore.[52]

The northern half of the state was a New York City market before the trade territory farther south had made any appreciable shift. For example, the commission firm of Biglow and Gibson advertised that they would make cash advances on produce to be sent to Buffalo, New York, and Boston. The firm cited references in those three cities and in Rochester as well.[53] In 1846 a Chicago farm paper carried advertisements by fifty Chicago firms and thirty-five New York houses, the latter group offering every type of goods. Among the advertisers was a New York hotel, which invited the patronage of travelers from the Chicago area, and two Boston firms—a hotel and a drygoods establishment. Two Saint Louis firms announced their services, as did one New Orleans company.[54] Striking in the newspaper's advertising was the absence of announcements by Philadelphia and Baltimore houses. Northern Illinois belonged to New York City as a trade area, and the seaboard cities farther south clearly made no efforts to break the monopoly. Transportation was of course the basic reason for the lack of competition for this new and lucrative market. In 1845 steamers were plying between Buffalo and Chicago on a daily schedule, carrying produce and merchandise.[55]

Iowa lacked easy water connections with New York City and consequently followed Missouri's pattern of wholesale purchases. In 1836 merchants in Dubuque were purchasing wholesale supplies in all the Eastern markets, many orders coming through Saint Louis. O'Ferrall and Cox and William Bull and Company patronized Baltimore and Philadelphia, and S. Shepherd and Company bought in

---

52. Springfield *Illinois Herald*, May 3, 1832.
53. Chicago *Daily Journal*, January 8, 1845.
54. Chicago *Prairie Farmer*, June, 1845.
55. Solon Robinson, "A November Voyage Round the Lakes," *Daily Cincinnati Gazette*, November 19, 1845, in Solon Robinson, *Solon Robinson, Pioneer and Agriculturist, Selected Writings*, Herbert A. Kellar, ed., I, 538-44.

New York City.[56] In this town New York wholesalers had as many customers as Baltimore and Philadelphia. Firms in Bloomington and Burlington, as shown by local newspapers, still bought most of their goods in Philadelphia, but New York houses attracted a few such customers. Here again transportation accounted in large part for the market situation. The Bloomington steamboat register for the period from March 27 to April 1, 1842, shows landings by seven steamboats; all of them named Saint Louis as home port.[57]

An Iowa City paper, in quoting from Newhall's *Sketches of Iowa*, suggested that travelers entering the territory from the north could come by stagecoach from Chicago to Ottawa, Illinois, by riverboat from there to Peoria, and by larger boat thence to Saint Louis. At that port steamboats for the upper Mississippi were always available. A shorter overland route from Peoria, Illinois, to Burlington in the Iowa Territory, by way of the tri-weekly stage was also available.[58] As transportation by overland freight was more expensive than by water, merchants of the area probably preferred the route that started in Chicago. If goods were to come through Saint Louis, Philadelphia was as good a place to buy as New York City and the Great Lakes route was unacceptable as a means of shipment. For these reasons, merchants of Iowa, although as close to the lakes as to Saint Louis, continued their trade with Philadelphia, since the necessity of freighting goods overland from Chicago destroyed the overwhelming supremacy held by the lakes route in northern Illinois.

Convenient and low-cost transportation, then, was a basic factor in the rivalry among merchants in the Eastern cities for Mid-America's markets. New York City, because of the ease of its trade routes, dominated the markets in northern Illinois; Philadelphia, because of freight costs from Chicago, held the supremacy in Missouri, Iowa, and southern Illinois, although New York gradually increased her share in all of these localities.

Obviously, shipments to Mid-America were sent by water routes whenever possible. Goods from New York went up the Hudson and out to the Great Lakes by the Erie Canal. If destined for Missouri, they were then sent south to Pittsburgh and brought down the Ohio River; for the northern sections served by that city, the lakes offered the best route. Baltimore and Philadelphia provided two routes, both widely used. Goods were freighted either to Wheeling, Virginia, or to Pittsburgh, since the Ohio River was accessible at both points.

56. *DuBuque* (Wisconsin Territory) *Visitor*, May 11, June 1, and August 17, 1836.

57. Bloomington (Iowa Territory) *Bloomington Herald*, April 1, 1841.

58. *Iowa City* (Iowa Territory) *Standard*, June 10, 1841.

Evidently, competition between those cities kept freight rates equal, for a merchant in 1834 explained in a letter that costs from Philadelphia to Wheeling were the same as from Baltimore to Wheeling.[59] Twenty years earlier, Joseph Hertzog wrote his partner at Saint Louis that the goods he had purchased to be sent West would be loaded for Pittsburgh or Wheeling by the end of the week, but his letter expressed no preference for either route.[60] As a matter of fact, many shippers employed both cities as a point of embarkation. James Aull generally sent part of his goods through Pittsburgh and part through Wheeling, as did Temple and Smith. The latter company sometimes expressed a preference for the Wheeling road and sent all the supplies for their own store at Saint Louis by that route. Many of their customers used the Pittsburgh route, however. Once goods reached a port on the Ohio, the route for the rest of the journey was determined. From any port on the Ohio River the Ohio-Mississippi-Missouri waterways were followed to the landing nearest the point of consignment.

An alternative route was, however, available. It was possible to ship merchandise down the Atlantic Coast and up the Mississippi River by way of New Orleans, thus avoiding the expense of freighting goods across the mountains. Eastern papers contained many advertisements that promoted this all-water route of shipment. Typical of these was an announcement of a new line of five packets sailing between New York and New Orleans, with vessels leaving each port every two weeks; masters of the vessels would, without charge, care for the forwarding of goods.[61] One company even proposed to remedy the problems involved in transferring cargoes from coastal ships to river steamboats at New Orleans by having steamboats tow the sailing ships up the river.

Heavy goods frequently traveled by way of New Orleans before the series of canals and improved roads lessened freight charges over the mountains. For instance, Scott and Rule at Saint Louis, in the spring of 1829, announced the arrival of their "more light and valuable" articles by way of Pittsburgh, the "domestic, queensware, and other heavy articles" being expected shortly from New Orleans on the steamboat *North America*.[62] Individual attitudes toward the major cities affected some merchants' decisions. However, although Joseph Hertzog thought New Orleans was a "dreadful hole," he in-

59. Letter of Robert E. Carrothers to Robert Garrett at Baltimore, dated Philadelphia, March 29, 1834, Garrett Family Papers.
60. Letter of Joseph Hertzog to Christian Wilt at St. Louis, dated Philadelphia, July 9, 1811, Joseph Hertzog, Letters.
61. *New York Evening Post*, December 23, 1826.
62. *St. Louis Beacon*, April 13, 1829.

structed Wilt to send lead shot east by that route.[63] Lighter and more valuable goods of this company, like furs, were sent by way of Pittsburgh. But with the few exceptions noted, alternative routes were lacking or remained undeveloped. Land transport did not compete with water transport until the railroads bridged and tunneled the natural obstructions.

It is impossible to estimate the cost of transporting goods from the East for the whole of the Western area. Charges were of course different for every locality and varied with the season of the year. Thus, low water on the Ohio might cause a 20 per cent increase in rates. There was a general tendency for rates to decline from year to year as the routes of travel improved and better and faster means of transportation developed. The costs were never reduced to any figure comparable with the low rates that prevail today, however. An example of freight rates in 1830 from Pittsburgh to towns on the Missouri River 100 to 200 miles above Saint Louis will illustrate the heavy toll exacted for transportation. Goods traveling between those points covered over 1,000 miles and underwent as many transshipments as supplies destined for any other area in Mid-America. Because of the costs entailed with warehousing and handling at many points, the figures for shipping from Pittsburgh to Mid-America represent the highest rates borne by merchandise. James Aull of Lexington, Missouri, had a large supply of merchandise ready for shipment at Pittsburgh in the spring of 1830 and, in planning for its transportation west, exercised extreme care to cut the charges wherever possible. Necessarily, the goods loaded at that port were transferred at Saint Louis. Added to loading costs were the insurance charges and the steamboat freight. Despite Aull's care to lower his transportation charges, he estimated the cost from Pittsburgh to Lexington at one-fourth of his total investment in the goods.[64]

High transportation charges were not the merchant's only problem, by any means. An appalling variety of accidents could happen to any shipment of goods, and every merchant who remained in business any length of time suffered some calamities. The experiences of some representative firms are worth recording. James Wier at Lexington, Kentucky, was one of the more fortunate merchants, as he was never faced with a loss that threatened the existence of his business. Still, he underwent anxieties and losses: A cargo of hemp that he shipped to Philadelphia by way of New Orleans in 1804 was damaged at sea

63. Letters of Joseph Hertzog to Christian Wilt at St. Louis, dated Philadelphia, May 2 and May 4, 1811, Joseph Hertzog, Letters.

64. Letter of James Aull to Tracy and Wahrendorff at St. Louis, Missouri, dated Lexington, Missouri, April 12, 1830, Letter Book B, Aull Collection.

and had to be sold at sacrifice prices. In 1811 he shipped 6,000 pounds of yarn on a river steamboat to New Orleans, only to learn after the vessel sailed that the master of the boat and of his shipment was a man of extremely bad character, suspected of stealing several cargoes of goods. Wier sent descriptions to agents in Natchez and New Orleans with instructions to take possession of his goods wherever they were found, and, as a result of his precautions, he recovered the yarn. In 1814 all the hardware he had bought at Pittsburgh failed to arrive, and a box of drygoods belonging to another Western firm was delivered to him instead. In November of 1816 a box of much-needed goods did not arrive with his other goods from Pittsburgh, and he complained bitterly about the resulting loss of business.[65]

Nor did the improvements in transportation that developed by the thirties guarantee to the merchant protection of his goods. Shipping difficulties contributed to James Aull's decision to reduce his business in 1836. The record of his shipments is that of a series of disasters. In 1829 he purchased $10,000 worth of goods in the East, which he insured with the Ohio Insurance Company at a cost of $769.97. Although equal to almost 10 per cent of the value of his purchases, the premium was amply justified by later events. Aull accompanied his goods home and supervised their loading on the steamboat *Talma* at Pittsburgh for the journey to Saint Louis. The vessel carried merchandise valued at $150,000, goods destined for stores at Chariton, Franklin, and other places above Saint Louis on the Missouri River. Eighteen miles from Saint Louis the vessel caught fire. In order to prevent complete destruction of the ship and cargo, the captain ordered a hole to be chopped in the boat's bottom, which allowed it to sink in the shallow water near the bank. The hole was caulked, the water pumped out, and the vessel then proceeded to Saint Louis under her own steam. All the passengers, including James Aull, worked with the crew in the frantic and successful endeavors to save the ship.

Aull's goods had been submerged only a little over two hours, but groceries and drygoods were considerably damaged by the muddy water. In spite of his heavy insurance the accident was costly for Aull. A court of three arbitrators at Saint Louis fixed his losses at $3,500, but a later compromise with the insurance company reduced the amount to $2,500. During the course of negotiations and pending a settlement, he necessarily traveled, at some expense, to Saint Louis and to the offices of the insurance company at Cincinnati,

65. An account of these misfortunes is given in various letters contained in James Wier's two letter books.

Ohio. Although his goods were two months late in reaching his stores, the resulting loss in trade was not considered a factor in determining the amount due him from the accident.[66] Insurance could cover the damage to the goods, but not the other losses from delays, trips, and other vexatious incidents involved in steamboat disasters.

Aull sustained additional losses in 1832. Low water in 1831 had caused freight rates to advance sharply, and Aull decided to make contracts in the future before shipment, in order to avoid such fluctuations. With this purpose in mind he hired the steamboat *Otto* in 1832 to carry his goods from Pittsburgh. The contract specified that the boat would carry 80,000 pounds of goods at $1.50 a hundred, 250 barrels of flour at $1.50 a barrel, 30 barrels of vinegar at $2.00 a barrel, 15 barrels of beans at $1.25 a barrel, and 3,000 pounds of soap for $25. But low water prevented the *Otto* from reaching Pittsburgh when Aull was ready to start homeward. He was under pressure to get his goods into his stores at an early date: The soap had to reach Fort Leavenworth at a contracted date, and the other goods were needed for the spring trade. Under these circumstances it was impossible to wait for the *Otto*. The low stage of the Ohio had boomed freight rates, so he was forced to pay more than his original contract had specified in order to have his goods transported in time to meet his contract and stock his stores. Aull owned a small interest in the *Otto*, and, as he planned to hold the boat liable for any losses sustained in chartering another vessel, he left the flour for sale at Pittsburgh and purchased another lot in Louisville. This transaction resulted in a saving of $100. In spite of his efforts to arrange a favorable freight rate, however, the rate to Lexington was 45½¢ a hundred higher than that called for in the contract with the *Otto*. Rates on the flour were $2.15 a barrel higher and on the beans 50¢. The *Otto* refused to stand the loss, and Aull finally referred the matter to a board of three arbitrators at Saint Louis, which assessed one-sixth of the loss against the boat.[67] The experience convinced Aull that a contract made in advance of shipment was no hedge against fluctuating freight rates.

In 1833, foreseeing a business depression, Aull decided to purchase fewer goods. He asked Anthony Beelen, a Pittsburgh dealer, to arrange for the shipments west, as Aull had decided to economize

66. The story of the *Talma* disaster is in a letter to Tracy and Wahrendorff at St. Louis, dated Lexington, Missouri, May 22, 1829, Letter Book B, Aull Collection. It was also reported in the Fayette *Missouri Intelligencer*, March 27, 1829.

67. Letter of James Aull to Edward Tracy at St. Louis, dated Lexington, Missouri, May 21, 1832, Letter Book 1830–33, Aull Collection.

also by omitting the winter trip east and had placed his orders by letter. He expected the freight from Louisville, Wheeling, and Pittsburgh to total 50 tons, and he thought Beelen should be able to negotiate for a boat to bring the goods from Pittsburgh at $1.50 a hundred. His letter suggested the line of argument to use to get the best rates. The owners of a vessel of from 100 to 125 tons could easily find other goods to finish out the shipment, and, if not, Aull was willing to purchase an additional 60 barrels of rye whiskey to increase the load. The trip from Pittsburgh to Saint Louis could be made in eight days and from Saint Louis to Fort Leavenworth in another eight. The vessel's charges would average approximately $100 a day for the trip to Lexington, and Aull would gather a return cargo of beans, pork, flour, and candles. Traders at Fort Leavenworth might also provide some freight for the return journey. Furthermore, shipments to the West would be greatly curtailed in 1833; in such circumstances, the owners of any boat should be glad to obtain whatever business they could—so Aull argued.[68]

Beelen contracted for the steamboat *Trenton* to bring the goods from Pittsburgh, but, in keeping with Aull's hard luck, the *Trenton* was lost in the Missouri River about 12 miles above its mouth. The Atlantic Insurance Company had insured the goods purchased in Philadelphia and readily paid the full loss on them, but Aull's agent in Saint Louis had been unable to get insurance there on the goods purchased at points other than Philadelphia, since insurance companies in the Mississippi Valley did not write as many types of insurance as the firms farther east. Aull had asked Beelen to obtain insurance on the other goods, so he assumed that the whole shipment was covered. Beelen had failed to act, however, and Aull soon discovered that only the articles loaded at Philadelphia had been insured. Here is an instance that explains why so many men made the long trip eastward each year to buy their goods in person. Personal buying and arrangements for shipment lessened the chances for such egregious errors as victimized Aull.

Some of Aull's goods were recovered from the wreck and sold in Saint Louis, thereby reducing his loss to $4,297.36. Beelen paid $3,000 of this balance, and the two men agreed to divide equally any further returns from the salvage of the *Trenton*. Aull's cash loss was thus theoretically reduced to $1,300, but the injury to the firm was incalculable. As to the goods he was supplying under contract to Fort Leavenworth, their delivery, by contract, was to be made by a certain

68. James Aull to Anthony Beelen at Pittsburgh, dated Lexington, Missouri, February 14, 1833, Letter Book 1830–33, Aull Collection.

date. All these provisions were lost in the river, and although insured, Aull suffered serious loss. He had to purchase replacements in Saint Louis at higher prices, a loss of $500. His four stores did not receive supplies until four months after other firms in his vicinity were stocked, and the delay cost him much trade. His brother went to Saint Louis immediately after the disaster to see what could be done to salvage goods and costs, and Aull wrote urgent letters to wholesalers in the East to rush a new supply of goods. In the end he, too, was compelled to leave his business and go to Philadelphia to expedite shipments. This journey consumed the whole summer, and he did not reach home until August.[69] The loss of the goods and business was a serious matter to the firm, and from 1833 to the dissolution of the partnership in 1836 Aull was crowded to make payments for wholesale goods rapidly enough to sustain his credit standing.

To outsiders the care exercised by merchants in shipping goods and in seeking low freight rates often seemed miserly and overly cautious. In 1827 a resident at Prairie du Chien, Wisconsin Territory, expressed this attitude. He was eagerly waiting confirmation of his appointment to a government job and was displeased because the mails were delayed. The local postmastership was held by a merchant who had been in the East, buying goods. The office-seeker's anxiety turned to wrath when an army officer informed him that the merchant was aboard a steamboat only a short distance down the river, with his own merchandise and the community's mail, waiting for the ice to go out before coming up the river. In his impatience, the hopeful citizen dispatched a complaint to Ninian Edwards in Illinois: "I am apprehensive that the whole is made subservient to the convenience of a merchant and that while I am tortured with suspense, he is calculating cent per cent, and hiring *cheap payable in mdse.* You know payments in that way are not as *imperitive,* as *silver or Gold.*"[70] According to his view, the merchant should have hired a carriage and rushed the mail to its destination. Perhaps he might have done so, but his cautious progress was based on experiences that other people only dimly comprehended. Communication and transportation were neither swift nor safe, and the merchants realized these facts more acutely than any other class in the West.

69. Letters of James Aull to Siter, Price and Company at Philadelphia, dated Lexington, Missouri, April 13 and October 16, 1833, Day Book 1833–35, Aull Collection.

70. Letter of Joseph N. Street to Ninian Edwards at Belleville, Illinois, dated Prairie du Chien, December 26, 1827, Ninian W. Edwards Papers.

THE WESTERN MARKETS

As indicated, the East did not monopolize the wholesale trade in Mid-America. Certain advantages were common to all wholesale centers located west of the Alleghenies, but each of these towns also had distinct advantages of its own. This generalization is somewhat less true of the cities along the Ohio River, principally Pittsburgh, Wheeling, Cincinnati, and Louisville, for these profited greatly from the common good fortune of being on the line of communication between West and East. They were on the western side of the mountains, located on the waterway that was, in the early period, the principal means of access and in daily contact with Western trade through the forwarding business. Many Eastern firms deposited goods with them to be sold on commission, and through this procedure the forwarding firms were able frequently to quote prices that compared favorably with those in larger centers.

The dealings of the firm of Lane, Knox, and McKee at Wheeling illustrate the manner in which such business often developed. Originally in the forwarding business, the company had handled the goods shipped by Temple and Smith of Philadelphia to its store in Saint Louis. From this operation Lane, Knox, and McKee moved to the practice of keeping on hand a supply of drugs from the Philadelphia firm, to sell on commission to Western merchants passing through Wheeling.[71]

In some cases the river towns competed with the East without direct outside support. Such a city was Pittsburgh. Like Wheeling, it was full of commission and forwarding firms that always had available a large supply of goods on consignment from Eastern houses. In this respect Pittsburgh was merely an extension of the Eastern markets, but in the production and sale of ironware it was a primary market. The first iron furnace west of the Alleghenies was constructed in 1789 near the town, and Pittsburgh soon became known for its metal goods. Throughout the period under review, even after freight rates dropped in the thirties, merchants purchased supplies in Philadelphia or New York in every line except iron goods, which they bought at Pittsburgh on their return journey. Accordingly, in 1828 James Aull bought most of his supplies in Philadelphia, but obtained three tons of ironware from Anthony Beelen at Pittsburgh on his way home. The purchase included axes, rolled iron, nails, log chains, spades, skillets, kettles, pots, and pans.[72]

71. The relation of the two companies is recorded in Temple and Smith's Letter Book 1818–22.

72. James Aull to Anthony Beelen at Pittsburgh, dated Lexington, Missouri, May 22, 1828, Letter Book B, Aull Collection.

Western merchants also bought whiskey, flour, and similar products that were processed at Cincinnati and Louisville, as they passed through on the journey home.[73] The saving in transportation costs caused merchants to buy as many items as possible in the river cities. Joseph Hertzog attended directly to purchases in Philadelphia for his nephew at Saint Louis, as Hertzog lived on the seaboard, but in 1812, when Andrew Wilt was ready to start west with a supply of goods, Hertzog directed him to make many purchases in the river cities: Whiskey was to be bought in Pittsburgh; gunpowder there or in Kentucky; writing and wrapping paper in Kentucky; country sugar and additional supplies of tinware at Cincinnati; cheap whiskey and linen in Kentucky; and ropes, cordelles, and fishing lines wherever cheapest, perhaps in Cincinnati.[74]

The extent of the market served by the towns on the Ohio River is shown in the advertisement of W. F. Hopkins in Cincinnati, Ohio, which appeared in a Saint Louis newspaper in 1835. Bolting cloth and "French Burr Blocks" constituted Hopkins' offering. Papers at Pittsburgh, in a large number of Ohio towns, in Kentucky towns such as Maysville and Louisville, in Saint Louis, and in Indiana and Illinois were asked to copy the advertisement.[75]

New Orleans merchants also shared in the wholesale trade of the Mississippi Valley, although their markets for goods other than groceries extended principally into the Southwest. John and Matthew Cartwright of San Augustine in the province of Texas bought their drygoods and groceries from a number of firms in New Orleans.[76] James Cochrane at San Felipe da Austin in the same territory was also a customer of the Louisiana city.[77] New Orleans was of course the closest market, and goods from that place were landed at Matagorda, Indianola, Anahuac, and Velasco on the Gulf Coast and freighted inland to the Texas merchants.

Although connections in the Southwest with Eastern cities were very rare in the early period, in Arkansas Territory Frederic Notrebe advertised as early as 1821 that he had just returned from Philadelphia with drygoods and groceries.[78] Even Notrebe, however, bought

---

73. Joseph Hertzog to Christian Wilt at St. Louis, dated Philadelphia, March 30, 1812, Joseph Hertzog, Letters.

74. Joseph Hertzog to Andrew Wilt at Philadelphia, dated Philadelphia, April 1, 1812, Joseph Hertzog, Letters.

75. St. Louis *Missouri Argus*, December 18, 1835.

76. Memorandum of purchases in Account Book of Matthew Cartwright 1833–35, Matthew Cartwright Manuscript Collection.

77. San Felipe da Austin *Telegraph and Texas Register*, various numbers for 1835.

78. *Arkansas* (Arkansas Territory) *Gazette*, January 6, 1821.

most of his goods in New Orleans, as evidenced by an advertisement in the summer of 1821 that announced his return from New Orleans with a supply of groceries and drygoods.[79] Advertisements of Saint Louis and Pittsburgh firms seldom appeared in the pages of the *Arkansas Gazette*, a circumstance that indicates there was little connection in the area with the supply routes for Missouri and Kentucky. In the earlier years New Orleans enjoyed almost a monopoly on the wholesale business in the area, although New York City gradually increased her share. In the issue for December 23, 1834, for example, J. DeBaum was advertising drygoods and shoes from New York City, as was also Ubait and Dunn, who claimed to have made purchases directly in that market.

Although the New Orleans drygoods trade area was limited, few cities in the United States had a wider wholesale grocery market. Merchants who bought drygoods and fine groceries to the eastward frequently got their coffee and sugar in New Orleans. James Aull ordered 15,000 pounds of sugar and 10,000 pounds of coffee in one lot from there in 1833.[80] Missouri, Illinois, and Iowa merchants found New Orleans grocery prices too attractive to resist, and even Wisconsin merchants bought supplies there: Theodor Rodolf at Mineral Point, in Wisconsin Territory, advertised "family groceries from New Orleans" in the *Miner's Free Press* on December 22, 1840.

New Orleans of course kept a share of the wholesale drygoods trade in her immediate vicinity. She held no particular advantage, however, because her supplies came on consignment from Eastern firms. For instance, Jacob Grove at Philadelphia was interested in the cotton trade, and through this connection he began to send large quantities of drygoods to New Orleans for sale by commission houses.[81]

But New Orleans was at an advantage in many ways in her struggle for a share in the wholesale grocery trade. Most of the produce of the Middle West was shipped by merchants, and New Orleans handled more produce than any other large city. Consequently, merchants came to her markets to trade their own or their customers' produce. Evidence of this trading appears in the price quotations of New Orleans commission merchants in many sets of business papers left by merchants in Mid-America. Through these quotations storekeepers learned that coffee and brown sugar were available at very low rates in New Orleans and white sugar could be had on as favor-

79. *Arkansas* (Arkansas Territory) *Gazette*, July 28, 1821.

80. James Aull to Breedlove and Company at New Orleans, dated Lexington, Missouri, April 3, 1833, Day Book 1833–35, Aull Collection.

81. Jacob Grove, Day Book and Journal 1838.

able terms as in the East. Such prices were practical because New Orleans was closer to the source of supply; sugar production in Louisiana jumped from 30,000 hogsheads in 1827 to 200,000 in 1844.[82] Large wholesale firms along the Atlantic seaboard bought coffee, cocoa, and sugar from Central and South America. New Orleans merchants purchased in the same market, and, as the source of supply was closer to New Orleans, her merchants were able to quote good prices. Here was one exception to the general rule that cities on the Atlantic seaboard were closer to foreign markets than were the other wholesale centers.

Merchants in Saint Louis were interested in the wholesale trade as early as the 1820s, since the city's geographical location favored such a development. The surrounding country was strongly dependent on her, even more so than were the trade areas of cities in other Mid-American states like Ohio. There, goods came down the river and were distributed from any one of the half-dozen cities along the bank or were even carried up tributary streams to the merchants. Goods might also come over the National Road to the cities of the interior or by way of the Great Lakes to those farther north. But Saint Louis was on the only line of transportation to the upper Missouri-Mississippi region. Population was not sufficiently great in the more northerly sections of Illinois to support good overland routes before the fifties, although some importations were made in that way. Therefore, the Mississippi remained the chief highway for the north central country, as the Missouri did for the more westerly trade. The Mississippi was shallower just above Saint Louis, so the city became a point of transshipment, and her merchants took full advantage of the fact to control the flow of goods to the hinterland.[83] This pattern of transportation lasted until the railroad era, when rail transport weakened the position of Saint Louis in Iowa and southern Illinois and strengthened Chicago's growing dominance in the fifties.

Both Saint Louis and Chicago were located then, as they are now, directly in Mid-America. While geography created difficulties for wholesalers in getting goods, it also gave them certain trade advantages. As already indicated, transportation of supplies from the seaboard was a dangerous and risky undertaking. While the wholesalers recovered their costs from the merchants who bought supplies in Saint Louis and Chicago, they also served their customers by supplying goods when they were needed. These wholesale centers also

82. Ulrich B. Phillips, *Life and Labor in the Old South*, 120.

83. Ellen C. Semple and Clarence F. Jones, *American History and Its Geographic Conditions*, gives a clear picture of the geographical advantages of St. Louis.

drew many small merchants who operated on too little capital to justify trips eastward to buy goods. Even for those who bought in the East, it was impossible to include in one order everything that would be needed for the ensuing twelve months, so they replenished stocks from the nearer wholesale houses.

Burrows at Davenport, Iowa, favored Cincinnati as a trading center, but in the fall of 1845 he discovered that he would run short of goods before navigation opened in the spring, so he visited Saint Louis to fill his needs.[84] James Aull found it easier to buy small orders to replenish stock in Saint Louis than at a distance of 1,000 miles to the eastward. He might buy $30,000 worth of goods in Philadelphia as his basic supply, but the stock was never sufficient to last out the twelve months; consequently, he was a valued customer of Tracy and Wahrendorff at Saint Louis. His letter books for 1829 show small orders to them for salt, tar, rum, molasses, almanacs, coffee, and whiskey. In 1830 he purchased fine coffee in Philadelphia, but it was so late in arriving, he ordered 1,500 pounds from Tracy and Wahrendorff to fill his customers' needs until the supply arrived from the East. In 1832 he wrote to Saint Louis for a stock of "Charley's Mission" almanacs and "Christian Almanacs." Three or four letters a month went to Tracy and Wahrendorff, ordering supplies to serve until goods arrived from the East, replacing defective goods had caused Aull to seek connections in that city, and, because more readily than anticipated. It is worth noting, too, that Tracy and Wahrendorff first established their connection with the Aulls through acting as forwarding agents for them at Saint Louis. The fact that Saint Louis was the logical point of transshipment for goods had caused Aull to seek connections in that city, and, because it was the most advanced wholesale center close at hand, he bought a great many supplies there. The patterns of growth and marketing of that one firm are typical of numerous concerns in the Saint Louis trade area.

Saint Louis merchants exploited their advantages. Most of the merchants, around 1820, advertised both wholesale and retail business. The small size of a company might be a handicap but not an insurmountable barrier to sales at wholesale. In 1820 Nathaniel D. Payne was advertising drygoods, groceries, and hardware at both wholesale and retail, and his announcement was typical of those issued by Saint Louis houses.[85] Saint Louis firms were already concentrating on the wholesale trade even in this early period, evidently. Paul and Ingram, who had connections with an Eastern house, ad-

84. J. M. D. Burrows, *Fifty Years in Iowa*, 70-71.
85. St. Louis *Missouri Gazette and Public Advertiser*, August 2, 1820.

vertised that they had purchased goods at auction in Philadelphia in the summer months, and they addressed their announcements directly to "country merchants."[86]

The story of wholesaling in Saint Louis for the next thirty years emerges in the records of the various houses, which show tendency to become exclusively either wholesale or retail, to concentrate on one line of goods, and to seek direct connections with European and Eastern sources of merchandise. In 1836 McKee, Stewart and Lind were in the drygoods business; they sold entirely at wholesale and offered liberal terms to Missouri and Illinois merchants.[87] But the rarity of such companies at that period is indicated by the fact that the novelty of being an exclusively wholesale business in one line could be used as the chief sales appeal. Year by year such companies increased in numbers, and the boast of the firm's maintaining resident partners in the East substituted for focus on one line as a selling point. By the time Saint Louis could no longer rely on frontier conditions to ensure a share in the wholesale trade she was ready to claim it through an efficient wholesale organization.

Obviously, wholesale and retail trading in the Saint Louis area in the fifties was much different from what it had been thirty years earlier. Around 1820 Saint Louis houses were still wholesale and retail concerns that advertised their goods very much as those who bought their stocks in the East proudly announced the fact at the head of their advertisements. An issue of a Saint Louis paper in 1855 shows the great change that had occurred since the twenties. The caption "Importers and Wholesalers" was now as common as the heading "Wholesalers and Retailers" had been a quarter of a century earlier. Many firms were concentrating on one line of goods. Barnard, Adams and Peck dealt in drugs, Carr and Buchanan handled books and paper, R. P. Hahenkamp sold groceries, D. H. Lackman marketed fancy and variety goods, and Z. F. Wetzell and Company imported and wholesaled drugs. A few firms advertised both wholesale and retail in one line of goods, but the old general wholesale and retail store was gone.[88]

Conditions in the smaller towns had changed quite as basically as in Saint Louis. In an issue of a Columbia, Missouri, paper in 1855 not a single local firm advertised goods on both wholesale and retail terms, and only one merchant announced that his goods had been imported from the East.[89] Clearly, the smaller towns had lost their

86. Franklin Missouri Intelligencer, December 9, 1820.
87. St. Louis Missouri Argus, April 8, 1836.
88. St. Louis Daily Missouri Republican, March 1, 1855.
89. Columbia Weekly Missouri Statesman, November 16, 1855.

wholesaling business to Saint Louis by that time. Furthermore, the absence from advertisements of indications of the goods' origin was evidence of the general tendency to buy in Saint Louis. In 1820 Saint Louis and the Eastern cities competed for the business of merchants in the small towns surrounding Saint Louis; by 1850 this element of merchandising, too, had changed. Saint Louis wholesalers bought their goods along the seaboard, as they had in former times, but the out-state merchants relied on Saint Louis for their supplies. The larger merchants in the cities of Mid-America had become middlemen between the seaboard houses and the storekeepers of the smaller towns. No longer did the average mrchant feel it necessary to buy directly in the East.

In 1840 the population of Iowa Territory was only 43,000 people, but in 1860 it stood at 517,875.[90] Settlers moved into northern Illinois in larger numbers also at the same time. The rapid development of Chicago reflected the growth of this trade territory. That city was not mentioned in the Census of 1830, but it could boast a population of over 100,000 in 1860.[91] Rails connected Chicago with the East in 1853, and as the railroads extended into Illinois and Iowa, the competition of Chicago with Saint Louis became more and more severe. Saint Louis had established rail communication with the East by 1855, but the coming of the railroad meant the end of the advantages that city had formerly enjoyed from her fortunate location for river traffic. Chicago's competition with Saint Louis for leadership in Mid-America was already evident in the fifties, but the rivalry was not to become acute until after the Civil War.

The railroad's penetration of the region completely revolutionized the techniques of wholesaling and ended the pioneer period of merchandising in Mid-America. No longer did the merchant buy the bulk of his supplies for the year at one time; no longer was it necessary for him to visit the seaboard; no longer did he risk the loss of his goods. The railroad brought the goods he now could order as he needed; it brought the traveling salesmen to him, so it was possible for him to spend all his time attending to business at home; and the greater safety of rail transport relieved him of the worries he had faced in the days of river transportation. Thus, the railroad, as an improved means of transportation, ushered in the day of modern merchandising.

90. Irving B. Richman, *Ioway to Iowa, the Genesis of a Corn and Bible Commonwealth*, 162, 237-38.

91. Johnson and others, *Commerce of the U.S.*, 235.

THE WEST AS SOURCE OF GOODS

In the early days of bartering goods for produce, storekeepers welcomed every opportunity to dispose of accumulated produce close at home, if they could be sure of payment in time to cancel their own debts. One important outlet that satisfied both needs was created by the presence of national forts in the West. These installations needed varying quantities of foodstuffs for the troops, and every year the government advertised for supplies in papers throughout the country.[92]

An advertisement in the St. Louis *Missouri Republican* for July 26, 1827, is representative of these notices. It announced that the office of the Commissary General of Subsistence at Washington would receive proposals for provisions for the specified forts until the first day of October, at which time contracts would be let. Jefferson Barracks, a post near Saint Louis, would require 150 barrels of pork; 325 barrels of fresh, fine flour; 20,800 gallons of good-proof whiskey, each barrel to have at least 16 good hoops; 1,450 bushels of good, sound beans; 22,800 pounds of good, hard soap; 10,400 pounds of good, hard-tallow candles, with cotton wicks; 400 bushels of good, clean salt; and 6,000 gallons of good cider vinegar, each barrel to have at least 16 good hoops. The items were to be delivered in four installments, and the dates specified were the first day of June, September, and December of 1828, and March, 1829. Cantonment Gibson, 150 miles above Fort Smith, Arkansas, would require 300 barrels of pork, 625 barrels of flour, 4,000 gallons of whiskey, 275 bushels of beans, 4,400 pounds of soap, 2,000 pounds of candles, 100 bushels of salt, and 1,500 gallons of vinegar, the specifications as to quality and containers being the same as for the Jefferson Barracks contract. In this instance, the whole shipment was to be delivered at one time. The advertisement set forth the needs of other posts in similar detail, these varying from the examples cited only in the quantities ordered.

The specifications compelled packers to meet rather rigid standards, the government agents being the sole judges as to whether these conditions were fulfilled. For example, in the packing of pork only one hog was allowed to the barrel, and only certain cuts of meat. The statement that only one head could be included leads one to suspect that shipments in the past had revealed hogs of unusual anatomical structure. Specifications for containers were equally exact. Barrels were to be made of "seasoned heart of white oak" and boxes

92. Lewis E. Atherton, "Western Foodstuffs in the Army Provisions Trade," *Agricultural History*, 14 (1940), 161-69.

built in sizes convenient for transportation. Shipments were to be inspected for approval only after delivery, and the contractor was held accountable for all expenses until the goods were safely placed in such storehouses as the quartermasters at the various posts should designate. Furthermore, the government reserved the right to alter quantities of any article advertised, even to the extent of eliminating items before a contract was signed. After an agreement was made, the government could still change the quantity of each delivery by one third on 60 days' notice.

Such conditions called for caution in bidding. The reserved right of the government to alter a contract made bidders hesitate to offer low prices on some costly article in the hope of balancing this item against other provisions that could be purchased cheaply. An alteration of quantities could destroy all profit if it affected the bidder's most lucrative items. On the other hand, an especially high price on some one article could cost the merchant loss of the whole contract.

As a means of immediately limiting the field to responsible people, the government required all new bidders to send proof of their reliability along with their estimates. Furthermore, those who received contracts had to give security for the fulfillment of their obligations. In only one respect, perhaps, did government regulations appeal to suppliers, and that was in the manner of payments. These were made in drafts either on the War Department at Washington or on some branch in a seaboard city, an arrangement that changed in the thirties, however, to payment in drafts drawn on banks in the trader's own locality. With drafts on Eastern banks often at a premium in the West, a recipient, if he did not need the money to pay for goods he had bought in the East, could sell his draft to some merchant who was making payments there. Drafts on Western banks did not carry this advantage, but at least the trader knew that his claim would be honored in acceptable currency.

In general, the contract bound the trader in every aspect of the transaction. He alone took the risks of transporting the goods to their destination, and an accident could easily involve him in a heavy penalty for failure to make delivery on time in addition to the loss or damage of the goods. Transportation was slow in the West, and the 60 days' warning of a reduction in the items to be furnished was sometimes insufficient. For example, a Saint Louis trader who was provisioning a fort 300 miles up the Mississippi might have dispatched his supplies before he received notice that they would not be needed in the amounts originally specified. None the less, merchants eagerly sought such business and the bidding generally was keen, no matter how distant the fort might be from the established routes of travel, for these contracts offered an extensive market to traders. Every year the government purchased large orders for the garrisons at Snelling, Crawford, Winnebago, Leavenworth, Gibson, and other posts in the West.

Not all bids were submitted directly to the War Department in Washington. Some classes of contracts were made at towns located near the forts. Such an agreement was reported to the quartermaster general in Washington by the acting quartermaster at Fort Leavenworth in 1834. Notices that bids for a supply of corn were to be received at Liberty, Missouri, on a specified day in August appeared in local papers during the summer. On the designated day the quartermaster at the fort visited the town to consider the estimates that had been submitted. All proved to be exceedingly high; the price of corn in the open market indicated collusion among the traders. The quartermaster rejected all offers and entered into an agreement with a trader who had not entered a bid. When the quartermaster would not accept the proffered bids, the traders individually sought to supply the corn at much reduced rates, but the officer stood by the contract he had made.[93] The officer sent a record of the whole affair to Washington for final decision. An opinion handed down from the Attorney General's office indicated that the officer had acted well within his rights, as the War Department's regulations granted men in the field the right to reject bids when there was evidence of an attempt to defraud the government. Contracts for small purchases of the type just described frequently went to people who resided near the forts, since contractors who lived at a distance did not consider them worth the trouble.

On the larger subsistence contracts there was a wide geographical distribution until the late 1820s: Traders situated in Washington, D.C., and Fredonia, New York, provisioned Green Bay and Detroit and other installations along the Great Lakes. The contracts for posts situated as far west as Jefferson Barracks, near Saint Louis, went to contractors as distant as Cincinnati, Ohio.

Indeed, Pennsylvania, Ohio, and Virginia men seem to have held a majority of the contracts for provisioning the Mississippi Valley posts as late as 1829. Missouri and Illinois merchants and traders engaged less frequently in such operations, although in both states there were many firms whose business patterns were well suited for participation. Inhabitants of what are now the states of Arkansas, Iowa, Wisconsin, and Michigan apparently devoted little attention to the trade.

93. Letter from Lt. J. Freeman, acting assistant quartermaster at Fort Leavenworth, to Gen. Thomas Jesup at Washington, D.C., August 20, 1834, in the Post Records of Fort Leavenworth.

Kentucky was something of an exception in the West, as a number of contracts went to her merchants.[94] Although it is probable that Eastern men bought part of their supplies in the West if they had contracts for forts in that region, the fact remains that traders to the eastward were the principals in the majority of the transactions.

The Army provisions trade shifted, however, in favor of the West around 1830. From then on, local traders increased their share in the larger contracts year by year. Once familiar with the methods of dealing with the government, Western men discovered that they held the advantage over their competitors to the east. Since they were closer than Eastern traders to the points of delivery, they could underbid foodstuffs shipped from the East, an advantage that was intensified by high freight rates. Furthermore, Easterners could not rival the contacts of their Western competitors when purchasing directly in Western markets.

Western merchants found the government business especially helpful. Inasmuch as they were marketing farm crops in the ordinary course of their dealings, contracts for provisioning forts supplemented their other activities nicely. There are numerous examples in the War Department records of the shifting of contracts to Western firms. In 1829 Jefferson Barracks was, as remarked earlier, provisioned by an Ohioan, but the contract for Fort Armstrong went to a man in Exeter, Illinois, and those for Crawford and Snelling to a Saint Louis bidder.

Some merchants engaged in the business of supplying forts only occasionally. Bad luck on one contract might cause some to withdraw permanently from the competition, and others might bid only in the years when local conditions promised unusual profits. Others engaged in the trade with great regularity. Representative of the latter practice were Hill and M'Gunnegle who, in addition to their interest in insurance companies, steamboats, and the commission and forwarding business, regularly submitted bids on the Army's needs in their locality. In 1829 they transported a detachment of troops to Fort Leavenworth, for which service they received $115 a day. The following year, they won a contract to carry merchandise to Fort Armstrong. From this beginning, they branched out to sharing the provisioning of Jefferson Barracks with a Pittsburgh firm in 1832, but they monopolized the business each year from then through 1837. As the barracks were only about 30 miles from their Saint Louis warehouses, they held a decided advantage in the bidding for supplies.

94. Copies of Contracts, Subsistence Department, Fiscal Year 1825–26 to 1828–29.

The effects of the trade on Western life can best be judged through the perspective of local merchants who participated. J. M. D. Burrows of Davenport in Iowa Territory found his one venture very profitable, while James and Robert Aull of Lexington in Missouri lost heavily in their one direct venture into the trade. Consequently, the records of these two contracts well express the range of local mercantile reaction to the government business.

Burrows' contract was made in 1841. At this time and for some years to come, his community was hard pressed financially. The land within the territory had just been brought into the market by the government, and much of the available cash went to the land office. As a result, farmers bought very little from the local merchants and that little generally on a year's credit. In 1841 Burrows figured that wheat and pork production in his community would be double the output of past years and felt that he must find a way to market these products if he expected to have any trade at his store. Advertisements in the St. Louis *Daily Missouri Republican* for supplies at Fort Snelling and Fort Crawford opened for him a possible outlet for the local produce. Burrows decided to submit bids for both wheat and pork, on the theory that success in the venture would help his own business and also bring money for circulation in his community. The latter consideration appealed also to two local men, who accordingly agreed to go bond for him. When he submitted his bid, Burrows asked the government to notify him at Cincinnati if he were successful. It was necessary for him to visit that city to purchase merchandise for the next year, and he hoped also to obtain there items for the contracts that he could not procure locally.

While in Cincinnati, Burrows learned that he had received the Fort Snelling contract and began to make plans for fulfilling the agreement. On his return he was surprised to learn that another merchant, John Atchison, had been in Davenport for three days, anxiously awaiting his return. Atchison had received the contract for Fort Crawford and wanted to buy the Snelling agreement from Burrows, more for the profit on the transport of the goods than on the goods themselves. He owned the *Amaranth*, a steamboat operating on the upper Mississippi, and he saw a chance to profit from the additional business. Burrows was not especially eager to sell to him, but he finally agreed to surrender the contract for a $2,500 bonus and the right to furnish the pork, flour, and beans at the stipulated price, less transportation. The government, having been notified of the transaction, insisted that its agreement was with Burrows and that he would be held accountable for fulfillment.

Burrows immediately started to purchase the needed foodstuffs. His supplies were ready for delivery when he was notified that the pork quota would be increased by one third. As the slaughtering season was almost at an end, gathering the extra quantity entailed considerable travel in the surrounding territory. Burrows managed to find the additional supplies, however, only to have the amount reduced to the original figure. As the contract date approached, Atchison loaded the provisions on board his boat and prepared to leave for the fort. Burrows had been warned that Atchison was in financial difficulties, so he required him to pay for the goods before leaving. In that way he was fully protected in the unusual step he had taken in selling his contract to another man.

The venture proved successful in every way. Burrows had been in business only a short time, and the money from this deal enabled him to expand his store. All the items returned a profit, especially the pork, which brought a third more than it would have cleared in the open market. A heavy decline in the market price of provisions had set in before delivery was made, and the farmers from whom he had bought his foodstuffs were very favorably disposed toward him because of the excellent market he had provided.[95]

Not all contracts terminated so happily for the traders involved. The Aulls of Lexington, Missouri, found it profitable to act as surety for men who supplied the forts in their vicinity. Although they had cooperated in this way with Joel Turnham on the business at Fort Leavenworth for several years, they felt that he was a poor manager, and in 1834 they entered their own bid to supply $7,000 worth of provisions at the fort. Turnham won the contract and got other men to serve as bondsmen, thus eliminating the Aulls from the share of the profits they had enjoyed in preceding years. Considerable rivalry had now developed between the men, and in 1835 the Aulls entered a bid sufficiently low to win the contract. The brothers figured that a number of factors would operate in their favor. James was constructing a flour mill 8 miles from Independence, Missouri, on the Little Blue River, and by grinding his own flour he hoped to profit heavily on that item. Salt was available in Saline County, at no great distance from Lexington, and the pork and beans locally. These items would cost little to transport, and the brothers counted on them to reduce the expense of filling the contract.

Fast work had been required at the last minute to obtain the business. The bid had been advertised in a Saint Louis paper on July 11, but the Aulls did not see a copy of the notice until September. The time was then too short to ask for permission to use the names of

95. Burrows, *Fifty Years in Iowa*, 42-48.

the Saint Louis merchants whom they intended to give as surety. Consequently, their bid offered these men as bondsmen without their knowledge. As they were business friends of the Aulls, they readily acquiesced in the arrangement when notified of the circumstances. The delay in getting the bid off to Washington colored the whole transaction. The equipment for the Independence mill failed to arrive in time for the firm to grind its own supply of flour, so it was necessary to purchase flour in Boonville, Missouri, 70 miles down the Missouri River. The brothers paid $4 a barrel, which left little room for profit on the contract price of $4.50 at the fort, since freight, insurance, and labor costs ate heavily into the narrow margin on which they were operating. The government inspector at the fort reduced this margin still more by docking them $35.44 at the time of delivery, since the flour graded *fine* and not *superfine*, as the contract specified.[96] They had purchased the soap from Irwin and Whiteman in Cincinnati, and the bill for its transportation added greatly to the costs. The soap, too, failed to satisfy the inspector. Because of the softness of the article, he reduced the estimated weight by one twelfth before he would accept delivery.

To add to the embarrassment of the firm, the bean crop in Missouri failed, and the nearest source of supply was Philadelphia. Fortunately, in these circumstances the War Department pursued a liberal policy. On December 20, 1834, the government offered Aull the option of furnishing 82 bushels of beans and 520 pounds of rice, if the price of the latter was reasonable. This substitution reduced the amount of beans to one-third the contracted figure. Aull made the mistake of setting too high a price on the rice, however, and was required to fill his quota of beans.[97]

The Aulls were not alone in their situation. Contractors throughout the Mississippi Valley were affected by crop failures in 1835. Hill and M'Gunnegle asked to be released from the penalty for non-delivery of beans at Jefferson Barracks, but were informed that the War Department did not have the power to do so. Several harder cases of a similar nature had already come up for consideration, and all had been held to the penalty. The letter that brought the depart-

96. Letter of the Commissary General of Subsistence, Washington, D.C., to James Aull at Lexington, Mo., January 25, 1836, in the Correspondence of the Commissary General of Subsistence, Letter Book No. 11. The account of the Aull contract, except for the information from the War Department records, is substantially the same as that given in Lewis E. Atherton, "James and Robert Aull—A Frontier Missouri Mercantile Firm," *Missouri Historical Review*, 30 (October, 1935), 3-27.

97. Commissary General of Subsistence to James Aull, December 20, 1834, in Letter Book No. 10; February 1, 1835, Letter Book No. 11.

ment's decision to the firm also offered the gratuitous advice that some merchants had applied to Congress for relief, but without success.[98] This firm had counted too much on government leniency, and its attempt to escape a bad bargain illustrates why it was necessary for the War Department to insist on penalties when merchants did not fulfill contracts. All contractors had been offered the option of substituting rice for part of the beans, but some preferred to run the risk of penalties, in the hope of escaping completely. The Aulls at least played fair by ordering beans from Philadelphia and taking the loss occasioned by heavy freight rates.

Before the Aulls could deliver their goods, the government exercised its option of reducing the contract one third in the prospect that troops would be absent from Leavenworth during the year. Unfortunately, the Aulls already had most of the provisions at the fort, awaiting the day of delivery. Late delivery would have meant a penalty, but in overstressing safety, they suffered a loss that was probably just as great as the penalty. The government was well within its rights in making the reduction, but the change caused an additional loss on the contract. Eighty bushels of the beans originally purchased in Philadelphia were shipped back down the Missouri River and sold in Saint Louis.

These experiences illustrate the difficulties government bidders faced, in the same way Burrows' venture pictures the most successful deals. The returns on most contracts, of course, fell somewhere in between. The continued growth of interest in government contracts and the sharp competition to obtain them show, however, that they were considered excellent business ventures by the Western mercantile class. The War Department pursued a lenient policy whenever possible. For example, in 1831 frost injured the corn crop in the region around Fort Leavenworth, and a reduction in the number of animals at the post occurred at the same time. The post quarter-master was willing to tear up the contracts he held for corn and to make new ones. Yet, whenever injury would accrue to the government for nonperformance of contracts, the traders were held to their agreements.

Another outlet for produce taken in barter by the merchant in Mid-America was the Santa Fe trade, and it was among the safer gambles undertaken by residents of the West. Violence on the trail was not unknown, however. The use of military escorts for shippers attests the dangers that threatened those who engaged in the

98. Commissary General of Subsistence to Hill and M'Gunnegle at St. Louis, May 20, 1835, in Letter Book No. 11.

trade.[99] Troubles intensified during the years 1846 to 1848, the period of the United States' war with Mexico. Normally, active hostilities end all trade between the warring countries, but, in spite of the dangers involved, American goods continued to move to Santa Fe markets during the struggle.

The disastrous expedition of Samuel Owens and James Aull to Santa Fe in 1846 illustrates in many ways the obstacles to trade that were created by the wartime conditions. The experiences of these two traders were not in all respects typical of the problems encountered by merchants during the war, but they do illustrate the risks every merchant undertook when he sent goods to the Southwest. Some merchants disposed of their goods in less time than did Owens and Aull, some escaped the necessity of serving in the Army, and few merchants suffered their violent deaths. The story of Owens and Aull departs from the usual run of experience in that they encountered greater troubles than the average trader faced.

Owens and Aull were experienced, knowledgeable merchants. They had been in business in western Missouri for a number of years. From 1831 to 1836, James Aull, whose records have furnished many details for this discussion of the frontier merchants' methods and who has been mentioned a number of times earlier in this account, headed the firm of "James and Robert Aull," with stores at Lexington, Liberty, Richmond, and Independence, Missouri.[100] His wide and frequent travels to the East and South extended also, on occasion, to the West. Trappers, government purchasing agents, Indian missionaries, and Santa Fe traders were among his customers, and these men gave him a wide acquaintance with frontier life. In the early 1830s he invested in steamboats plying the Missouri River, opened a rope walk at Liberty, Missouri, and built his own flour mill. The decline of Aull's enterprises, the dissolution of his partnership with his brother Robert in 1836, and his concentration on the Lexington store alone for several years thereafter will be discussed later.

To a man so recently in the very center of affairs, management of one store must have been dull, for Lexington was rapidly losing its favored position in Western trade to Independence. The records of Aull's business during this period are fragmentary, and it is impossible to estimate the reduction in the volume of his trade.[101] The

99. Lewis E. Atherton, "Disorganizing Effects of the Mexican War on the Santa Fe Trade," *The Kansas Historical Quarterly*, 6 (1937), 115-23.

100. Atherton, "James and Robert Aull."

101. Letter books, invoice books, and account books for the firm of James and Robert Aull are complete for the years 1831–1837. A gap exists in the letter book of Robert Aull, covering the period from November 20, 1847, to November 13, 1851, Aull Collection.

one store, however, could not reach the trade area formerly served by the chain, and this handicap, coupled with the decline of Lexington's role in the Santa Fe trade, limited his business activities to a relatively small field. In these circumstances it was only natural for his interest to turn to the direct trade with Santa Fe, an enterprise with which he was well acquainted. In the 1830s, while Lexington still had hopes of competing with Independence for the trade to the Southwest, Aull had sold goods to the traders annually. In 1832 he sent his own agent to Santa Fe with a supply of merchandise. His primary reason for not personally continuing the trade after that time came from the difficulty he experienced in disposing of goods in Santa Fe in time to meet his credit obligations in the East.[102] Thus, his mercantile experience and his knowledge of the Santa Fe trade, gained over a period of years, were sufficient to give him every prospect of success in the venture he was undertaking with Owens.

By 1844 Owens had purchased Robert Aull's interest and had become the sole proprietor of the store at Independence. By that time he had become known in the Santa Fe trade, with the reputation of being a kind and liberal man who would "furnish wagons, teams, provisions, and general outfit for credit" to those who engaged in the trade to the Southwest.[103] As an Independence merchant Owens naturally became interested in that trade, and he found a ready partner in his former employer James Aull, who saw in the Mexican trade an opportunity to enter once more the main current of Western commerce. The men formed a partnership and set out for Santa Fe in the spring of 1846 with a $70,000 stock of goods.

They chose for their venture the least propitious time in the history of the Southwest. Mexican animosity toward the United States was at explosive strength as a result of the annexation of Texas; rumors of war had become increasingly current. For the traders, the outbreak of war meant that the entry ports for goods in the Santa Fe market would in all likelihood be blockaded. If war developed, the merchant might find himself in enemy territory, his goods a free prize to a population that, in peacetime, was willing to pay a high price for American products. To forestall such a circumstance, one group of traders left Independence early in May, 1846, and by rapid travel reached Santa Fe in forty-five days. Trouble developed, however, when they journeyed south to Chihuahua; the traders were held

102. James Aull, Letter Book, January 3, 1830, to February 14, 1833, entry dated November 3, 1832, Aull Collection.

103. James J. Webb, *Adventures in the Santa Fe Trade 1844–1847*, edited by Ralph P. Bieber, 42 and 274. Webb mentions the fact that Owens occasionally sent goods of his own, but gives no estimate of the extent of this business.

prisoners there for a time before being allowed to start the sale of their goods. Men of English, German, and French nationality received preferred treatment, so at least one American trader, in order to benefit by these easier circumstances, traveled as assistant wagonmaster for a Prussian Jew, with his goods under the man's protection.[104]

The group of traders Owens and Aull joined did not leave Independence until the latter part of May. They had traveled only 300 miles when they were overtaken by a detail from S. W. Kearny's command, which required them to wait at the Pawnee Fork until the main body of Kearny's troops arrived. Kearny was following the orders of the War Department, which were based on the belief that the merchandise would be confiscated in Santa Fe if military protection were not provided. The remainder of the journey was then made in the rear of the United States troops, with progress so slow that the party did not reach Santa Fe until August. A peaceable commercial undertaking had thus become involved in the Mexican War, valuable time had been lost, and disposal of the goods had been plunged into the greatest uncertainty. On the other hand, military authorities thought the least the traders could have expected, had they been allowed to proceed without protection, was detention in Santa Fe. In such a contingency the Mexican merchants would have preceded the Americans to the southern markets and would have placed them at a disadvantage in the disposal of their wares.[105] The merchants did not concur in these views, but were helpless to alter the course of events.

Kearny's protection ended in Santa Fe, and the traders then set out for the markets of Chihuahua. The caravan camped for two weeks near the ruins of Valverde, however, in hopes of obtaining news of conditions to the south. There they were overtaken by a detachment of Col. A. W. Doniphan's regiment of Missouri Volunteers, under the command of Captain Walton, and were required to wait until Colonel Doniphan arrived.[106] The period at Valverde preceding the arrival of the troops was not pleasant, since rumors of an impending attack by Mexican forces kept the group in a state of alarm. The traders, who exceeded three hundred in number, had formed a corral of their wagons for defense. But such measures did not conceal the fact of their helplessness, should an army attack

104. This trader was James J. Webb, and he relates the event in his *Adventures in the Santa Fe Trade*, 180, 263-64.

105. "Report of Committee on Claims," *House Reports*, 30th Cong., 1st sess., No. 458, 1-2.

106. "Report of Committee on Claims," 2-3.

them. Furthermore, the patriotism of the United States citizens did not appeal to the foreign traders among them when the governor of Chihuahua tossed in an apple of discord by instructing the merchants to dismiss American drivers in favor of Mexicans, with the assurance that those who did so could bring goods into Chihuahua free of duty. Most of the Mexican and English traders complied with the order, but the Americans remained adamant. The internal dissension within the group was heightened still further by the offer of the British agent in Chihuahua to have the caravan proceed under his protection, a scheme that especially appealed to the English traders but was resented by the Americans.[107]

The arrival of Doniphan put an end to the arguments, and the traders followed his troops into El Paso del Norte and took advantage of their arrival there to make a few small sales. But military restrictions proved irksome to the merchants, some of whom attempted to escape Doniphan's control and others of whom got into difficulties with him over endeavors to communicate with Chihuahua.[108] Doniphan finally decided to push on to that city, but rumors of superior Mexican forces in the area caused him to order the creation of a "Traders Battalion" of two companies, to be commanded by "Major" Samuel Owens, Aull's partner.[109] Doniphan's actions were irregular, at least. The Colonel was in command of only a Volunteer regiment, yet without authority from the War Department, he designated a group of Santa Fe merchants as soldiers. The Mexicans might easily have seized them and their goods later, on the clearly legal grounds that they were a military expedition, and they could have dealt with them summarily under military law.

The general story of the battle of Sacramento, fought in February, 1847, lies outside this narrative. It is important here because of the consequences for the firm of Owens and Aull. Few Americans fell in the battle, but Major Owens was among the casualties. The various stories of how he met his death differ widely. Doniphan reported that he lost his life by excessive rashness—riding up to a redoubt filled with armed men and continuing to fire his pistols until both he and his horse fell under the return fire.[110] James J. Webb was told by one of Owens' men that the Major might have courted death because of family troubles; he had shaved and dressed carefully in clean

107. John T. Hughes, "Diary," Thursday, October 26, to Friday, December 4, 1846, in John T. Hughes, *Doniphan's expedition and the conquest of New Mexico and California,* edited by William E. Connelley.

108. Hughes, "Diary," January 1, February 4, 1847.

109. "Report of Committee on Claims," 4. The order was issued February 9, 1847.

110. St. Louis *Daily Missouri Republican,* June 18, 1847.

clothes just before the battle. Webb also reports that only the horse was killed in the first firing, and Owens was pinned beneath it. The Mexicans were then able to kill Owens and strip him of his valuables.[111] William E. Connelley cites the story that Owens was killed by the spears of the Mexicans, and that his seeming rashness is to be explained as the result of the machinations of a cabal among the officers of the United States forces that stopped the general charge by the troops in order to give an officer named Reid the honor of winning the battle. Still another account pictures the Major as leading a charge, shouting, "Give it to them, boys! They can't withstand us," and falling two minutes later with a grapeshot through the forehead, so close to the gun that the fire burned his clothes.[112] Indeed, Samuel Owens died as many different deaths as there are sources reporting it. His funeral was in harmony with his importance. Burial took place "with great pomp" in Chihuahua after that city was occupied on March 1, 1847. His "coffin with trimmings" cost $70—only slightly more expensive than the wax candles, an item of $65.[113]

The burden of caring for the goods of the firm now fell to Aull. After Chihuahua was occupied, the traders were free to dispose of their goods, their objective when they left Independence ten long months before. They were not yet free of danger, however, for if Doniphan should depart the merchants would be at the mercy of the Mexicans. Consequently, they presented a petition to Doniphan, asking him to make known his plans, a request he was unable to fulfill until he received orders from his superior officers. This uncertainty increased the willingness of the merchants to sell at sacrifice prices on a market that would have been sluggish, even in a normal year, as the result of such heavy importations of goods.[114]

But James Aull was unwilling to be stampeded. For several years in the 1830s he had fought an annual battle to get his goods through from Philadelphia in time to serve the spring trade of four stores, and in spite of the primitive transportation he had almost always won. Schooled to expect difficulties, he was unwilling to admit defeat. So he set to work to sell the goods of Owens and Aull as quickly as possible, but only at prices that would pay dividends on the venture. Even the slow journey to Chihuahua he had turned to profit; the account book of the firm shows numerous sales made to

111. Webb, *Adventures in the Santa Fe Trade*, 274-75.

112. Hughes, *Doniphan's expedition*, note 107. Connelley gives a number of versions by men who participated in the battle.

113. Owens and Aull, Day Book, containing invoices of goods from February 14, 1846, and letters and entries from January 28, 1847, entry dated March, 1847, Aull Collection.

114. Hughes, *Doniphan's expedition*, 453-55, 465-66.

the troops under whose protection Aull traveled. On April 3, 1847, for example, he was able to send pay accounts of officers and drafts for Army supplies in excess of $15,000 to Rich and Pomeroy at Santa Fe, to be forwarded to his brother Robert at Lexington. Some of the money he earned as middleman for the troops, for, despite his difficult situation, he bought provisions from the Mexicans and quoted pork and mutton to the Army at profitable figures. Nor were the profits gathered in such perilous circumstances to remain idle after they were delivered in Lexington, for James instructed Robert to invest the proceeds in Treasury notes at 5 and 6 per cent interest if they could be obtained at par.[115] Dangers from a state of war apparently did not deter him from embracing any opportunities created by the predicament in which he found himself.

Meanwhile, the sale of his goods continued. By taking a note he was able to sell a load of goods to Santiago Ulivarri at San Miguel for $1,260. By the last of May his brother-in-law E. W. Pomeroy, at Santa Fe, was able to send $16,000 to Lexington, and at about the same time, Owens' nephew Harrison left for Independence with 75 mules, 6 wagons, and $1,250 in money.[116] Obviously, the goods were being liquidated rapidly, but a second major catastrophe was now to descend on the firm.

Doniphan had finally received orders from Gen. Zachary Taylor to join him at Saltillo. What were the traders to do? If they remained at Chihuahua, they would be without protection; if they accompanied the troops, there was small prospect of disposing of their goods. Doniphan attempted to help them by negotiating a treaty with Governor Trias to provide for the neutrality of Chihuahua, but his effort failed. On April 25 Doniphan ordered the evacuation of the city, and by April 28 all had obeyed except a very few traders who were unwilling to sacrifice their goods. Among the latter was James Aull. His friends in Santa Fe realized his precarious position, and Pomeroy, in his letter of May 29, 1847, could give Robert little assurance of his brother's safety. Persons of influence in Chihuahua had promised protection, but they were unwilling to answer for the mob. Misgivings must have filled the minds of the merchants who elected to remain in the city as they watched the departure of Doniphan's force on the morning of April 28, 1847—"The army and a part of the traders were moving off in the direction of Saltillo, while a bustling train of merchants were hurrying out at the other end of the city in the direction of Santa Fe; the skulky Mexican soldiers and lawless rabble rejoicing at our departure from the capitol, and

115. Owens and Aull, Day Book, Aull Collection.
116. E. W. Pomeroy to Robert Aull, May 29, 1847, Aull Collection.

Mexican girls dressed as men accompanying their sweethearts on the road to Saltillo."[117]

Shortly after Doniphan left, the remaining traders agreed to pay the legal rates of duty on the imported goods, in return for which they were to receive the protection of the Mexican authorities. On the evening of June 23, however, while alone in his store, James was attacked by four Mexicans and fatally stabbed in the back. Most of the available money and goods were taken.[118] The act was motivated solely by the hope of plunder, and the municipal authorities made what recompense they could by apprehending the culprits and giving James an honorable funeral. But the second of the two partners had now met his death, and the property of the firm was in danger of being confiscated.

The Mexican authorities appointed a "depository" for the goods and from June to August they were stored in two rooms for which the heirs of the estate were charged rental of 25¢ a day. The "depositary," John Mandri, proved himself to be a good bookkeeper. He collected $4,323.19 from the sale of wagons and harness and from debtors of the estate. His accounts show that he paid out exactly the same amount for translating, customs, fines for illegal inclusion of powder and whiskey in the goods, transportation, and rent.[119] While these charges depleted the profits expected from the sale of the goods, his negotiations and the return of some money were certainly better than the confiscation of the goods—a possibility that threatened for a time.

On August 8 Pomeroy with several others left Santa Fe for Chihuahua to settle the estate. Apache Indians had been terrorizing the Mexicans along the route, and Pomeroy's party was attacked, but they managed to escape with the loss of only three mules and $300 worth of provisions. Good fortune continued with them, and they were able to obtain possession of the firm's goods in Chihuahua about the middle of October. The goods proved to be principally lienzo, bleached goods for which there was little demand. The partners had originally planned to sell these farther south, but, as there was now no hope of getting permission to make the journey, Pomeroy and his companions opened two retail stores in Chihuahua.[120] By November 15 a third store was in operation, and they had sold $9,000 worth of goods.

117. John T. Hughes in the Liberty (Missouri) Weekly Tribune, July 3, 1847.
118. Hughes, Doniphan's expedition, 477.
119. Owens and Aull, Day Book, Aull Collection.
120. Joseph P. Hamelin to Robert Aull, October 31, 1847, Aull Collection. Hamelin was a clerk for James Aull.

A Doctor Connelley, who had engaged in ventures with Owens in Chihuahua in 1843, was appointed legal representative for the estate under a bond of over $150,000. Power of attorney was necessary if the estate was to be kept out of the courts, and Pomeroy urged that someone travel in the interest of the firm from Lexington to Pittsburgh to get the Mexican consul there to certify the papers. The situation at Chihuahua was grave. The difficulty of communication with the outside world is shown by the fact that copies of Pomeroy's letter were sent out by way of Santa Fe and by Vera Cruz, in the hope that at least one letter would get through. Pomeroy closed his urgent request with the words, "Remember that we are in H–11 and wish to be transferred to a better place."[121] In spite of the appeal for haste the papers were not ready until March 4, 1848, at which time the required authorization was sent to Chihuahua.[122]

The Mexicans permitted the sale of the goods to continue, however, and by January, 1848, the estate was liquidated, with the exception of 40 bales of bleached cotton—Pomeroy dispiritedly estimated that there was enough of this article in Chihuahua to supply the demand for two years. Other than this item, the goods sold at an excellent price. The cost of the original outfit was $70,000. Duties and expenses connected with the liquidation brought the total investment to $100,000. Pomeroy hoped to realize a net profit of $30,000 from the expedition, but when the books were closed, the venture barely cleared expenses.[123]

Owens and Aull left Independence in 1846 with reasonable expectations of disposing of their goods in six months at an excellent profit. Conditions created by the war lengthened the time to two years, took the lives of the two men, and destroyed the prospects of a profit. Only prompt action on the part of friends of the men in Santa Fe prevented the last possible financial disaster, the confiscation of the cargo. On the other hand, had the Owens and Aull expedition been forced to halt at Santa Fe, the two men might have returned home, having lost only their fortunes.

121. E. W. Pomeroy to Robert Aull, November 22, 1847, Aull Collection.
122. Robert Aull to John Potts, March 4, 1848, Letter Book V, Aull Collection.
123. Robert Aull to Siter, Price and Company, July 14, 1848, Letter Book V, Aull Collection.

CHAPTER IV
BUSINESS ORGANIZATION
AND METHODS

The corporate form of organization was unimportant in Western merchandising before the Civil War. Capital was scarce in the West, and residents found sufficient opportunity for investments without turning to the corporate forms of business. Nor did merchandising require large sums of money in that period; $5,000 or $6,000 sufficed to purchase a good stock, and much of this stock could be obtained on credit. Those who operated from three to eight stores could do business on $50,000 capital.

If the savings from large-scale organization seemed desirable, operation of three or four stores was sufficient. A liquid capital of $50,000 permitted cash purchases, which reduced the cost of goods by 25 per cent, according to the estimate made by many merchants. The firm could send one partner to the East each year to buy supplies at the auctions in New York and Philadelphia, and no cheaper means of acquiring goods existed. A mercantile unit of this size could own its own steamboat for carrying stocks and trading produce to and from its stores and thus effect considerable saving in transportation, a charge that sometimes totaled 25 per cent of the value of the goods. Advertising was so standardized that most merchants ran the same advertisement, unchanged, through many issues of the local newspaper—a saving that small stores might enjoy as well as the larger firms. The operation of more than one store reduced labor cost by very little, since every unit required one or two clerks at the least.

On the other hand, certain inherent difficulties appeared as soon as firms expanded to three or four locations. Even when junior partners operated the new stores, the senior partner frequently encountered problems. Since communication was slow, the junior partner generally was free for long periods from personal direction by the senior member of the firm. Letters helped to maintain contact, but the junior partner could conceal many irregularities when letters were the only form of supervision. Under such circumstances, honesty and character were of greater importance than business ability, and in the recommendations written for young men who had worked for merchants these qualities understandably received the greatest emphasis. Nor is it remarkable that the largest units seldom exceeded three or four stores.

Although a common form of organization, the partnership suffered in reputation because each partner was liable for the transactions of the other, a situation that the State of New York sought to remedy by creating "limited partnerships" in manufacturing and merchandising. Under this form, regular partners carried on the business and were liable for the debts of the firm as had been partners in the old form. In addition, however, it was possible for special partners to participate; partners of this category contributed money to the business but were not liable beyond the amount of money they subscribed. Such partners could not permit the use of their names in the conduct of the business and could not withdraw any of the capital during the life of the partnership. They were privileged to examine the records and to advise the actively engaged partners, but they could not transact any business for the firm. Violation of this restriction made them liable for the debts of the firm to the same extent as were the general partners.[1]

This New York statute was widely copied in the West, although Missouri and Kentucky prohibited limited partnerships. In some states the statute was modified, as in Wisconsin, which modeled its law on New York's but permitted a partner to receive interest and profits on the money subscribed during the course of the partnership, provided such payments did not reduce the amount of the original capital.[2] These statutes marked the transition from the partnership to the corporation, in which the limited-liability clause is a characteristic. The chief advantage of the limited partnership was its attractiveness to investors; an investor was much readier to subscribe money to a firm when his liability for its debts was limited to the amount he contributed than when his liability equaled that of the active partners. The limited partnership well suited an economy in which money was seeking investment and the corporation form had not as yet matured. The West had little capital that was not in actual use under the supervision of its owner, and this circumstance, combined with the small scale of the business operations, prevented limited partnerships from achieving general acceptance in the region before the Civil War.

1. James P. Holcombe, *The Merchants' Book of Reference for Debtor and Creditor in the United States and Canada*, 137-40.
2. Holcombe, *Merchants' Book of Reference*, 264-66.

The simpler forms of partnership agreement can be divided into two classes—silent partnerships and those in which all the members actively participated. In the silent partnership one man generally furnished all or most of the capital. The junior partner conducted the business in his own name and received a share of the profits as return for his labor and the capital he had invested. This type had certain distinct advantages. For one factor, it permitted Western firms to maintain connections in the East; the silent partner there furnished the goods for the store and, by virtue of his residence near the source of supplies throughout the year, was able to purchase stock at the lowest prices and to the best advantage. As noted earlier, one of the commonest appeals in the advertising of the period revolved around this point—the purchase of goods in the Eastern markets at advantageous prices. For example, Paul and Ingram at Saint Louis, in a large advertisement in the Franklin *Missouri Intelligencer* in 1820, informed merchants of the surrounding territory that they had arrived home with drygoods and hardware purchased for cash at auction in Philadelphia—the cheapest means of acquiring supplies. This method of buying would continue in the future, they announced, their having established a partnership connection with a firm in Philadelphia.[3] Almost twenty years later another Saint Louis firm was using the same selling points. Isaac Burnet and Company advertised goods for sale as cheaply as they could be purchased by going East, as a member of the firm was in the wholesale drygoods business there and he purchased most of their goods at auction.[4]

Nor was the practice followed solely by wholesale houses. Christian Wilt opened a store in Saint Louis in 1811 with goods purchased in Philadelphia by his uncle Joseph Hertzog. Hertzog's arrangement with his nephew illustrates another reason for the widespread use of the silent-partnership form of organization—the need of the younger men for capital to start in business. Wilt's father had given him $1,500 to invest, and there was a prospect of this amount being increased to $2,000 if the son showed ability; but Joseph Hertzog supplied most of the capital for starting the business. On his part, he was willing for Wilt to have an equal share in the business when he could raise the money, or the percentage could stand as it was; Hertzog had full confidence in the future of Saint Louis as a profitable business center. On Wilt's part, by managing the firm in Saint Louis and devoting his full time to clerking, he received a larger share of the returns than his capital stock alone would have earned.[5]

3. Franklin *Missouri Intelligencer*, August 5, 1820.
4. St. Louis *Daily Missouri Republican*, April 6, 1837.
5. Joseph Hertzog to Christian Wilt at St. Louis, dated Philadelphia, April 6, 1811, Joseph Hertzog, Letters.

Sometimes the junior member furnished no capital at all. Jones's fictional account relates the story of an established merchant who formed a partnership with an enterprising young man, furnished all the goods, and gave the younger partner half the profits for operating the store.[6]

Men like Ninian Edwards who were busy with politics, farming, and land speculation found the silent partnership useful in conducting their mercantile ventures. Edwards entered such an arrangement with James Mitchell at Belleville, Illinois, in the twenties. Edwards furnished Mitchell with goods worth $10,000 and paid the transportation charges to Saint Louis; both shared the cost from there to Belleville. Mitchell provided the building and paid the costs of vending the goods for one year, beginning October 1, 1821. At the end of the year they divided the profits equally. Edwards also permitted Mitchell to construct a brick house, which Edwards was to purchase at cost. The contract further specified that Mitchell would not be held liable for bad debts and unavoidable accidents if he exercised care in conducting the business.[7] Such arrangements enabled older and more experienced merchants to branch out to other stores or to devote time to other enterprises; for younger men they provided opportunity to start in business at an early age and with larger stocks of goods than they could purchase with their own resources.

Characteristically, no matter what the distance, the older men attempted to keep a guiding hand on the business by correspondence. Edwards made all purchases for the stores in which he was interested; Joseph Hertzog could not let his nephew Andrew Wilt leave for the West without a four-page letter of minute instruction: Wilt must keep a record of his journey from Philadelphia to Pittsburgh, presumably for Hertzog's use, should he make the trip, and almost certainly to keep that young man's mind on business matters and away from his fellow passengers on the stage; in Pittsburgh he must board at a respectable place and not lounge around the town with companions; when not engaged in business he should converse with business friends of the firm; further, he should assume a little importance in his manner, as such an air did not hurt a man.[8] Andrew was a young man starting on his first journey west with goods. Such being the case, his uncle's instructions were somewhat more minute and elementary than those usually given to clerks and junior partners.

6. John Beauchamp Jones [Luke Shortfield], *The Western Merchant*, 18-20.
7. Ninian Edwards to James Mitchell at Belleville, dated Belleville, Illinois, August 11, 1827, Ninian W. Edwards Papers.
8. Joseph Hertzog to Andrew Wilt at Philadelphia, dated Philadelphia, April 1, 1812, Joseph Hertzog, Letters.

Still, advice was freely given: advice to advertise, to cultivate some important business or political figure, to grasp every opportunity to expand business—excepting, always, the granting of wide credit; such was the tenor of the letters to junior partners. When, as happened in some cases, they became despondent over business or wanted to move to another location, the senior partner offered encouragement and praise for their work. Most of the letters, however, must have conveyed the idea to the junior partner that his senior would have acted just a trifle more astutely in the matter under discussion.

More widely used was the active partnership, in which the names of all members were openly employed. James and Robert Aull operated stores at Lexington, Richmond, Liberty, and Independence in Missouri from 1831 to 1836, hiring clerks in all places except Lexington, which was their headquarters, to conduct the business, but excluding them from investment in the firm. The Aulls exercised close supervision over all the stores, although Robert remained at Liberty much of the time to handle the business there. Clerks made lists of needed goods, but James personally took care of the orders and made the annual trips east to purchase supplies. Both brothers supervised book accounts and indicated the amount of credit individuals should receive, but James saw to the collection of long-outstanding accounts. Samuel Owens, "head man" at Independence and the most capable of the clerks, entered the business as a partner with Robert when the original company ceased as a brotherly partnership in 1836. Owens' career was financially successful, as indicated by his joining James in the venture to Santa Fe and Mexico in 1846. The undertaking, which represented an investment of $70,000, yielded a financial profit, but, as related in Chapter III, ended in personal disaster for both partners. Because of his ability, Owens was allowed considerable leeway in conducting the Independence store. There the brothers provided him with a bookkeeper at $250 a year to relieve him of the routine work on accounts and to enable him to devote more time to the general business. But Owens' achieving partnership was an exceptional career, and although he was a partner, James Aull continued to make the decisions on matters of policy for the other stores.[9]

A variation in this form of active partnership was the arrangement in which the name of the local junior member was linked with that of the senior partner in the place where the store was located. This form was widely used by the Lammes, a family that came to Missouri from Kentucky and engaged in merchandising on a large scale in the twenties and thirties. They operated stores at Liberty, Franklin, Inde-

9. Lewis E. Atherton, "James and Robert Aull—A Frontier Missouri Mercantile Firm," *Missouri Historical Review*, 30 (1935), 3-27.

pendence, and Columbia, and the junior partner's name was connected with the firm's in each town.[10] In this company a senior member of the firm attended to wholesale purchases in the East in the
same way as the Aulls, but the conduct of business was not as closely
centralized as the Aull system. Joseph Webster and John R. Crandall
at Dubuque in Wisconsin Territory organized their business on the
same basis. They were partners in a store in Dubuque and operated
in other towns with junior partners. Thus, the firm's name was Swan,
Webster and Company in Middletown, and Webster, Hill and Company at Spoon River in Illinois.[11] The contracts under which these
companies operated varied little, if any, in form from the partnership
agreement in which a silent partner provided the financing. The operating partner in both types might be closely supervised, or he might
enjoy a wide discretion in business matters. The silent partnership
probably allowed the operating partner broader latitude in general.

Far more numerous than these partnerships and usually involving
much less capital were those that operated a single store. Both members gave full-time service to the business and contributed to the
capital stock. This type was a generally practiced form of organization, individual ownership of stores being somewhat less common
than today. In part, the prevalence of this type of ownership resulted
from relatives' cooperating in business ventures. George Lichtenberger, a merchant at New Harmony, Indiana, well illustrates the
pull of family ties in such a matter. Lichtenberger was in business for
himself. He regularly received letters from a relative in Illinois,
apparently his wife's father. This man was an experienced tradesman,
but obviously was dissatisfied with his situation and eager to locate in
the same town with his daughter and her husband. In a letter in 1846
he asked if Lichtenberger considered himself permanently located
and suggested the possibility of the two families moving to "Ioway or
Wisconsin," where business and family relationships could be much
closer.[12] The correspondence available to the historian does not indicate the outcome of this particular proposal, but the practice of relatives pooling their resources to start a business enterprise was not
uncommon.

Most of the contractual agreements for partnerships were brief and
left many details to an oral understanding between the members.
For example, John and Matthew Cartwright each subscribed $2,000
in 1834 to a joint venture in merchandising in San Augustine in the

10. Fayette *Missouri Intelligencer,* December 25, 1829.

11. *DuBuque* (Wisconsin Territory) *Visitor,* June 22, 1836.

12. P. Saltzman to George Lichtenberger at New Harmony, Indiana, dated at
Buffalow Grove, Illinois, some time in 1846, Letters to George Lichtenberger.

province of Texas. Their contract was not detailed, but they obviously prospered under it, for each subscribed $3,500 in 1835 to renew the agreement.[13] Alonzo Pearson and Erasmus D. Sappington started business with even less capital; each contributed $1,000 to form a partnership in Saline County, Missouri, in 1829, with the understanding that the business was to continue for three years and was not to be moved without the consent of both parties.[14] Claiborne F. Jackson, Democratic governor of Missouri at the outbreak of the Civil War, and Moss Prewitt entered a partnership in Franklin, Missouri, December 1, 1829. Prewitt invested $5,000 and Jackson $2,500. Jackson agreed to pay Prewitt 10 per cent a year on Prewitt's extra investment but had the option of increasing his share to $5,000 at any time, thereby ending the interest charges. Both were to devote full time to the business, and the profits were to be divided equally at the end of the year. As a protection against either member jeopardizing the property of the other, they agreed that mutual consent was necessary for either to go security, whether personally or for the firm. All goods used for personal and family consumption were to be charged at cost, plus 6 per cent. The contract was to run for two years unless terminated after three months' notice by one of the partners.

This latter provision was typical of partnerships. The terminal date provided time to make adjustments in the partnership, increase capital, or advertise to customers that the partnership was terminated and all debts owed to the firm due at once. Businesses frequently used the notice of dissolution of partnership and the consequent need for all accounts to be settled as a means of hurrying collections, even though the partnership might continue under a new contract. In this particular case Prewitt and Jackson quit business before the two years were up, and Jackson entered a partnership with Samuel Miller at Arrow Rock, Missouri, under a four-year agreement. Each man invested $3,000 and their agreement entitled Jackson to receive $500 a year for operating the store if Miller did not participate actively. This connection proved more enduring than Jackson's with Prewitt; the partners renewed their contract in 1835 for another four-year period.[15] As these illustrations show, the contract was not a long legal document. The agreement consisted of a stipulation about the

13. Contract of John and Matthew Cartwright, Matthew Cartwright Manuscript Collection.

14. Contract of Alonzo Pearson and Erasmus D. Sappington, April 11, 1829, Governor M. M. Marmaduke Manuscript Collection.

15. Contracts of Claiborne F. Jackson with Moss Prewitt, December 1, 1829, and with Samuel Miller, September 22, 1831, Dr. John Sappington Manuscript Collection.

amount of capital to be contributed by each partner, a brief statement of the duties of each member, and the length of time the partnership was to obtain. Beyond these conditions, the agreement frequently made no other specifications.

So long as the members remained friends, as they usually did, such a contract was all that was needed; but there were times when all parties wished for detailed wording. Ninian Edwards seems to have had his share of difficulty with contracts, even though he was a lawyer. In 1816 Edwards furnished goods to a son-in-law of Col. Auguste Chouteau who planned to engage in business in Saint Louis. Edwards furnished the capital and the other partner managed the store, both sharing in the profits. In 1822 the affairs of the partnership were settled, with Edwards agreeing to take 20 per cent of the profits, in so far as he was entitled to a share of the profits, and to take back all goods that had not been sold. Edwards felt that he should have received a 25 per cent profit, and he requested Chouteau, who was interceding for the son-in-law, to ask any Saint Louis merchant if he were grasping in accepting only 20 per cent. The son-in-law had agreed to the arrangement, had also rectified a $2,000 mistake against Edwards in the matter of invoices, and had, as well, canceled further demands for unspecified interest and premium charges. He failed to keep his agreement, however, and Edwards instituted a law suit, which Edwards won, but at a cost of $500 to himself. At this point Chouteau asked to arbitrate the case, the minor partner having instituted another suit despite his setback in the first. Edwards, obviously anxious to placate Chouteau, replied to his request in a long letter in which he set forth the reasons why the son-in-law would be no more successful in the second suit than in the first. Feeling that his case was sure to win at law, he refused to arbitrate.[16] Regardless of the outcome, such quarrels proved expensive to both parties, a fact that stands as one of the reasons why merchants found it unwise to expand business connections beyond the range of their immediate supervision.

In 1827 Edwards became involved in another dispute, this one with James Mitchell over the settlement of the partnership they had entered at Belleville in 1821. The contract seemed to be quite clear when drawn, but six years of business operations had caused the partners to arrive at many points of difference in its interpretation. Mitchell asked for half the profits, regardless of bad debts and other losses, basing his claim on that part of the contract which excused

16. Ninian Edwards to Col. Auguste Chouteau at St. Louis, dated Edwardsville, Illinois, October 13 and October 22, 1823, Col. Auguste Chouteau Papers.

him from liability for bad debts and unavoidable accidents if he exercised caution in conducting the business. Edwards called Mitchell's an unreasonable interpretation, and he secured the opinions of many merchants to support his views. He even sent a copy of the contract to Daniel Webster for an opinion and was comforted by Webster's assurance that he was in the right. Furthermore, he brought a number of charges against Mitchell. Goods had been charged to Edwards at higher than cost, whereas Mitchell had taken goods for his own use without adding even the transportation charges. He had failed to construct a store building according to specifications; had purchased real estate with the money of the firm without consulting Edwards and now wanted him to take possession of the land at the original cost, even though it was worth much less; and had hired men to sell goods from the store, charging Edwards with half the cost. Mitchell had cheated Edwards in their joint operations in bank notes and had taken his share of profits from the store in goods figured at the invoice price, again without adding transportation charges. The partners submitted the dispute to Edward Tracy and William Rule, Saint Louis merchants, as referees. Tracy and Rule decided that Edwards' capital should be the first obligation against the firm. After that obligation had been discharged, Mitchell was to get half of the nominal or gross profits—a decision in his favor, as gross profits left the bad debts to Edwards. In several other charges the referees ruled against Mitchell, but in the end he signed the referees' decision and agreed to settle partnership affairs as rapidly as possible or forfeit a penalty of $4,000.[17]

The right and wrong of such disputes cannot be determined from the fragmentary records. Generally, only one side of the case appears in the letter books and documents. The question of right is not important here, however, for the cases serve to illustrate the troubles that disturbed the conduct of business in even so simple a form as the partnership agreement.

THE PRODUCE TRADE

From the time of his arrival in a frontier settlement, the Western merchant engaged in the produce trade, as has been discussed in preceding chapters. Such involvement was necessary first, as a means of increasing sales to Western farmers, who needed to barter produce for goods, and second, as a means of paying for goods purchased in the East. In a real sense the Western storekeeper was an integral part

17. Ninian Edwards to James Mitchell at Belleville, dated Belleville, Illinois, August 11, 1827, and other entries, Edwards Papers.

of the three-cornered trade relationship that characterized American economic life before the Civil War. During that period the South produced cash crops suitable for export in large quantities, and these were handled by Eastern merchants and commission men, who in return supplied the South with merchandise. The West also relied on the East for merchandise and other manufactured products. Lacking in cash crops that could command an immediate sale in European markets, the West made up for the deficiency as far as possible by serving as a source of foodstuffs, mules, and forage for the South. Credits established in the South in this manner could be transferred to Eastern merchants to pay for finished goods purchased there. By taking the farmer's crops in exchange for merchandise the Western merchant supplied the farmer with goods from the East, and by sending farm crops to the Southern market, he was able to meet a large percentage of his bills in the East.

Even though this system was beneficial to the West, farmers and merchants alike frequently complained against the flow of cash and credits to the East. A citizen of Franklin, Missouri, in 1821 wrote to the editor of his paper to comment on the hard times and scarcity of cash. He was sure, however, that there was sufficient money in the country, if only it were properly handled; the West exchanged its money for "imported finery and foreign gew-gaws" instead of developing its own factories. The letter pointed to the four or five stores in Franklin as horrible examples of the prevailing system. Each of these annually remitted $12,000 to $15,000 to the East, exporting cash and leaving the local community short of currency. A system of domestic manufacture would end dependence on other sections and keep the money at home, according to the writer.[18]

Several years later, during the hard times in 1837, a merchant wrote to the editor of a Saint Louis paper and threatened Eastern wholesalers with the loss of the Western market if they were too insistent on collecting accounts. His ire had been aroused by an announcement in a Philadelphia paper that two agents were to be sent west to collect in specie the debts due Eastern wholesalers. In the writer's estimation, such a course would have been reprehensible at any time, but he considered it downright villainous when the object was to remit the money to England in order to sustain banks there. He asked the Easterners to consider that steamboats now came from New Orleans in seven and eight days. Only habit explained why merchants in Cincinnati, Saint Louis, Louisville, and Nashville continued to buy at second hand in New York and Philadelphia instead of directly in France and England. "Let our wealthy western

18. Franklin *Missouri Intelligencer*, April 23, 1821.

merchants consider such a possibility."[19] In spite of all the grumbling, however, the West continued to rely on the three-cornered relationship with the other sections.

The system of bartering produce for store goods was universal in the West. Merchants realized the necessity of this practice as a means of moving their stocks of goods, and mercantile account books reveal its importance. A farmer very frequently settled his bills by bringing in produce to balance the charges against him. For instance, James Aull took three barrels of whiskey from Aaron Overton at $11.33 a barrel, and two more at a slightly higher price, thus canceling Overton's account; another customer paid in beeswax; a third brought in a supply of tow linen, for which he received credit at 25¢ a yard; another farmer settled his account with tallow and country sugar. Produce was not the only medium of exchange. Services might also be bartered. One farmer paid his bill by hauling goods; another brought in a load of oak planking. Cutting brush and grinding an axe were the means of settlement for one man who had nothing in the way of produce to offer. Scythe stones were the medium of payment for another.[20]

The same trading practices prevailed in other sections of the frontier. The account books of Jared Warner indicate that between 1849 and 1859 few men settled their bills with cash. Moses Hicklin paid in cash, pork, and flour; George Engle paid in cash; Benjamin Brown paid in wheat and flour; Samuel Rosencrants paid part of his bill in wheat and gave a note for the remainder; John Bureingame paid his account by working for Warner, by one coonskin, and by rafting and boating.[21] Warner's accounts exhibit more uniformity than those of many merchants in that he received a large part of his payments in pork and wheat; other storekeepers frequently accepted payment in a variety of ways.

Moses Payne at Columbia, Missouri, accepted much produce in exchange for goods. In 1830 Cornelius Short brought him a dozen eggs, which were rated at 4½¢. In return, Short bought a "bonnet and trimmings" at $3.75 and promised to bring enough bacon to town the next week to satisfy the account. As Payne valued bacon at 4¢ a pound, Short was required to supply 92½ pounds to pay for the bonnet.[22] Elisha and Gilbert Read at Chicago pursued the same course in their trading practices. They accepted a wide variety of

19. St. Louis Missouri Argus, May 26, 1837.

20. James Aull, Ledger, Independence, Missouri, beginning 1827, James and Robert Aull Manuscript Collection.

21. Jared Warner, Ledger 1849–59, Jared Warner Manuscript Collection.

22. J. M. and A. M. Payne, Day Book 1830–31.

items and services in payment for their goods. Abnor Bristol paid his bill of $2.12 with cash and a whippletree; Walter Chambers received $3.37 credit for chopping 13½ cords of wood, and he also applied 15½ bushels of wheat on his bill; Ebenezer Ford chopped 42 cords of wood and butchered hogs for the Reads; Walter Chambers cut saw logs and did one day's work with his team; Hamilton Dickerson made a pair of pantaloons; Simon Read brought in two hogs; John Jeffry paid in unspecified work; John Mack paid with 3½ barrels of cider; and Mr. Perry settled by bringing in 2½ bushels of pease.[23]

Merchants doing this kind of business obviously accumulated a great deal of produce in a short time. Earlier in this study it has been noted that they often processed the produce before shipping it to the larger cities to pay wholesale bills. Burrows at Davenport, Iowa, bought some goods in Saint Louis and New Orleans for which he could pay directly by sending flour from his mills to the two cities. James Aull built up credit in the same manner. In his order for 15,000 pounds of sugar and 10,000 pounds of coffee from James Breedlove and Company at New Orleans in 1833 he explained that he hoped to pay for the whole amount from the proceeds of a shipment of bale rope—processed from the hemp he had accepted in exchange for goods. Shipments of large quantities of bagging and rope enabled him to meet many such bills without the necessity of transmitting money. He also used smaller shipments of honey, beeswax, furs, pork, and tobacco to the same end.

Joseph Hertzog owned a lead-processing factory at Saint Louis, and the extent to which he relied on shipments from this enterprise to reduce money remittances is evident from a letter to a New York commission house in 1811. The New York firm was holding a consignment of Hertzog's lead, and he was anxious to have it sold, since lack of ready money threatened to halt his accustomed spring shipments to his Western store. It was now March, and he had expected to receive $5,000 in money from sales of lead by the first of February.[24] James Wier at Lexington, Kentucky, shipped tobacco, cotton, yarn, bagging, and rope to New Orleans and the eastern cities, as his letter books between 1806 and 1824 show. Shipments from his hemp factory were impressively large, and they frequently were consigned to Philadelphia, New York, and Baltimore commission houses.

This double value to the merchants—increased sales to farmers through the barter system, and the use of farm crops to discharge

23. Elisha and Gilbert Read, Account Book 1818–59.
24. Joseph Hertzog to David and Philip Gum at New York City, dated Philadelphia, March 30, 1811, Joseph Hertzog, Letters.

remittances to the East—caused the storekeepers of Mid-America to develop a regular system for handling the produce they accumulated. The value to the farming class of the merchants' role as middlemen emerges in a dispute that developed in Missouri in 1821. Farmers near Franklin became disgusted with the local merchants over their efforts to defeat state banking legislation and for their unwillingness or inability to handle the shipment of farm crops. As the farmers saw it, the merchants were unwilling for them to have either state money or the returns their crops would bring. These two sources were the only means they saw of getting the funds necessary to purchase the supplies they needed. And they were right in their analysis, even though they were doing their local merchants an injustice in assuming that they did not want to accept farm crops in payment for supplies. William Lamme and R. S. Barr and Company, the largest local merchants, advertised that, because of the hard times and lack of cash in the country, they would take farm crops and give receipts for them. They would also advance the cash necessary to ready the produce for market, pay the freight, and personally attend to selling the products. The farmers would receive pay in specie as soon as the crops were sold and would be charged only the legal rate of interest for any money advanced, plus 5 per cent commission on the sales.[25] Ill feeling continued, however, and the farmers decided to form a cooperative enterprise to handle exports.

This decision resulted in formation of "The Missouri Exporting Company," which prepared articles of incorporation by October, 1822. The organization was to begin operations with a capital stock of $20,000, divided into $20 shares. At the time a farmer subscribed, he was to pay $1 for each share purchased, the balance being due as the directors ordered, although never at a rate greater than $4 a share every three months. The organization was a democratic farm movement, as evidenced by the provision that permitted only one vote to a member no matter how many shares he owned. The company elected its directors at a meeting in Chariton, Missouri, on the first Monday in December; in order to be eligible to serve, each director was required to own 25 shares. The directors were to appoint a man experienced in merchandising to handle the organization's business, but he must hold $1,000 in stock. The company was to declare dividends once a year and was to limit its business to "commercial transactions generally"—a rather vague statement of the organization's scope. In exporting crops, those of stockholders were to receive preference over those of nonmembers, and produce was not to

25. Franklin *Missouri Intelligencer*, July 16, 1821.

be sold at retail unless the purchaser's note had sufficient endorsers to make it safe.[26]

By December 17, 1822, the company was ready to transact business. One of its officers asked members to submit lists of the kinds and quantities of produce they would have ready for export in the spring and summer. The company asked for bids for the construction of flatboats, since two or more would be needed on the first of each month from March to July.[27] No further notices appeared in the local papers, and it is probable that no marked success was achieved by the enterprise. Conditions in Missouri continued to improve during the twenties, a circumstance that lessened the farmers' animosity toward the mercantile class.

The wide range of products accepted in exchange for goods has already been indicated, different localities doing their largest trade, as might be assumed, in produce peculiar to their area. Some merchants accepted farm crops solely because it was the only way they could do business in the community, and for that reason they usually exchanged goods for produce, a practice that forced the farmer to look elsewhere for the disposal of a cash crop. In almost every community of any size, however, there was at least one merchant who would buy from the farmer for part cash and part trade. David Lamme needed rags so badly for his new paper mill in Missouri that he advertised for them, offering 3¢ a pound for linen and cotton rags and 1¢ a pound for other kinds. Although he owned a store, there was no mention of barter—the operation of the new mill immediately created a demand.[28]

L. P. Marshall at Franklin, Missouri, owned a large warehouse on the river and was in a favored position for collecting and shipping produce. To increase this business he advertised for hemp, offering to pay half in cash and half in goods.[29] John Adams at Edwardsville, Illinois, in 1832 was offering $1 in merchandise or 87½¢ in cash for good castor beans. His desire to obtain the beans caused him to offer goods in advance to responsible people, payment to be made when their crops were harvested.[30] There was no doubt that merchants preferred to pay in goods from their shelves and used every means to persuade their customers to accept their terms. In many cases, however, opportunities for profit or immediate need caused them to lose no time in making cash purchases when produce came to market.

26. Franklin *Missouri Intelligencer*, October 29, 1822.
27. Franklin *Missouri Intelligencer*, December 17, 1822.
28. Columbia *Missouri Intelligencer*, January 11, 1834.
29. Fayette *Missouri Intelligencer*, January 22, 1830.
30. Edwardsville *Illinois Advocate*, June 5, 1832.

As the quantities of produce collected by individual storekeepers assumed appreciable size by the end of the year, commission firms in larger places competed for the privilege of handling the shipments. New Orleans commission companies often mailed quotations to stores in the Mississippi Valley. A list of prices sent to E. D. Sappington at Jonesboro, Missouri, by Renfro, Breedlove, and Richeson of New Orleans in 1825 was typical. The statement contained a full analysis of the probable price range for all crops during the coming season. Detailed discussions of the tobacco market as well as of bagging and twine, pork, flour, whiskey, lard, and furs informed the merchants of the propects for trade. The listing paid some attention also to articles like beeswax and ginseng, which seldom were shipped in large quantities. According to the circular, sales of corn, beef, and pork were largest in the spring, at which time the planters, having realized the proceeds of their own crops, were ready to purchase foodstuffs in quantities. The report also listed exchange rates on Eastern cities.[31]

Representative shipments of James Aull from his store at Lexington, Missouri, indicate the range and quantity of produce handled by merchants in smaller towns. On April 1, 1828, he shipped 1,058 muskrat, 496 raccoon, 16 otter, 32 mink, 24 wildcat and fox, and 60 deer skins to Saint Louis. In the next month Aull shipped an unstated amount of beeswax to a commission firm at Philadelphia; Saint Louis houses had not offered as much as he thought the shipment was worth. In June he proposed sending 200 raccoon skins to a store in Franklin. His proposal included the expense of hauling the furs to Franklin and waiting until November for his money if the Franklin merchant would pay a shilling each for the lot. The same month, Aull shipped 2 hogsheads of tobacco to New Orleans, consigned to James Breedlove, a member of the firm that sent the circular to Sappington at Jonesboro. A letter to the commission firm of Tracy and Wahrendorff at Saint Louis directed them to pay the freight on the shipment to New Orleans and to oversee the transfer of the tobacco to another boat. Early in the autumn he sent 9 barrels of beeswax to Franklin by wagon, whence they were shipped by keelboat to Saint Louis; Tracy and Wahrendorff handled the transfers at that city and sent the produce on to Breedlove at New Orleans. There the goods were transferred to a coasting vessel and consigned to Robert Toland in Philadelphia, to be sold and the proceeds placed to Aull's credit. Aull valued the shipment at $318.20, in the hope that, by sending the beeswax to the eastern city he would get 20¢ for each pound.

31. Circular in John Sappington Collection.

In October he sent a barrel of honey to a Judge Tod, for which service a Franklin firm credited him with $15. On November 5, Aull dispatched a wagon to haul 3,000 pounds of freight to Saint Louis and bring back a load of merchandise. Part of the freight bound for Saint Louis comprised 8 barrels of beeswax, which Aull directed Tracy and Wahrendorff to sell. In April of 1829 Aull shipped 9 barrels of beeswax to James Breedlove at New Orleans, and in May he sent 70 muskrat and 9 otter skins by keelboat to Tracy and Wahrendorff, who were to dispose of them in Saint Louis.

Before starting East to buy goods in 1830, Aull dispatched more beeswax to Tracy and Wahrendorff—21 barrels in this lot. They were to hold the shipment until he reached the city. His records show that he disposed of four packages of the same product in Saint Louis the following spring. In April of that year he shipped aboard the steamboat *Trenton* 12 bales of hemp, 1 barrel of tallow, and 2 hogsheads of tobacco. Tracy and Wahrendorff were to load the tallow and beeswax he had sent them earlier in the year and ship the whole lot to New Orleans. The November shipment consisted of 68 barrels and kegs of honey and 8 barrels of beeswax from Lexington and 673 gallons of honey and 6 barrels of beeswax from Liberty. Tracy and Wahrendorff were to insure the beeswax and send it to New Orleans for sale. The honey presented difficulties. Aull was afraid it would leak out of the containers, so he asked the Saint Louis firm to sell as much of it as they could to the small grocers there. The rest could be shipped up the Ohio River if freight rates were not too high. In 1831 and 1832 Aull also sent raccoon, fox, otter, and deer skins to Tracy and Wahrendorff.[32]

Aull's shipments of goods and produce resulted partly from direct purchase and partly from barter for goods. The records of other storekeepers in the West vary from his only in the type of article received in the barter process. Taken collectively, the records illustrate the Westerners' methods of marketing their crops. The merchant's role was clearly that of basic agent in enabling the Mississippi Valley region to build up credits in Southern and Eastern markets to pay for merchandise. The great majority of such men considered the produce trade only as a sideline, but a few like J. M. D. Burrows at Davenport, Iowa, finally turned to it as their principal occupation.

In the early years Burrows disposed of produce taken in barter by selling to the trading posts up the river. Fort Snelling, Prairie du Chien, and Snake Hollow were his best markets. At Snake Hollow he exchanged bacon, flour, and beans with the Indians for feathers

32. Aull letter books covering the period, Aull Collection.

and beeswax, which he sold in Cincinnati. In the spring of 1814 he was able to dispose of all his produce in one sale to the American Fur Company at Prairie du Chien.[33] Finding the produce trade profitable, Burrows enlarged his enterprises and in the spring of 1844 tried a venture in New Orleans. Potatoes were quoted at $2 a bushel in that market, but were selling for only 50¢ at Davenport. So Burrows loaded a flatboat with 2,500 bushels and decided to send another boat also with a cargo of pork, bacon, beans, oats, corn, and brooms. The boats were dispatched in the care of men hired for the trip, and Burrows kept track of their progress through reports from steamboat captains who passed them coming up the river. When the boats were nearing the mouth of the Illinois River, he took passage on a steamer and caught up with them as they approached Saint Louis. There he attempted to obtain insurance for the trip down river, but discovered that the Saint Louis companies did not write policies on flatboats. This information was an unwelcome surprise. Since he had traded mainly with Cincinnati in the past, he had always been able to insure cargo on such vessels. Two days of anxious negotiation ensued, and finally, through personal friendship with a director of one of the Saint Louis companies, Burrows was able to secure a policy.

The company insisted on his accompanying the boats to their destination, however—a trip he had not originally intended to make. The journey would keep him away from his business for two months, but he could not afford to allow the boats to proceed without insurance—all of his available capital was tied up in the shipments. So Burrows made the journey, arriving in New Orleans after six weeks of river travel. When he reached there, the city was full of potatoes, the high prices that had prevailed earlier in the year having attracted shipments from France. His potatoes were unsalable. The best alternative was to trade his cargo to the captain of a Bermuda-bound vessel for 8¢ a bushel delivered on board ship. He accepted payment in coffee.[34] The loss suffered by Burrows was caused by the slow transportation prevailing in the West—the same factor that wrecked so many merchants in their estimates of wholesale orders.

Burrows was not discouraged from undertaking other ventures. In the winter of 1845 he bought breadstuffs to the limit of his capital. The commission firm of Henning and Woodruff at Saint Louis had told him to buy $100,000 worth of wheat, either for himself or on their account, in the expectation that a deficiency in the English market would cause a great increase in price. Burrows decided to

33. J. M. D. Burrows, *Fifty Years in Iowa*, 33-41.
34. Burrows, *Fifty Years in Iowa*, 58-60.

employ his own money and reap the whole reward, and he made trips throughout the surrounding territory during the winter to buy. Before time to start shipments the Mexican War broke out and prices tumbled. Rumors that privateers were operating on the ocean caused insurance rates to rise until they equaled 10 per cent of the value of the goods.

Burrows had bought flour at from $4 to $4.50 a barrel and wheat at 60¢ a bushel. He sold some of his holdings in Saint Louis, where the flour brought $2.25 a barrel and the wheat 40¢ a bushel. But the market there could not absorb all his supply, so he shipped the rest to New York City. The flour soured on the ocean voyage, so it brought $1 and the wheat 20¢. Burrows was virtually penniless as a result of the venture, and Henning and Woodruff at Saint Louis were also heavily involved. Fortunately, Woodruff's brother-in-law, E. K. Collins of New York City, who owned the Collins Shipping Line and was quite wealthy, carried the commission firm through its crisis. The company, in turn, helped Burrows, Billings at Beardstown, Illinois, and Walker of Burlington, Iowa—all of whom had been engaged in the enterprise.

Unsettled international conditions caused prices to continue low during the summer and early winter months of 1846, and the partners all decided to enter the market again. This time they were able to obtain grain at very low rates, since other buyers near Davenport gladly sold all their grain to Burrows. Prices advanced rapidly in the spring months, and the commission firms that had remained in the business cleared up their losses of the previous year and built a good reserve of capital besides.[35] R. M. Prettyman, Burrows' partner in the mercantile business at Davenport, decided that such violent shifts from profit to loss and back again were not to his liking, so he decided to sever his connection with Burrows' commission enterprise. In the end they agreed to continue as partners in the store, with Burrows conducting the produce business on his own capital. The connection was of value to Burrows because he frequently bought grain half for cash and half in trade, which enabled him to make a double profit on the grain bartered for merchandise. The arrangement suited Prettyman, as it freed him from the risks of the produce business and still gave him an easy way of disposing of produce taken in exchange for goods.

After 1850 Burrows engaged in the milling and meat-packing business, but a series of fires and other calamities cost him heavy losses in the sixties. He is representative of the merchants in the smaller places who gradually shifted to the produce trade. Most of these men

35. Burrows, *Fifty Years in Iowa*, 61-69.

retained their stores, however, to profit from bartering goods for produce. Elisha and Gilbert Read of Chicago operated a general store in the twenties but concentrated more of their time and energies on farming, lumbering, and the sale of foodstuffs in the thirties. Their day book shows that they did considerable mercantile business in the later period, selling goods to men who worked for them in the enterprises and taking produce in exchange for supplies from their stores.[36] Jared Warner's tax assessment for 1850 listed three houses, a sawmill, barn, smithshop, 80 acres of land, a storehouse, another mill (probably lumber also), merchandise, logs, and cash—the whole being valued at slightly more than $5,000.[37] An earlier account book indicates the way this property was probably handled, as it contains the record of his interests in lumbering and the provisions trade. Numerous men worked for him, and he paid one-third of their wages in cash and two-thirds in provisions. For example, on April 18, 1843, Ezra Rice was employed at $15 a month, $5 paid in cash and the remainder in trade.[38] Later entries show that Ezra took drygoods and coffee as well as meat for his $10. These supplies were drawn from Warner's store as needed.

By their own accounts, it is clear that local merchants varied in the degree to which they engaged in the produce business. Some accepted only as much as was necessary to hold their customers, others went over to that line of activity completely. But all were involved to some extent; the barter system was universal in that period and region. Furthermore, the economic life of the West—built, as it was, around the collecting and processing of raw products and the exchange of these for manufactured goods in distant markets—gave rise to the development of forwarding and commission houses in all the larger towns in the Mississippi Valley.

The functions of commission and forwarding naturally went together. Merchants who bought goods in distant markets had to rely on forwarding organizations to handle the transfers, freight, and insurance incurred in bringing goods to the West. In that period transportation was not organized on a national scale, and it was impossible to ship supplies any great distance without employing several different companies in the process. Nor was there any guarantee of regularity in the schedule on which these small groups operated. Even if a merchant personally accompanied his goods, he saved time by engaging the services of forwarding companies at the points of transfer, where they were fully acquainted with the organization of

36. Elisha and Gilbert Read, Account Book 1818–59.
37. Jared Warner, Day Book 1849–54, entry on last page.
38. Warner, Day Book, 1836–49.

transportation. These firms also owned warehouses in which goods consigned to their care could be stored until shipping arrangements were complete. Furthermore, they maintained connections with similar companies in other cities, which assured them of a share of the business passing through their own city. Companies in different towns consigned goods to their associates' care, a practice that contributed to a more efficient handling of shipments. Men who had such connections were also well equipped to carry out commissions. Merchants were in daily contact with them and in their frequent visits to the warehouses were likely to see goods or produce left for sale. The forwarders had the space for storage and were acquainted with conditions in other markets. Consequently, many forwarding companies combined the two functions. Many indeed carried a stock of goods on their own account and added the business of merchandising to their other functions.

No other group of businessmen in the West could boast of the wide trade connections developed by the commission and forwarding groups, unless it was the fur companies. Henning and Woodruff, the Saint Louis company with which Burrows dealt, was a branch of James E. Woodruff and Company of New York, which maintained another office in New Orleans under the name John D. Woodruff and Company. Vairin and Reel at Saint Louis operated a branch house in New Orleans under Julius Vairin and owned a large warehouse on Water Street in that city. The firm offered to make liberal advances on goods consigned for sale in Saint Louis or New Orleans. In addition to this service they engaged in the wholesale and retail trade in drygoods, hardware, and saddlery.[39]

Tracy and Wahrendorff of Saint Louis carried a supply of goods for wholesale and retail trade. The scope of the forwarding and commission activities of this company is apparent from the amount of business James Aull transacted with them. In addition to their merchandising business, they served as agents for several insurance companies, and Tracy was on the board of directors of an insurance concern that had its headquarters in Saint Louis. In 1823 the firm held the agency for two steamboats that plied between Pittsburgh and Saint Louis; an advertisement by the company in that year offered freight downstream at a $1 for 100 pounds. Allen and Grant were their agents at Pittsburgh, an association that gave them a direct connection with that city.[40] Even in the smaller towns such men frequently maintained wide connections. A. Dinsmore at Burlington,

39. Advertisements of the firm appeared frequently in the *Missouri Republican* between 1832 and 1835.
40. St. Louis *Missouri Republican*, December 10, 1823.

in Iowa Territory, advertised a commission and forwarding business in 1841 and gave references in Saint Louis, Pittsburgh, and Philadelphia.[41]

Hill and M'Gunnegle at Saint Louis owned stock in local insurance companies and were agents for others. They advertised their "extensive warehouses" at the steamboat landing, where they conducted a commission and forwarding business. They offered liberal cash advances on goods consigned for sale. John G. Stevenson handled their business at New Orleans, and the firm offered to advance money on goods consigned to him from Saint Louis if the products were insured and nonperishable. They also held agencies for a number of steamboats running down the Mississippi to New Orleans, up to Galena, Illinois, and up the Ohio to Louisville, Kentucky. Hill and M'Gunnegle advertised free handling of goods shipped on these steamboats, except for actual costs involved in making transshipments. They placed extensive advertisements in the local papers to publicize the goods they had for sale on commission. One week's advertisements in a biweekly paper listed coffee and Madeira wine, 144 kegs of powder, coal grates, feathers and glass, flour and cider, ground alum salt, cotton yarns, New Orleans sugar, paper, whiskey, and dried peaches—each of the announcements referring to a separate consignment. The coffee and sugar came from New Orleans and the paper from the Phoenix mills in Cincinnati.[42] If a manufacturer wanted to invade the West directly, he found commission firms an easy way to introduce his goods into the stores of the region.

These companies had a set system of rates, and Western and Eastern chambers of commerce frequently published standard charges for their own localities. In Philadelphia and New York in the late thirties the charge for selling merchandise was 2½ per cent, the same rate that prevailed for buying and shipping goods to other places. Commission houses charged 2½ per cent for buying and holding goods subject to a merchant's call, but they performed this function without charge if the merchant supplied them with funds before goods reached them and became subject to payment. The rate for obtaining insurance was .50 per cent, but the fee rose to 2½ per cent for adjusting and collecting insurance losses. The standard rate for receiving and forwarding goods was .50 per cent.[43] In the West higher charges generally prevailed for all these services. For instance,

41. Burlington (Iowa Territory) *Hawkeye and Iowa Patriot*, April 15, 1841.

42. *St. Louis Beacon*, May 6 to May 13, 1830.

43. B. F. Foster, *A Practical Summary of the Law and Usage of Bills of Exchange and Promissory Notes*, 115-16.

a 5 per cent commission was allowed for selling merchandise, just double the rate prevailing in the East.[44]

The large volume of business resulted in good profits for such companies. James L. Applegate received some excellent commissions, even though he was located on the upper Missouri River, 200 miles from Saint Louis. John Atchison of Galena, Illinois, sent him 12,000 pounds of lead, which he sold at 5¢ a pound. Atchison received $520 for his lead, and Applegate $30 for making the sale. Christy, Gentry and Company of Lexington, Missouri, consigned 100 bales of hemp to Applegate, which he sold for $1,600. From this amount he deducted $30 for freight, $10 for insurance, $25 for drayage, and $80 for his commission.

Goods coming from a distance bore much heavier charges. William T. Saunders of New Orleans shipped 25 hogsheads of sugar, 2,000 sacks of salt, and 150 boxes of raisins by the steamer *Alex Scott*. The goods brought $6,097.50, but were subject to charges of $948.37; Applegate received $304.87 as his commission for the transaction. Other charges were $72 for drayage, $16.50 for insurance, and $5 for labor.[45] The total charges compared favorably with the 20 to 25 per cent charged for moving goods from the seaboard to the Saint Louis area. There was no escape from the enormous costs connected with shipping merchandise, no matter what the procedure. Commission and forwarding agents expedited shipments and relieved merchants from the necessity of personally accompanying every box of goods they moved from one place to another, and they charged well for these aids. They did, however, perform a real service.

BILLS, EXCHANGE, AND CURRENCY

Sam Hildeburn, a Philadelphia jeweler, in a letter to a wholesale house in Birmingham, England, in 1816 expressed the banking views held by most Eastern and Western merchants.[46] After explaining that his remittances would be slow for a time, he called attention to the opening of the Second United States Bank in July of that year. He hoped the bank would equalize exchange among the states, "now a serious evil." He reported that bank paper throughout the West, even within ten miles of Philadelphia, was presently at a discount of

44. J. E. Thomas, "Commercial Summary," in St. Louis *Missouri Argus*, January 27, 1837.

45. Sales listed in Lisbon Applegate Manuscript Collection. The sales are not dated. Applegate was probably located near Chariton, Missouri, as he received some of his mail there.

46. Hildeburn and Woolworth to Birmingham, England, dated Philadelphia, May 25, 1816, Hildeburn and Woolworth Letter Book.

at least 12 per cent, and even more in many places. Under such conditions the Western merchant could not think of making purchases, "that being the true cause I believe of the stoppage of business."

During much of its existence the bank justified the hopes of men like Hildeburn. It facilitated remittances to the East and exercised a restraining hand on the excessive issuance of notes by banks located in the different states.[47] With the disappearance of the Second U.S. Bank in the thirties the state banks once more issued paper money in quantities so large as to drive the notes below par value. The merchant knew the exchange value of notes issued by local banks and could accept them in comparative safety, but his transactions were complicated by the daily presentation of notes drawn on banks in other communities and other states. The weaker banks were anxious for their notes to travel a long way from home, for the danger of their being presented for redemption was lessened by distance. Missouri merchants received paper of banks in Tennessee, Kentucky, Illinois, Ohio, and Virginia in payment for goods. Sometimes these notes were worth only 20¢ or 30¢ on the dollar, and to accept them for any more meant just that much loss. In some instances, merchants were offered—and accepted—notes of banks that had already failed.

The farming class, which constituted most of the customers in Western stores, was not well posted on financial matters and often accepted payment in notes at values considerably higher than their actual worth. It was not a pleasant duty for the merchant to tell a customer that his bank notes were worth less than their original value, but such action was frequently necessary. The merchant could not be overly cautious, for if he did not offer all that the notes were worth, some competitor got the business. So it became necessary for the storekeeper to keep well posted on the exchange value of notes issued by banks over a wide area if he wanted to keep his customers and at the same time remain solvent. Even a reputation of having the most exact and up-to-date knowledge of the value of a bank note was no shield against the ire of the farming class, which held that money was money and that any reduction below the face value was robbery.

The passing of notes of insolvent banks and counterfeiting added to the merchants' problems, since the great variety of dies in use made these practices rather easy. An episode that terminated favorably for the merchants involved was recorded in a Detroit paper in

47. See Ralph C. H. Catterall, *The Second Bank of the United States.* Catterall undoubtedly gives too flattering a view of the bank's contribution to the solution of the exchange problem between East and West. Mercantile records indicate that difficulties existed, even at the peak of the bank's operation.

1829. A stranger to that place gave a number of $5 bills, supposedly drawn on a bank at Morristown, Pennsylvania, to various stores in exchange for merchandise. The notes were counterfeit, but they were accepted without question except by the proprietor at the last store visited by the man who was passing the money. The storekeeper left the customer waiting while he went out to ascertain the value of the bills, and his prolonged absence finally made the man uneasy. Leaving the merchandise and some good money he had received in exchange for his counterfeit notes, he fled from the store. The returning proprietor witnessed his departure and, with a crowd of citizens, pursued him to the steamboat *William Penn,* which was tied up at the town's wharf. Along with an accomplice, who was discovered in the search of the boat, he was lodged in jail to await action by the courts.[48] Only through the alert action of the last merchant visited were the businessmen of the town saved a sizable loss.

Even specie constituted a problem in some areas. Many Mexican dollars from the Santa Fe trade appeared in Missouri, and merchants received these, in due course, from their customers. In 1829 James Aull wrote to his agents in Saint Louis to ask them the value of Mexican dollars and how to detect counterfeits. Four months later he sent to Saint Louis 117 Mexican silver dollars, which he had taken in at 92¢ each. He instructed his agents that if they could get the same value for them, they were to effect an exchange; otherwise he would take the money east with him and exchange it there.[49] There were no banks in many of the smaller towns in the early period, and merchants were forced to gather their information on currency values from newspapers and from acquaintances in the larger places or to rely on their own judgment as guide. But, even in such uncertain and changing circumstances, if a merchant was willing and able to devote much attention to the value of the money he handled, he could keep his losses at a minimum.

A transaction that involved much time and care was making remittances to the East. Although the Western merchant might consign produce to Saint Louis, New Orleans, or Cincinnati, he still was forced to buy exchange on Eastern cities in order to meet his bills in the seaboard centers. In those cases in which the shipments of produce were not sufficient to balance his accounts, it was necessary to send specie or notes to the nearest city where exchange could be purchased—a very difficult matter. James Aull even resorted to concealing silver in the heads of casks of beeswax he was shipping by steam-

48. *Detroit* (Michigan Territory) *Gazette,* July 23, 1829.
49. James Aull to Tracy and Wahrendorff at St. Louis, dated Lexington, Missouri, July 23 and November 16, 1829, Letter Book B, Aull Collection.

boat to Saint Louis. He marked the casks that contained money, and he notified his agents in Saint Louis to be on the lookout for the money. He frequently used this means to transport the Mexican dollars he took in trade; one shipment of freight in 1830 contained 900 Mexican dollars.[50]

Transportation of paper money presented problems also. The mails were notoriously unsafe for the shipment of valuables, so a common practice was to send money in two different mails when it necessarily moved by that means from place to place. The sender would cut the bills in halves, dispatch half of each bill by one mail and the other part by the following mail. In that way, if one mail should be lost, it was possible to redeem the remaining halves by presenting them to the bank of issue. As an example of this practice and its merits, on March 9, 1817, James Wier sent halves of $300 in bills to Philadelphia for use by a relative who was to bring goods to him. Two days later the remaining halves were dispatched in another mail. One may assume that both packets reached Philadelphia safely.

Such precautions were fully justified by adverse experiences. In 1828 James Aull directed his partner to mail $100 to him at Louisville, Kentucky, where he would pick it up on his way east. He left Louisville before the letter arrived, however, and it was advertised in the Louisville *Focus*, that being the manner of locating owners of unclaimed mail. The notice attracted the attention of a thief, who claimed the letter and cost Aull $100.[51] Money was sometimes sent to the larger cities in the care of travelers, that means being considered safer than the mails. Trustworthy wagon drivers also obliged merchants in the same way; on one occasion, Aull sent $3,000 to Saint Louis in the care of a wagoner he knew.

Aull's situation was typical of that of many merchants. His business was located 200 miles up the Missouri River from Saint Louis, the city where he purchased his exchange on Eastern cities. There were no banks in Lexington from which he could buy drafts, and postoffice money orders were unknown. Whenever his produce shipments to Saint Louis were insufficient to cover his purchases of exchange there, he had to transmit money by concealment in the goods or by messenger. The risk and awkwardness of transmitting money by the available methods kept the merchant continually on the search for safer means.

In such circumstances, it becomes clear why many merchants turned to banking as a career, for they personally had felt the intense need for such institutions in their own communities. Thus, Robert

50. James Aull, entry in Letter Book B.
51. James Aull, entry in Letter Book B.

Aull began to obtain and sell exchange on Eastern cities to merchants in his vicinity. After the death of his brother James he gradually expanded this business until he finally abandoned the mercantile trade to establish the first bank in Lexington, Missouri. The large number of merchants who went into banking in other communities demonstrates that the problems of exchange, deposit, and redemption of bank notes convinced the mercantile class of the need and value of banks in smaller places. Until these appeared, however, the merchant faced his problems alone and unaided.

Because the balance of trade was in favor of the East, the merchant had to pay a premium on the exchange purchased on Eastern cities. The demand was so great at times that exchange could not be obtained at all or only at premiums that bore heavily on the purchaser. Consequently, the mercantile class sought every means of obtaining drafts without buying in the open market. The government spent considerable money in the West on supplies for the Indians and government forts. Storekeepers eagerly sought to obtain the drafts given in payment and were glad to act as surety for government contractors in return for the privilege of using the drafts they received.

The Aulls backed William Ish on a contract to supply fresh beef to Council Bluffs in 1827 and J. H. Kennerly of Saint Louis on a transportation agreement with Fort Leavenworth in 1833. Hezekiah Simmons of Saint Louis secured the contracts to supply $17,000 worth of provisions at Prairie du Chien and Saint Peters in 1829; John O'Fallon and Scott and Rule, also of Saint Louis, served as his bondsmen. Joel Turnham of Lafayette County, Missouri, won large subsistence contracts for Fort Leavenworth in 1831, 1832, and 1833, for which the Aulls at Lexington served as surety.[52] The value of such arrangements to Western merchants is apparent from the correspondence connected with a contract for 1836. In June of that year the Quartermaster's Division notified Turnham and Arthur at Liberty, Missouri, that the amount of their delivery at Fort Leavenworth, $3,156.98, had been remitted by the Treasurer of the United States to Siter, Price and Company at Philadelphia, to be placed on their books to the credit of James and Robert Aull at Lexington, Missouri, as Turnham and Arthur had directed.[53] The transaction relieved the Aulls from the necessity of sending money the 200 miles to Saint Louis and then paying a premium for exchange on the East.

52. Copies of Contracts, Subsistence Department, War Department covering the years under discussion. Atherton, "James and Robert Aull."

53. Gen. George Gibson to Turnham and Arthur at Liberty, Missouri, dated Washington, June 8, 1836, Letter Book No. 12, 1836, Office of Commissioner General of Subsistence.

Turnham and Arthur, on the other hand, wanted provisions or currency in their own community, where they bought supplies to fill their contracts. The Aulls could furnish them foodstuffs taken in exchange for store goods or with money received on local accounts. Thus, both parties to the transaction profited. The War Department's copies of contracts show that in many cases merchants obtained the agreement to supply forts directly for themselves, thus securing a market for crops taken in barter as well as exchange to pay bills in the East.

In this process, government drafts for services in the West frequently returned East in the possession of a Western merchant and became the property of some seaboard wholesale house from which the Westerner bought supplies. Even so small a matter as the pension of a Revolutionary War veteran gave a merchant an opportunity to build up credit to the eastward. In 1832 Aull sent power-of-attorney for a veteran to his agents, Tracy and Wahrendorff; if they could secure payment of the pension, the money was to be placed to Aull's account with them.[54] In return, the pensioner received credit at the Aull store in Lexington.

Missionary societies and Indian agents were other sources of negotiable drafts. Merchants eagerly sought these because they were drawn on Eastern cities and were exchanged for goods or money in the local community. Gen. William Clark, Indian agent at Saint Louis, deposited $27,300 with Siter, Price and Company at Philadelphia in 1826. From January 17 to May of that year, he drew $12,645.22 from the fund, a considerable part of the payments being in favor of Saint Louis merchants.[55] Seemingly, these agencies with financial connections in the East recognized the merchants' problems and used their transactions for mutual advantages. James Aull profited from sale to the Harmony Indian Mission, located some 90 miles south of his store in Lexington, and he also found its drafts on the home missionary society in Boston a welcome aid in solving his search for exchange. Through his dealing with the mission, he was able in 1828 to send a draft for $1,000 on the home society to his creditors in Philadelphia.[56]

Merchants used every means to make payments without sending money or buying exchange at premium. The closeness with which

54. James Aull to Tracy and Wahrendorff at St. Louis, dated Lexington, Missouri, September 11, 1828, Letter Book B, Aull Collection.

55. Account of B. Pratte and Company from January to May, 1826, William Clark Papers; letters from agents with the various Indian tribes to Clark reveal that local Western merchants sold many supplies for the use of Indian tribes. William Clark Collection.

56. Atherton, "James and Robert Aull."

they watched for such opportunities is indicated in a letter from James Aull to a New Orleans commission house in 1820. Aull had heard that some men from his part of the state were on their way to New Orleans with produce. He asked the commission house to locate them, secure their surplus cash, and invest it in 7,500 pounds of sugar for the Aull stores. Aull, in exchange for the traders' cash, would issue in their favor drafts on the mercantile house in their home community.[57]

Commission and forwarding houses purchased exchange for their customers who resided in the surrounding territory. If the merchant was known to be a responsible man, this service was often executed on a credit basis. Commission firms, however, charged a set rate for effecting such transactions. In addition, exchange and commission brokers set up offices in the larger centers. These men ultimately became bankers, usually passing from exchange agents to full-fledged bankers by gradual stages. L. A. Benoist's advertisement in a Saint Louis paper in 1837 throws light on the general nature of the business. In a notice headed "Exchange and Commission Brokers," Benoist announced a discount service at the lowest rates on the notes of all solvent banks in the United States. He would accept the notes of insolvent banks at the highest current price and would collect drafts, notes, and bills on favorable terms. Benoist stated that he could transmit funds to most of the principal cities of the United States, and he offered drafts on Philadelphia and Baltimore in sums suitable to any customer. He would also purchase drafts at sight or on time at very small discounts. Another advertisement by Benoist in the same paper offered 4 per cent interest on demand money left with him, and as high as 6 per cent on deposits for 90 days.[58] All these services were needed by the average merchant during the course of the year, and such houses as Benoist's probably had no trouble in obtaining business.

CREDIT AND ACCOUNTS

Fordham, writing in 1817, estimated the price of goods in the West to be twice that prevailing in England. Lack of capital and other factors that he did not understand caused trade to be exceedingly profitable, in his estimation. He found that merchants considered 75 per cent to 100 per cent to be a fair mark-up, 50 per cent barely acceptable, and 25 per cent as insufficient to keep a man in

57. James Aull to James N. Breedlove at New Orleans, dated Lexington, Missouri, May 17, 1830, Letter Book B, Aull Collection.
58. St. Louis *Daily Missouri Republican*, April 6, 1837.

business, since other enterprises in the West offered better opportunities. Corroborating evidence to support this flattering view is not lacking. Jones estimated gross profits of merchants in Missouri around 1831 at 100 per cent, and John Symmes was very much disturbed at the action of the Army board which set his "net" return at only 50 per cent on the goods he retailed at Cantonment Davis on the upper Missouri River.[59] But the picture of profits is far too idyllic when viewed solely on the basis of the percentage of mark-up on the wholesale price. Certainly, transportation disasters and other risks attendant on merchandising in a frontier community reduced the net gain.

Credit extension, for example, constituted a serious problem for most storekeepers. Everyone wanted to buy on time because wealth was just around the corner. The farmer's optimism made him a good customer when he was purchasing on credit, but it failed to support him in the same role when time arrived for payment. Western merchants were fully aware of the situation and did all they could to promote cash payments. They offered their goods at much lower prices for cash, but the farmer found it cheaper to buy the goods on credit and not pay at all. In 1838 Cordell and Company at Jefferson City, Missouri, advertised that they had adopted a strictly cash policy in their business. They explained that credit sales entailed a 10 to 15 per cent increase in prices, to which must be added 10 to 15 per cent more for bad debts, and this burden rested on the consumer. Under the cash system they were then instituting, they expected to be able to reduce all prices from 20 to 30 per cent.[60] The advertisement was not just a sales talk to entice customers to the store, for merchants agreed among themselves that a cash system would effect a substantial reduction in costs.

But the logic of the matter could not prevail against the Westerner's need for credit. Almost twenty years before this time the Lammes at Franklin, Missouri, had attempted to conduct business in the same way that Cordell and Company now advertised. In 1820 William Lamme advertised a new stock of goods from Philadelphia, which he intended to sell for cash at his stores in Franklin and Richmond; prices would be reduced to very low levels, in keeping with the new cash policy. To expedite transactions under the new system he promised to take Kentucky and Tennessee state bank paper at par.

59. Fordham, letter dated Shawanoe Town, Illinois Territory, November 15, 1817, in Extracts from Letters, John C. Symmes Papers, 1791–1817, Draper Collection. Symmes's profit was not really net, for items like clerk hire were not considered.

60. Jefferson City (Missouri) *The Jeffersonian*, April 21, 1838.

In return for these concessions, he announced that he expected customers to call and settle all outstanding accounts by the first of July. Those who had bought goods at Richmond would find copies of their accounts there and at Franklin, to facilitate the process of transferring to the cash basis. Obviously, Lamme was serious in his intention to establish the cash system.

In 1823 Lamme advertised another shipment from New York and Philadelphia, and once again he announced his intention of adopting cash sales. He was sure his old customers would forgive the move to a cash basis, in the light of his liberal credit policy in the past and because of the very low prices at which he sold his goods. The notice plainly showed that he had made little headway in the intervening years in installing the cash system that he had planned to adopt in 1821. Two years later, in another advertisement, Lamme announced the opening of a new store at Liberty, Missouri, where he offered the stock of merchandise for "fair prices" for cash or in exchange for beeswax and furs. The announcement carried the information that Mr. Hickman, one of his partners, was now in the East buying goods, and the merchant needed funds to pay for the supplies. Consequently, it was necessary to ask those in arrears to pay their bills. The advertisements are evidence that the five-year battle to adopt the cash system had failed, in spite of Lamme's announced intention "not to deviate" from his cash policy.[61] From time to time a merchant found his business jeopardized by heavy book accounts and strained credit standing in the East. Then he would try to insist on cash sales, but such systems worked only in theory. In actual practice the merchants discovered that there was no escape from the credit system.

Though defeated in their efforts, merchants continued to emphasize cash transactions. Scott and Rule at Saint Louis announced a heavy shipment of goods from the East in 1829. These supplies were offered at extremely low prices to customers who had cash, lead, or beeswax to exchange. Good acceptances or approved, indorsed notes payable at the Saint Louis branch of the Bank of the United States were also acceptable. But "none others need call," as the embarrassment of the firm, occasioned by credit losses and the lack of punctuality on the part of customers, prevented the store from pursuing a liberal credit policy any longer. Outstanding accounts must be closed at once, or the debtor would be subject to suit.[62] No announcement could have been more forceful, but later advertisements indicate that

61. Franklin *Missouri Intelligencer*, May 27, 1820, September 2, 1823, and December 2, 1825.
62. *St. Louis Beacon*, April 13, 1829.

Scott and Rule had resumed the credit system. Another Saint Louis firm, Paul and Ingram, advertised over a two-year period that they sold for cash and could offer extremely low prices under that system. Early in 1822, however, they attempted another approach. At the time, state bank paper was below par. Local citizens were complaining of the low rate at which merchants accepted such money in exchange for goods, and Paul and Ingram saw an opportunity to continue the cash system and still maintain their sales. Accordingly, they announced their willingness to accept Missouri loan office and bank paper and bills of Illinois banks at a good rate in exchange for merchandise. They explained that this policy was workable because the money was to be used to purchase farm produce.[63] But they, too, eventually resumed the sale of goods on credit. Necessity and inclination endeared the system to the customers, and the mercantile group, in order to retain their business, had to acquiesce. They continued to preach the philosophy of cheap prices for cash but transacted most of their business on credit.

Jones paid considerable attention to the problem of credit in his description of the mercantile system. On the opening day a small store might expect a cash sale of $75 and only $25 on credit, but as time progressed the men entitled to credit would arrange for it and such sales would form a greater part of the total business. At the end of two months such a store would probably have transacted $1,200 worth of cash business and have $1,500 on its books.[64] His estimate, which is fictional, is that 45 per cent of the sales were for cash.

Actual business records show Jones's to have been a rather high estimate. One account book of an unidentified merchant shows sales of $439.94¼ cash and $1,072.10¼ credit from May 28 to June 30 in 1832. Here, slightly less than a third of the business was for cash. In July, sales increased on the cash side, for in that month 45 per cent of his business was for cash. The autumn months brought a slump. In September cash sales totaled $95.70 and credit $210.69¼; October's figures show $169.98¾ in cash sales and $433.07¼ in credit.[65] These figures place the business of the firm heavily on the side of credit sales. The amount of specie taken in across the counter was even less than the figures indicate. Some "cash" customers paid immediately in plank, beeswax, corn, hominy, or flax; others hauled goods for the store or made chairs for the proprietor. All these ac-

63. St. Louis *Missouri Gazette*, January 9, 1822.
64. Jones, *The Western Merchant*, 49 and 70.
65. Account Book 1832-36, of an unidentified merchant in the town of St. Helena, location not given.

counts were entered as cash sales, which greatly reduces the percentage of business transacted for actual cash.

Moses Payne at Columbia, Missouri, was a careful, Christian merchant who ended his career as a wealthy man, but the credit accounts at his store were large. In the fiscal year ending June 1, 1829, he did $17,202.47 worth of business, only $6,710 of this being for cash. The next year his sales totaled $46,361.80, but much of the gain came from sales on credit, only about a fourth of the goods being sold for cash.[66]

James Aull blamed the credit system for his need to close out his chain stores. Business had increased yearly, but uncollected accounts rose as rapidly. As early as 1832 Aull decided to contract his stock and clear the firm of debts. At that time the value of his stock of merchandise amounted to $35,000, probably a third of which was still unpaid for in the East. A letter to Siter, Price and Company at Philadelphia in 1833 shows him to have been motivated by a policy of caution. "We are extremely anxious," wrote Aull, "to be free from debt believing that there will be a change of times for the worse and that a prudent man should prepare for it. In this country a universal credit system is pursued and as we have been engaged in business for a number of years we have a large amount credited out. We have determined that 1 Jany 1834 will find J. and R. Aull out of debt."[67]

But the policy was difficult to put into practice. During the winter term of the circuit court in Independence in 1835 Aull was able to collect only $500. Yet, he held notes against men living in the vicinity for $25,000 and had as much more on his books.[68] He was not unaware of the economic forces operating in the country at the time and, in spite of his heavy burden of debt, suggested to two other merchants that the present would be a good time to speculate. In a letter to Edward Tracy and William Glasgow at Saint Louis he commented on the fine price of cotton and the great increase in banking capital. He felt that there would be a reaction, but not for a year or two at least, and the group could temporarily afford to expand. The letter was strongly prophetic of the panic of 1837—"as to banks so many of them have been created so lately and apparently on such good foundations that they will hold up for a few years longer and will continue to facilitate trade as they have done. It is, therefore, our opinion that we might venture into steamboat or other speculations

66. J. M. and A. M. Payne, Day Book 1830–31.

67. James Aull to Siter, Price and Company at Philadelphia, dated Lexington, Missouri, January 21, 1833, Letter Book 1830–33, Aull Collection.

68. James Aull to E. and A. Tracy at St. Louis, dated Lexington, Missouri, February 28, 1835, Day Book 1833–35, Aull Collection.

at the present with some degree of certainty of making money at the same time preparing for any storm that may come some two or three years hence."[69] With this idea in mind Aull made some investments, but worry over failure to collect outstanding debts caused him to decide to dissolve the chain of stores on January 1, 1836. The company was solvent, and Aull weathered the panic of 1837 successfully in his store at Lexington. His letters on the eve of the depression reveal him as having a good grasp of economic matters. Yet he, too, had found it impossible to escape the credit system, and it had jeopardized his business.

In a letter to his Eastern agents he estimated the outstanding claims of the firm at $150,000 and explained that dissolving the chain of stores would give him an excellent excuse to bring pressure to bear to collect these debts.[70] The stock of merchandise in the four stores probably never exceeded $50,000, and yet in five years' time the firm had allowed its unpaid book accounts to rise to a figure three times that amount. Aull's situation was simply another instance of the credit system triumphing over an intelligent and cautious merchant.

Storekeepers lacked the services of credit rating bureaus, but after a merchant was in business for a time he became well acquainted with the economic status and honesty of the farmers in his community. For this knowledge, a new merchant had to rely on the advice of some reputable local man. When Jones and his brother went up the Missouri River to open a new store in a strange community they had no knowledge of whom to credit. The brothers had boarded with a farmer while getting ready for the opening of the store and had observed that he was a responsible man and well acquainted in the community. Consequently, they obtained from him the name of every farmer in a radius of 15 miles whom it was safe to credit.[71] It was a simple device for credit rating, but it probably proved an excellent guide in a region where every man was acquainted with the affairs of his neighbors.

Wholesalers who dealt with merchants in the East and in parts of the South could benefit from the information gathered by the credit rating bureaus, but even for these areas, the bureaus were few and informal in their methods. Prior to the panic of 1837, a merchant's reputation for financial reliability depended mainly upon recommen-

69. James Aull to Tracy and Glasgow at St. Louis, dated Lexington, Missouri, July 4, 1835, Day Book 1833–35, Aull Collection.

70. James Aull to Siter, Price and Company at Philadelphia, dated Lexington, Missouri, February 6, 1836, Letter Book 1835–38, Aull Collection.

71. Jones, *The Western Merchant*, 49.

dations from local citizens, the judgments of lawyers who were acquainted with suits for collection, and the attitudes of other merchants in the area. The enormous number of bankruptcies that occurred during the panic of 1837 demonstrated a pressing need for more accurate information concerning the financial resources of applicants for credit. Consequently, more firms became active in developing systematic methods of obtaining reliable information for credit rating purposes.

A beginning had been made as early as 1827, when Sheldon P. Church, operating from New York City, had begun to make credit reports to some of the larger Eastern wholesale firms. With the recognition that such reports were now essential, more firms employed credit rating agencies, some of which corresponded with legal firms in the various communities and others with representatives who traveled through an area to gather such facts and impressions as reflected on a merchant's business methods and reliability.[72] The notes made by Peter Mallett, who traveled through North Carolina to rate individual firms for the benefit of his own commission house, Krider and Mallett of New York City, list some of the factors on which the ratings depended.

> Fayetteville: G. M. Ross. No capital, not much of a business man, doing but little & must eventually sink. [On a later trip, in 1849, this firm was marked "failed."]
>
> Warsaw: W. Pierce. No. 1 & making money.
>
> Silesville: M. P. Siles. Lord of all he surveys and no. 1.
>
> Elizabethtown: J. Bryan. Has sold his old stock & will commence again. Capital 8 or 10,000. Undoubted credit, shrewd, prudent & understands himself, though too fond of his *Bitters*. Prompt.
>
> Snow Hill. Green County. G. S. Pridgen. Years few. Capital moderate. Extent of trade 8 or $10,000. Business habits good has made money & is a close prudent man.
>
> Chas. Harper & Son. Capital 20 or $25,000. In business many years & made money. Extent of trade 8 or $10,000. Business habits & good character.
>
> Greenville, Pitt Co. Wm. Barnard. A shrewd old Frenchman. Years 15. Capital 70 or $80,000. Business habits good. Character good. Trade 15 or $16,000. Is perfectly safe.
>
> Cooper & Strong. Capital moderate. Business habits tolerable. They are *Yankees* & have recently moved here. Is well enough to let them alone.

72. Lewis E. Atherton, "The Problem of Credit Rating in the Ante-Bellum South," *The Journal of Southern History*, 12 (1946), 534-56.

Tarboro. Bowditch & Howell. Not in business long & but few know their circumstances. H. is a mean scotchman & B. a contracted Yankee.

Washington. Wm. Barnard & Son. Years 2 or 3. Capital 75 or $80,000. Wm B. the father is the capitalist. Son a lawyer by Pro- & no business man. Business carried on chiefly by his clerk. They do a large business.

Newbern. C. Kelly. Years few. Capital moderate. A prudent close, penny saving old Fellow, enjoys public confidence & credit at home. Good for what he buys.

Wm. G. Bryan. Years 12. Capital not much. Quite embarrassed though has strong friends. Business habits & character good. Is P. M. Magistrate etc. Doing a fair business. I would rather not sell him.

F. Pearce. Years 6 or 8. Failed in Swansboro a few years ago & compromised at 50 cents. Capital considerable. Is doing a large business, principally Groceries. Extent of trade 8 or $10,000. Business habits & character good & had Public confidence. Is close & prudent.

Chapel Hill. J. C. Holmes. Greatly overrated in N.Y. Capital small & by no means a desirable customer. Habits Good. Quite active & attentive to business & appears to be doing well. But there is a deficiency somewhere.[73]

Following the Civil War, business houses in the North and in Mid-America began to employ the credit rating agencies or to adopt their methods, in recognition of the risks their less accurate financial information incurred. In the period and area on which this study centers, however, competition between merchants and the seasonal flow of money peculiar to an agricultural economy forced them to extend credit almost indiscriminately and, in too many instances, unwisely.

So many wholesalers pursued the policy of granting six months' credit without interest and then charging 6 to 10 per cent to the payment date at the end of twelve months that the practice was almost universal. The merchant signed a note at the time he purchased his goods and the wholesaler expected payment when the note fell due. This general policy on the part of wholesalers reacted on the credit policy of Western storekeepers. As goods purchased on credit cost no interest for six months, the merchant was disposed to allow his retail customers the same length of time to pay. All debtors were

73. Peter Mallett, "Credit Rating Book of North Carolina Firms," in Peter Mallett Papers. Quoted in Atherton, "Credit Rating in South," 547-48.

expected to settle their accounts twice a year, January and June being the usual times for settlement. The widespread application of this policy emerges from examination of numerous account books. For example, Perry Wilson and Company at Fort Madison in Iowa Territory arranged with a Mr. Webster to trade with them and to pay his account twice a year. The agreement specified that, if Webster paid in produce, he must deliver it early enough to permit shipment before navigation closed.[74]

Many merchants used the pages in the back of their day books to write out notes for the amounts owed them by customers. The prevalence of this policy of asking for notes on all unpaid balances in January and June indicates that merchants considered the debts better secured thereby. Large numbers of customers balked at this policy, if the amount of attention given the matter of credit is any indication of customers' attitudes. Merchants did not hesitate to dun their customers by letter. James Wier of Lexington, Kentucky, wrote to a debtor at Louisville in 1826 and enclosed a statement of his account. Wier expressed surprise that the account had not been paid, as the goods had been sold at an exceptionally low price. He was planning to go East soon to purchase goods and felt compelled to call on all friends for payment. He was hopeful that the Louisville customer would not fail him. The letter was not stringent in tone, but Wier wrote to a Louisville law firm the same day and enclosed an itemized statement of the account, with the explanation that the debtor probably would not pay in response to his letter. Even though the debt was small—a little over $36—he asked the lawyers to call on the debtor and obtain at least a note for the amount.[75]

Merchants used newspapers, too, as a means of dunning customers, but these appeals for payment were general in direction. Such notices appeared in greatest volume in January and June, but can be found in almost any issue of Western papers before the Civil War. Only three or four forms were common, for such advertisements were as stereotyped as the larger general advertisements. One of the most frequently cited reasons for requiring payment of debts was the merchant's intent to leave for the East shortly to purchase new goods and his need of money to meet his bills there. It was a perfectly legitimate appeal, as few storekeepers succeeded in paying for all the goods they had bought the previous year before leaving to lay in another supply. As the Western settler surely considered such journeys expensive undertakings, the merchant made full use of the

74. Perry Wilson and Company, Blotter 1842–43.
75. James Wier to Louisville, Kentucky, June 10, 1826, Letter Book 1816–24, Draper Collection.

argument. James H. Woods at Fayette, Missouri, in 1825 headed such a notice with "Money Wanted," and then he explained that he expected his customers to pay their bills at once so a member of the firm could leave for the East.[76] Morrison and Prentice at Dubuque in Wisconsin Territory announced in 1836 that all persons indebted to the partners were earnestly requested to make immediate payment, as one of the firm would soon leave for the East. "Money is said to answer all purposes; and it is well understood that stages and steamboats give no credit." The firm would accept lead and mineral as payment on accounts as well as "Sucker Paper and Nicholas Biddle."[77]

Another well-used announcement was built around changes in the firm. Such an occasion provided a good excuse for tightening down on delinquent debtors. O'Ferrall and Cox at Dubuque added a new partner in 1836 and used the change in membership as the basis for an advertisement that asked for the immediate payment of bills or the giving of a note to secure the account.[78] Such changes generally involved the starting of new company records; a new partner was seldom willing to buy an interest in old accounts. As a matter of fact, formation of a new partnership was, in the main, a bookkeeping matter that demanded no great haste in collections. Because the change might convince some customer that it was now time to settle, however, merchants never let this or any other opportunity pass without using it to collect their outstanding accounts. Even if the new partnership consisted of the same men as parties to a renewal contract, it was customary to ask debtors to settle up at the end of the period of business. It was in such circumstances that Cornelius and White at Columbia, Missouri, in 1834 advertised that the first term of partnership had ended and the business of said period must be settled at once, including accounts.[79]

Many merchants did not seek for an elaborate excuse to ask customers to settle but frankly announced that they expected payments. Such notices generally hinted at legal action and some plainly threatened such a course. C. B. Fletcher at Vandalia, Illinois, in December, 1826, warned his customers to pay their accounts by the twentieth of the following month. Failure to do so would result in the notes being placed in the hands of William Brown, a local

76. Fayette *Missouri Intelligencer*, April 11, 1825.

77. *DuBuque* (Wisconsin Territory) *Visitor*, June 1, 1836. "Sucker paper" meant depreciated notes of state banks and "Nicholas Biddle" the currency of the National Bank—so called after the president of that institution.

78. *DuBuque* (Wisconsin Territory) *Visitor*, June 15, 1836.

79. Columbia *Missouri Intelligencer*, January 4, 1834.

attorney, for collection.[80] Here was a merchant who handled the credit matter without undue consideration for the feelings of his customers. John Hogan at Edwardsville, Illinois, was another. On May 24, 1832, he started running a short announcement in the local newspaper that all persons indebted to his store since January 1 would be confronted by an officer after the first of June.[81] Such hardy spirits were few in number. Generally, if legal action was mentioned, it was done indirectly. As an example of this method of collecting overdue accounts, Boyse, Meler and Company in 1831 announced that Christmas was past and customers should pay their accounts. The firm hoped to avoid the "fashionable method" of collecting accounts by suit.[82] Some merchants attempted to handle the painful duty of collection in a humorous way. In 1840 a firm at Burlington in Iowa Territory requested all persons who knew themselves to be indebted to the store, either by note or account, to lay aside their bashfulness and boldly come forward and settle their debts: "We stand pledged at all times to do all in our power not to mortify them."[83]

The pattern of these various advertisements was repeated again and again in the newspapers in Mid-America. Notices generally ran for several issues; in some, the merchant threatened immediate and dire action against delinquent debtors on dates that had passed before the advertisement stopped appearing. Since newspapers were not published in all communities, some merchants had to take other measures to bring their customers to account. Jones's brother sent him out on horseback to visit all delinquent debtors. Jones spent the nights at the homes of settlers along the way, occasionally accompanied by one of the debtors for a part of the journey. One man had only 25¢ in cash, but he rode the route with Jones until he had succeeded in selling enough furs to pay his bill.[84] Such direct solicitation probably was more effective than short advertisements in the newspapers.

But some debtors withstood all appeals, and in the end the merchant had no alternative but to bring suit. Such was James Aull's situation in some instances. He asked any who could not pay to give a note, which he held for a while, generally six months to a year. At the end of that time he instituted legal action. Some debtors moved to other localities, and in such cases Aull asked the constable or postmaster in the distant community to institute court proceedings. A

80. Vandalia *Illinois Intelligencer*, December 23, 1826.
81. Edwardsville *Illinois Advocate*, June 5, 1832.
82. Jefferson City (Missouri) *The Jeffersonian*, January 6, 1838.
83. Burlington (Iowa Territory) *Hawkeye and Iowa Patriot*, October 22, 1840.
84. Jones, *The Western Merchant*, 115-16.

fee of 10 per cent seems to have been the usual charge for such services. Aull traced his debtors as far away as Kentucky and eastern Illinois to bring action against them. On July 21, 1829, he wrote to an acquaintance at Boonville, Missouri, 80 miles down the river from his store, and asked him to give the account that he enclosed to the constable of the township in which a Mr. Lillifield was living, a community 20 miles from Boonville. If Lillifield refused to give a note for the bill, which amounted to $27, Aull directed suit to be instituted; any money collected was to be placed to Aull's credit with a merchant at Franklin, Missouri.[85]

Another customer, a blacksmith by the name of Saul W. Mason, was credited for $77.88 at Aull's store at Liberty, Missouri. He gave a note for his bill and paid $20 on the account, but moved to Kentucky without making any further effort to settle the indebtedness. Aull sent the note to the postmaster at Lexington, Kentucky, and asked him to put it in the hands of an officer for collection. The note bore interest at 10 per cent, and Aull specifically instructed the postmaster to have the officer secure both interest and principal. In return for his trouble the officer was to keep 10 per cent of the amount collected.[86] In spite of such exacting attention to the credit problem, however, many merchants seemed unable to prevent their accounts from reaching figures that endangered their own business standing.

ADVERTISING

The pattern of mercantile advertisements was much the same throughout the Mississippi Valley. Merchants generally announced the origin of their goods if they were purchased to the eastward, since that factor had a decidedly favorable influence on customers. Following this statement of origin came a detailed list of goods comprising the stock, generally set in small type and crowded together as closely as possible. The advertisement generally closed with the statement that goods would be sold very cheap for cash and with a list of the items that would be accepted in barter. Many storekeepers believed in the efficacy of such advertisements, and Eastern partners in Western firms generally advised their young associates in the West to resort to the columns of the newspapers as a means of increasing sales. For example, Temple and Smith at Philadelphia advised their

85. James Aull to Robert A. Clark at Boonville, Missouri, dated Lexington, Missouri, July 21, 1829, Letter Book B, Aull Collection.

86. James Aull to the postmaster at Lexington, Kentucky, from Lexington, Missouri, at an unspecified date, Letter Book 1830–33, Aull Collection.

junior associate at Saint Louis in 1821 to advertise his stock of goods, as such action would be sure to help the business.[87]

Advertisements of commission men and forwarding agents varied somewhat from the announcements employed by regular merchants. They were more widely published, since their business covered a larger area and success in handling shipments required connections along all the water routes over which merchandise could be transported. Furthermore, the stock on hand necessarily changed frequently or the commission firm soon lost its business. One week the company might have a heavy stock of whiskey, the next, quantities of drygoods or groceries. Clearly, it was impractical for commission houses to run the same advertisement for long periods of time, as did regular merchants who bought large quantities of goods only once or twice a year. A most persuasive factor for continuing the same advertisement was that, if the merchant changed his announcement frequently, the costs increased. The only way to hold down rates in a business that demanded advertising over a wide area and required frequent changes in the announcements was to decrease the size of the advertisement. This procedure became universal with commission and forwarding men, so that their announcements frequently occupied not more than an inch of space.

Hill and M'Gunnegle at Saint Louis followed the practice of running several small announcements in one issue of a paper. On April 13, 1829, they had three such advertisements in the *St. Louis Beacon*, one limited to Poland starch, a second to leghorn bonnets, and the third to log chains. Such announcements generally stated the quantity of the articles for sale but offered little information in addition and varied from regular mercantile advertisements in form rather than purpose. In both types of notices, the chief aim seems to have been to bring the name of the company before the public and to list the goods offered for sale. Auction firms also employed the short advertisement because their stock changed as frequently as that of the commission men.

Advertising rates were figured on the basis of the size of the announcement and the length of time it ran. The editor of the *Missouri Herald* in the small town of Jackson in Missouri Territory in 1819 charged $1 a square for the first insertion and 50¢ for each additional time the same announcement appeared. His table of rates indicated no reduction for large advertisers.[88] Rates in Saint Louis papers in 1837 were $1 a square for the first insertion. If the notice ran for

87. Temple and Smith at Philadelphia to J. J. Smith at St. Louis, dated Philadelphia, November 21, 1821, Letter Book 1818–22.
88. Jackson (Missouri Territory) *Missouri Herald*, September 4, 1819.

some time, the average cost was greatly reduced, however. For five issues the average dropped to 60¢, and if the announcement ran for a month the rate dropped to an average of 33¢, only a third of the charge for one insertion. The reductions continued until a square that continued for one year cost a merchant slightly over 12¢, on the average. Saint Louis papers also gave special rates to advertisers who purchased a large amount of space and offered cheaper rates on announcements in daily papers than on those in weekly issues. Advertisers were expected to pay their bills twice a year, a further reduction of a third of the total being granted to those whose bills amounted to $50 or over for the year.[89] Such charges of course gave the best rates to advertisements that ran unchanged during many issues, a schedule prompted in great part by the cost of setting type. That similar charges prevailed throughout the Mississippi Valley is evidenced by the tendency of merchants to leave their notices unchanged for long periods of time, so that an announcement of "spring goods, just arrived" might run in August and September issues.

Newspapers in the large cities circulated widely in the surrounding territory, so their advertisements were directed only in part to local trade. As early as 1821 the *Missouri Gazette and Public Advertiser* had agents in twenty-six small Missouri towns and in Illinois. Many rural subscribers received their papers a month or six weeks late, which explains why advertisements were written in a manner to appeal to customers who would read them long after they were published.

Furthermore, goods were not received as frequently as today, and an advertisement of the supply of merchandise on hand covered the full stock of goods for sale several weeks or months in the future. This practice of course saved money because the notice continued in the same form for a longer period—and it was even more regularly used in the smaller communities. Merchants who visited the East bought the greatest part of their merchandise in one lot. The slow transportation caused long periods to intervene between orders, and merchants experienced difficulty in synchronizing advertisements with the seasons. Consequently, they contented themselves with advertising "spring and summer" and "fall and winter" goods. Even so, the notices did not coincide closely with seasons or events.

It is difficult to make an accurate estimate of the percentage of merchants who advertised. Even the larger firms varied widely in the emphasis they placed on newspaper announcements. Hill and

89. Rates agreed upon by a number of St. Louis papers. Printed in *Daily Missouri Republican*, April 6, 1837.

M'Gunnegle used the newspapers much more frequently than the firm of Scott and Rule, but amount of advertising is not a reliable measure of the size of the company. In this comparison, Hill and M'Gunnegle paid slightly more than $27 in state and county license fees in 1829, whereas Scott and Rule paid $60. The latter firm was obviously much the larger but, also obviously, placed less emphasis on advertising.[90] Many smaller firms used the papers only for special announcements such as those concerning a change in the firm. The opening of a new store generally called for an advertisement, even if the owners did not continue to advertise. With the chief value of the announcements confined to giving the location of a store and enumerating its stock of goods, it is likely that the notices published by new firms gave the best returns of any money spent for advertising. Certainly, almost all new stores publicized their business. When Muir and Ennalls opened a new store in Little Rock, Arkansas Territory, in 1825, their advertisement stressed that fact in all the issues of the local paper throughout the summer months.[91] Equally sure to call for a notice in the papers was the dissolution of a partnership or the closing of business. As recognized earlier, these notices were, in many instances, efforts to collect delinquent accounts.

Settlement of the business affairs of deceased merchants was matter for advertisement in the local papers. Samuel C. Lamme of Franklin, Missouri, was killed while on the return trip from a Santa Fe trading expedition, and David S. Lamme announced the terms of settlement for the estate in the *Missouri Intelligencer:* On December 10, 1829, the merchandise in the stores at Liberty and Independence, Missouri, were to be sold to the highest bidder on six months' credit, unless disposed of sooner at private sale. The announcement continued with further details: The stock at both places was described as fully suitable for the market in the "upper country." All sales for $10 and over would be on credit, but bond and security were required. Sales for less than $10 would be made only for cash. On December 15, 1829, the holdings at Franklin would be sold at public sale, including animals and equipment used by Lamme in the Santa Fe trade and the machinery and stock of tobacco on hand in a tobacco factory. Sales at all the places were scheduled to start at 10 and to continue until all goods were sold.[92] The merchandise of bankrupt firms also was advertised in the newspapers and was sold at public auction sales. Stores that ordinarily did not make use of the

90. *St. Louis Beacon*, May 27, 1830.
91. Little Rock (Arkansas Territory) *Arkansas Gazette*, July 5, 1825.
92. Fayette *Missouri Intelligencer*, November 20, 1829.

newspapers published notices of such extraordinary sales, although some failed to publicize even these occurrences.

Less than half of the Western merchants who lived in a community that boasted a newspaper seem to have advertised with any regularity. It would appear that only a third of the storekeepers in some localities advertised at all. The first newspaper at Dubuque in Wisconsin Territory claimed sixty stores for the town. Only about a third of them advertised in the first issue of the paper, however, and issues immediately following the first showed no tendency for the number to increase.[93] When the editor of the *Missouri Intelligencer* moved his paper from Franklin to Fayette in 1826, only one local merchant advertised in the first issue of his paper in his new location. At the time, however, Fayette had a population of 300, and the two mercantile establishments were supplemented by other tradesmen who could be classed as merchants, as they sold the articles they produced. These included a cabinetmaker, three saddlers, a silversmith, blacksmiths, and potters. Advertising gradually increased for the *Intelligencer*, but never more than a third of the tradesmen advertised with any regularity.[94]

While the newspapers were the chief means of advertising, merchants employed other avenues to some extent. In cities of any size there were city directories that listed the names and residences of the inhabitants and in many cases the business occupations also. The Saint Louis directory for 1836–1837 is typical of those printed elsewhere. Charles Keemle, the editor, argued that a directory was the best possible means of advertising, as copies were available in hotels, on steamboats, and in all public places. He obtained a number of advertisements from local firms, and these he displayed in the front of the book. They differed from newspaper advertisements in a number of ways. The lists of goods "just arrived" were not a part of the notices, since they were to serve for at least a year—longer, in many cases. The type was much larger than that used in the newspaper announcements; in some cases the name of the firm and the form of business was set up in half-inch type. All gave the name of the firm, the location of the business, and the services offered by the advertiser. Pictures of the building occupied by the store or of the firm's product or main item for sale appeared more frequently than in newspaper notices.[95] These advertisements compare in form with their modern descendants in telephone directories and resemble them much more closely than any other form of advertising of the time.

93. *DuBuque* (Wisconsin Territory) *Visitor*, May 11, 1836.
94. Franklin *Missouri Intelligencer*, June 29, 1826.
95. *St. Louis Directory for 1836–37*, Charles Keemle, ed.

Some publishers printed books that described the leading commercial houses in the city. Taylor and Crooks published *Sketch Book of St. Louis* in 1858, a work devoted to the history of various concerns, which stated their origins, development, and business advantages. The sketch of Wolff and Hopp informed the reader that the firm sold German, French, English, and American fancy goods, notions, and toys; the firm had entered business in 1835 and made rapid progress from the start; it was among the first to import directly from Europe, and a member visited Europe each year to buy supplies; Wolff and Hopp maintained fine store- and salesrooms, with extensive stocks of goods on hand at all times.[96] Descriptions of other companies were in an equally flattering vein, perhaps because the book was financed directly by local houses.

As early as 1850 handbills were being used to advertise business houses. Professional cards of doctors, who also owned drugstores, gave both office and home addresses and indicated the services rendered by the owner of the store. Manufacturing concerns used small cards in the same way.[97] Earlier still was the practice of printing advertisements on wrapping paper. Joseph Hertzog sent several reams of advertisements printed on half sheets of "newspaper" to his nephew in Saint Louis in 1813. Hertzog thought these would make good wrapping paper for small articles and shoes and would circulate widely in the country.[98]

Advertising played a smaller part in mercantile life in the pre-Civil War period than it does today. Then, its primary aim seems to have been to state the location, business, and services of a store or to acquaint the public with any changes in the structure of the firm. Little effort was directed toward increasing sales through creating new desires for goods. This is especially noticeable in the advertising of goods suitable for the various seasons and holidays. Merchants in the smaller towns scarcely attempted to publicize goods that might serve as Christmas presents or for other occasions. Even in larger towns like Saint Louis few merchants sought to increase their business through such means. The largest newspaper in Saint Louis, the *Missouri Republican*, carried only a scattering of small notices headed "Christmas and Holiday Goods" in its December issues in 1834. In part this was due to a limited concept of the powers of advertising; merchants apparently had no notion of the possibilities

96. J. N. Taylor and M. O. Crooks, *Sketch Book of St. Louis*, 330-33.

97. Examples of this type of advertising may be found in the St. Louis history collection of the Missouri Historical Society at St. Louis, folder marked "Advertisements."

98. Joseph Hertzog to Andrew and Christian Wilt at St. Louis, dated Philadelphia, April 27 and July 22, 1813, Joseph Hertzog, Letters.

of increasing sales by appealing to latent desires of customers; and the contemporary practice of turning every holiday into intense commercial campaigns to sell goods as gifts was not known. Such stimuli to business remained for a more enlightened age to develop. Mother's Day and all the other sacred modern observances, which create so much business through appeals to sentiment, were either still to be invented or were untouched by the pioneer merchant. The directly functional character of early advertising stands out fully when compared with the modern form.

Perhaps the most marked contrast is the almost complete absence of prices in early advertising. Merchants frequently advertised goods "cheap for cash" or stated that their prices were as reasonable as those to be found anywhere, but they neglected to give a schedule that could be used for comparison. Jones's explanation seems logical: Cash prices were nearly uniform among stores in a locality, and reductions were allowed only to purchasers of a quantity of goods; because credit sales involved risk, the merchant added to his charges proportionately. Dr. Greenleaf might be worth $25,000 and Mr. Gates $1,000, but even though both were good men, Mr. Gates might be slower to pay than Dr. Greenleaf. Consequently, he was charged a slightly higher price for the goods bought on credit. The prices quoted were confidential, to prevent hard feelings.[99]

Mercantile business records do not substantiate Jones's explanation, however. Another reason for the absence of prices in advertisements is that much of the business in the West was on a barter basis. Under such a system there was a tendency to arrange prices to meet the conditions of each transaction. But neither is this explanation entirely satisfactory, for merchants in the East, where the barter system was fast disappearing, also omitted mention of definite prices from their advertisements. If bartering had been the only reason for omitting prices, Eastern merchants would have been free to list their rates in the newspapers long before the Civil War. It is probable that the principal reason for leaving prices unstated was that storekeepers feared to announce their prices lest other merchants undersell them. As long as no merchant advertised his prices, others need not do so, either. More than likely, quoting prices was regarded as slightly unethical—unfair competition, contrary to the rules of the game.

A few merchants flirted with the idea, however. Parker, Barr and Company at Columbia, Missouri, in 1835 announced a stock of 20,000 pounds of coffee, which they would sell for 16-2/3¢ a pound retail. They offered, also, a large stock of iron at 6½¢ a pound. The

99. Jones, *The Western Merchant*, 49-50.

firm announced its intention of keeping supplies of both commodities on hand at all times.[100] Robert Ranken of Saint Louis, in May, 1833, advertised goods at 25 per cent to 75 per cent below prices charged by auction and commission houses. This offer became definite in June in order to close out spring importations. Young Hyson tea was quoted at 75¢ a pound and green coffee at 12½¢, calicoes at 10¢ to 25¢ a yard, and bed ticking at from 18¢ to 25¢. The later announcement repeated the earlier assertion that these prices were as much as 75 per cent below those charged by commission houses.[101]

George Leidig at Vandalia, Illinois, in 1829 advertised whiskey at 37½¢ a gallon by the barrel and 43¾¢ by the single gallon. He priced loaf sugar at 25¢ a pound. A list of other articles included in his stock was part of the advertisement, but with no definite prices.[102] Leidig's advertisements ran from November to January without any change in his price quotations. The higher rates for changing the form of announcements probably prevented him from altering prices during that time.

Other merchants undoubtedly met Leidig's prices, but Parker, Barr and Robert Ranken quoted figures that represented only slight advances, or none at all, over wholesale rates. Their prices were indeed bargains. Two of the notices are early examples of the modern practice of advertising "leaders" as a means of attracting trade—coffee and iron in the case of Parker, Barr and Company, and whiskey and sugar in Leidig's announcement. It is worth noting, however, that occasional advertisements of this type did not stampede other merchants into following the same practice. In none of the three towns did other merchants react by advertising their prices. Nor did these three firms seem to prosper greatly by their variations from the established custom; none of them increased advertisements in later issues. Price quotations and the use of leaders were not widespread practices until after the Civil War.

Merchants were much freer from the influence of manufacturers than they are today. Now, even small-town merchants find it necessary to carry several brands of breakfast food because of demand from customers who want to buy the brand approved by their favorite radio or television star or in their most familiar comic strip. Standard brands were unknown in the early period. Coffee and tea bore general trade names, so that every wholesale center carried supplies of Imperial Hyson, Young Hyson, and Gunpowder tea, for example. A merchant could buy these from any wholesale grocery house, since

100. *Columbia Patriot*, December 12, 1835.
101. St. Louis *Free Press*, May 16 and June 13, 1833.
102. Vandalia *Illinois Intelligencer*, January 3, 1829.

none promoted a special brand. The same condition prevailed in the drygoods line. Manufacturers and wholesalers left the advertising in the hands of the local merchants, and customers selected their purchases without previous bombardments in favor of some particular brand.

Patent medicines represented the only exception to this practice. Usually, the owner of the remedy wrote the advertisements and secured the testimonials to accompany them. For example, when Joseph Hertzog arranged for his nephew at Saint Louis to handle Dr. Dyott's patent medicines, the doctor paid the costs of manufacture, freight, and advertising and gave the retailer a profit of 20 per cent on all medicine sold.[103] And no producers were more willing to spend money on advertising than the manufacturers of patent medicines. Benson and Company at Franklin, Missouri, in 1829 advertised a supply of "Swaim's Genuine Panacea" with directions printed in Spanish and therefore suitable for sale in the Santa Fe trade. Like other merchants, they limited the advertisement to as small a space as practical, in order to lessen printing expenses. A week later, however, a full three-column announcement of "Columbian Syrup" appeared on the front page of the local paper, paid for by the manufacturer. The description of the medicine revealed its marvelous curative powers in any and all diseases and established its claims beyond argument by giving testimonials from grateful users of the product. The advertisement named Benson and Company as the sole agents for the medicine in the state of Missouri and the product's moderate price as $3 a bottle.[104] The issue of the paper for September 25 carried a full-page advertisement of the same product. Such extravagance could never be charged to a Western merchant, but patent medicine salesmen apparently found the practice profitable, since their advertisements showed no concern for the expense of advertising space.

Another marked contrast with modern advertising was the infrequent use of pictures. Even two- and three-column notices regularly appeared without any illustrations to break the monotony of the reading matter, and where pictures did appear they were generally only a symbol of the business advertised. A cut of the same pestle and mortar was used by merchants throughout the Mississippi Valley to head notices of drugs for sale. Leather workers frequently used the picture of a boot or a saddle. Metal workers employed the design of a still. As it was easier for skilled tradesmen than for merchants to

103. Joseph Hertzog to Christian Wilt at St. Louis, dated Philadelphia, April 25, 1811, Joseph Hertzog, Letters.

104. Fayette Missouri Intelligencer, August 14 and 21, 1829.

obtain some design symbolic of their business, such formalized pictures were limited mostly to the skilled trades. A picture of a chair,
a stove, a hat—anything that the workman produced—headed the
announcement.

In general, the early advertising was dreary, matter-of-fact reading
that served a limited purpose and was completely devoid of all the
customer appeal of modern advertising. Personality was lacking; one
advertisement was like all others. Between that dead level and the
modern form of individuality in advertising were many experiments
with new techniques, some of them in this early period. One experi-
menter was L. Deaver, who based his announcements on an appeal
to fashion. His "Emporium of fashion" obtained "elegant ready made
clothing" directly from the markets in New York City, Philadelphia,
and Baltimore. An arrangement with merchants in those cities enabled him to import goods once a month. In this way he planned to
keep Saint Louis supplied with the latest fashion, and his extensive
stock would permit purchasers a wide choice in making their selections.[105] The appeal to fashion was evidently successful, for Deaver
continued to advertise in the same vein over a period of years. Mark
Murry at Belleville, Illinois, advertised goods at only a 20 per cent
advance on Philadelphia prices. His policy of adhering to low charges
resulted from his desire to see Belleville advance as a city.[106] John
Hogan in the same state expressed the belief that "a nimble six-pence
is better than a slow shilling," and consequently he intended to sell
at a low price and rely on a large volume of trade for his profits.[107]
Despite the general decorum of advertisers, even the most extrava-
gant claims sometimes appeared in the newspapers of the day.
O'Hara opened a tailoring establishment in Franklin, Missouri, in
1820 and immediately announced a 20 per cent reduction over all
prices prevailing there; he would accept country produce on the same
terms as cash. O'Hara defied "even prejudice" to show that he could
not execute work as well as any man in the territory; his experience,
based on work in forty-two European cities, five years in Philadelphia
and New York, and two in Lexington, Kentucky, eminently fitted
him for his trade.[108] An occasional quotation of prices and the mention of some special advantage of location distinguished some advertisements from the usual run. But beyond these mild statements
merchants did not go. Custom and difficulties created by frontier
conditions served to hold advertising to very circumscribed purposes.

105. St. Louis *Missouri Republican*, January 2, 1835.
106. Vandalia *Illinois Intelligencer*, February 14, 1829.
107. Edwardsville *Illinois Advocate*, June 5, 1832.
108. Franklin *Missouri Intelligencer*, April 1, 1820.

SUMMARY

THE FRONTIER MERCHANT
IN MID-AMERICA

From the arrival of white settlers in sufficient numbers to support local stores to the beginning of the railroad age in the late fifties, merchandising in Mid-America remained much the same in its common practices. In general, the period was an age of little specialization, and merchants necessarily assumed a number of functions besides the purveying of goods to their western destinations and the disposal of farm crops taken locally in barter for marketing in the centers of trade.

Such variety of interests made merchandising an exacting and time-demanding occupation; but merchants also frequently held prominent positions in community life. They were richer, better read, and more widely traveled than the average Westerner, and, as businessmen, they found it advisable to take a leading part in the development of their localities. As middlemen between producer and wholesaler or manufacturer, they very early and in the absence of banking facilities became key factors in the growth of credit and exchange techniques. Their enterprise linked them to the fur trade and to the supply of the Western forts and thus built in Mid-America a firmer economy for the early settlers.

With the passage of time the dominance of Philadelphia and Saint Louis in the wholesale trade was challenged by New York and Chicago. Improvements in transportation, such as the Erie Canal, served to lessen the isolation of the West, even before the development of the railway. The growth of population, the development of wholesale centers in Mid-America, and specialization in various kinds of merchandise contributed to the gradual decline of the general wholesale and retail store. By the close of the period wholesale and retail functions were approaching final separation and one-line retail stores were becoming common. No longer was it necessary or common for merchants to go east to buy supplies. Banking facilities had improved over those available in the early years. The arrival of the railroads greatly accelerated the trends toward change, so that shortly after the Civil War merchandising methods contrasted markedly with those of the period under review. The frontier merchant in Mid-America occupies a niche in the history of the nation that is as unique and valuable as those held by the fur trader, farmer, and professional man.

BIBLIOGRAPHY

MERCANTILE RECORDS

American Fur Company. "Catalogue of Papers of American Fur Company, 1834–47," Grace Lee Nute. Typewritten manuscript. Newberry Library, Chicago. 6 vols.

Lisbon Applegate Manuscript Collection. State Historical Society of Missouri, Columbia.

William H. Ashley Papers. Missouri Historical Society, St. Louis.

James and Robert Aull, Manuscript Collection 1828–60. Historical Society of Lexington, Missouri. (Now in Lexington Library and Historical Association, Lexington, Missouri.)

Brown Brothers and Company, Papers 1825–80. New York Public Library.

Matthew Cartwright Manuscript Collection. State Historical Society of Texas, Austin. (Now catalogued as in Archives, Texas Collection, University of Texas at Austin.)

Col. Auguste Chouteau Papers. Missouri Historical Society, St. Louis.

William Clark Collection. Kansas State Historical Society, Topeka.

William Clark Papers. Missouri Historical Society, St. Louis.

Levi Coit, Letter Books 1804–16. Moses Taylor Collection, New York Public Library. 2 vols.

John F. Darby Papers. Missouri Historical Society, St. Louis.

Ninian W. Edwards Papers 1803–32. In the Autograph Letter Series, Chicago Historical Society. Vols. 48-52, inclusive.

Elias Pym Fordham, "Extracts from letters written on a journey to the western part of the United States and during a residence in the Illinois Territory." Edward E. Ayer Collection, Newberry Library, Chicago.

F. Frisel and Company, Journal from March 9 to October 29, 1818. State Historical Society of Missouri, Columbia.

Garrett Family Papers 1820–80. Manuscript Division, Library of Congress.

Jacob Grove, Day Book and Journal 1838. Historical Society of Pennsylvania, Philadelphia.

Hamilton and Hood, Letter Book 1824–39. Historical Society of Pennsylvania, Philadelphia.

Joseph Hertzog, Letters from Joseph Hertzog 1811–15. William Hertzog–Collins Collection, Missouri Historical Society, St. Louis.

Hildeburn and Woolworth Letter Book, 1815–18. Historical Society of Pennsylvania, Philadelphia.

George Lichtenberger, Letters to George Lichtenberger 1837–48. New York Public Library.

Lippincott and Company Manuscript Collection. Historical Society of Pennsylvania, Philadelphia.

Pierre Chouteau Maffitt Collection. Missouri Historical Society, St. Louis.

Peter Mallett Papers. Southern Historical Collection, University of North Carolina, Chapel Hill.

Governor M. M. Marmaduke Manuscript Collection. State Historical Society of Missouri, Columbia.

John O'Fallon Papers. Missouri Historical Society, St. Louis.

J. M. and A. M. Payne, Day Book 1830–31. State Historical Society of Missouri, Columbia.

Philadelphia firm, owner unidentified, Day Book E. Historical Society of Pennsylvania, Philadelphia.

Elisha and Gilbert Read, Account Book 1818–59. State Historical Society of Wisconsin, Madison.

Riggs Family Papers. Manuscript Division, Library of Congress.

Solon I. Robinson, Account Book 1840–53. Typewritten manuscript in possession of Herbert A. Kellar, McCormick Historical Association, Chicago. (Now in McCormick Collection, State Historical Society of Wisconsin, Madison.)

St. Helena firm, owner and state unidentified, Account Book 1832–33. Missouri Historical Society, St. Louis.

St. Louis—Early Days. Miscellaneous collection of interviews and clippings. Missouri Historical Society, St. Louis.

Dr. John Sappington Manuscript Collection. State Historical Society of Missouri, Columbia.

Smith and Glenn, Day Book and Ledger, 1827–30. State Historical Society of Missouri, Columbia.

John C. Symmes Papers 1791–1817. Draper Collection, State Historical Society of Wisconsin, Madison.

Temple and Smith, Letter Book. Ridgway Branch of the Franklin Historical Library Association, Philadelphia. (Now catalogued as in Library Company of Philadelphia Manuscript Collection on Deposit at Historical Society of Pennsylvania, Philadelphia.)

Wynant Van Zandt Papers. New York Public Library.

Jared Warner Manuscript Collection 1834–80. State Historical Society of Wisconsin, Madison.

James N. Weems and Benjamin Rawlings, Day Book 1818–22. Historical Society of Pennsylvania, Philadelphia.

James Wier, Letter Books 1805–24. Draper Collection, State Historical Society of Wisconsin, Madison. 2 vols.

Perry Wilson and Company Manuscript Collection 1836–49. Historical, Memorial and Art Department of Iowa, Des Moines. (Now called Iowa Department of History and Archives, Des Moines.)

REMINISCENCES, NOTES OF TRAVELERS, AND GAZETTEERS

Allen, D. C. "The Bonnet Show at Big Shoal Creek Meeting House, Clay County, Missouri." University of Kansas City Library, Kansas City. (Now the University of Missouri–Kansas City Library.)

Burrows, J. M. D. *Fifty Years in Iowa: being the personal Reminiscenses of J. M. D. Burrows, concerning the men and events, social life, industrial interests, physical development, and commercial progress of Davenport and Scott County during the period from 1838 to 1888.* Glass and Company, Davenport, 1888.

Darby, William. *The emigrant's guide to the Western and Southwestern sections and territories comprising a geographical and statistical description of the states. . . . Accompanied by a map of the United States. . . .* Kirk and Mercein, New York, 1818.

Duden, Gottfried, "Gottfried Duden's 'Report' 1824–27," trans. by William G. Bek. *Missouri Historical Review*, 13 (1919), 251-79.

Gazetteer of the state of Missouri. With a map of the state. . . . To which is added an appendix, containing frontier sketches, and illustrations of Indian character. With a frontispiece, engraved on steel. Alphonso Wetmore, compiler. Charles Keemle, St. Louis, 1837.

Gustorf, Frederick Julius. *The Uncorrupted Heart: Journal and Letters of Frederick Julius Gustorf*, trans. by Fred M. Gustorf, ed. University of Missouri Press, Columbia, 1969.

Hall, James. *The West: Its Commerce and Navigation.* H. W. Derby and Company, Cincinnati, 1848.

Jones, John Beauchamp. *Life and Adventures of a Country Merchant. A Narrative of his exploits at home, during his travels, and in the cities. . . .* J. B. Lippincott and Company, Philadelphia, 1882.

———— [Luke Shortfield]. *The Western Merchant, A Narrative, Containing useful instruction for the Western man of business* who makes his purchases in the east; also, Information for the eastern man whose customers are in the west: Likewise, Hints for those who design emigrating to the west. Deduced from actual experience by Luke Shortfield. Gregg, Elliot and Company, Philadelphia, 1849.

Neilson, Peter. Recollections of a Six Years Residence in the United States of America interspersed with original anecdotes, illustrating the manners of the inhabitants of the Great Western Republic. William Tait, Edinburgh, 1830.

Peck, John M. A new guide for emigrants to the West, containing sketches of Michigan, Ohio, Indiana, Illinois, Missouri, Arkansas, with the territory of Wisconsin and the adjacent parts. Gould, Kendall and Lincoln, Boston, 1837.

Rainey, Thomas C. Along the Old Trail; pioneer sketches of Arrow Rock and vicinity. Marshall, Missouri, Chapter of the Daughters of the American Revolution, Marshall, 1914.

Reminiscences of Chicago During the Forties and Fifties, Mabel McIlvaine, ed. R. B. Donnelley and Sons, Chicago, 1913.

The St. Louis directory for the years 1836–37 with a sketch of the city of St. Louis . . . , Charles Keemle, ed. C. Keemle, St. Louis, 1836.

Tanner, Henry S. The American traveller; or Guide through the United States. Containing brief notices of the several states, cities, principal towns, canals and rail roads, etc. With tables of distances, by stage, canal and steam boat routes. The whole alphabetically arranged, with direct references to the accompanying map of the roads, canals and railways of the United States. Published by the author, Philadelphia, 1834.

Taylor, J. N., and M. O. Crooks. Sketch Book of St. Louis: containing a series of sketches of the early settlement, public buildings, hotels, railroads, steamboats, foundry and machine shops, mercantile houses, grocers, manufacturing houses, etc. George Knapp and Company, St. Louis, 1858.

NEWSPAPERS

Arkansas (Arkansas Territory) Gazette, January 6, 1821, to July 12, 1836. Littlefield Newspaper Collection, University of Texas, Austin. (Now catalogued as in Newspaper Collection, University of Texas at Austin.)

Bloomington (Iowa Territory) Herald, 1840–41, 1846. Historical, Memorial and Art Department of Iowa, Des Moines. (Now the Iowa Department of History and Archives, Des Moines.)

Burlington (Iowa Territory) *Hawkeye and Iowa Patriot*, October 22, 1840, to April 15, 1841. Historical, Memorial and Art Department of Iowa, Des Moines. (Now the Iowa Department of History and Archives, Des Moines.)

Chicago *Daily Journal*, 1845 and 1849. Newberry Library, Chicago.

Chicago *Prairie Farmer*, 1845 to 1846. McCormick Historical Association, Chicago. (Now in McCormick Collection, State Historical Society of Wisconsin, Madison.)

Columbia *Missouri Intelligencer*, May 4, 1830, to December 5, 1835. State Historical Society of Missouri, Columbia.

Columbia (Missouri) *Patriot*, December 12, 1835. State Historical Society of Missouri, Columbia.

Columbia *Weekly Missouri Statesman*, 1855. State Historical Society of Missouri, Columbia.

Davenport (Iowa) *Democrat and Leader*, June 29, 1936. Iowa Department of History and Archives, Des Moines.

Detroit (Michigan Territory) *Gazette*, 1817 to 1830. Newberry Library, Chicago.

DuBuque (Wisconsin Territory) *Visitor*, May 11, 1836, to June, 1837. Historical, Memorial and Art Department of Iowa, Des Moines. (Now the Iowa Department of History and Archives, Des Moines.)

Edwardsville *Illinois Advocate*, June 5, 1832. Mercantile Library, St. Louis.

Fayette *Missouri Intelligencer*, June 29, 1826, to April 9, 1830. State Historical Society of Missouri, Columbia.

Franklin *Missouri Intelligencer*, April 23, 1819, to June 16, 1826. State Historical Society of Missouri, Columbia.

Galena (Upper Lead Mines, Illinois) *The Galenian*, May 16, 1832. Mercantile Library, St. Louis.

Iowa City (Iowa Territory) *Standard*, June 3 to October 22, 1841. Historical, Memorial and Art Department of Iowa, Des Moines. (Now the Iowa Department of History and Archives, Des Moines.)

Jackson (Missouri) *Independent Patriot*, December 23, 1820, to December 15, 1826. State Historical Society of Missouri, Columbia.

Jackson (Missouri Territory) *Missouri Herald*, 1819 to 1820. State Historical Society of Missouri, Columbia.

Jefferson City (Missouri) *Jefferson Inquirer*, May 29, 1845. State Historical Society of Missouri, Columbia.

Jefferson City (Missouri) *The Jeffersonian Republican*, 1831, 1833 to 1837. State Historical Society of Missouri, Columbia.

Liberty (Missouri) *Weekly Tribune,* July 3, 1847. State Historical Society of Missouri, Columbia.

Madison (Wisconsin Territory) *Express,* 1839 to 1841. State Historical Society of Wisconsin, Madison.

Mineral Point (Wisconsin Territory) *Miner's Free Press,* 1837 to 1841. State Historical Society of Wisconsin, Madison.

New York Evening Post for the Country, 1836. New York Public Library.

New York *The Evening Post,* 1826, 1830, 1835, 1840, 1850. New York Public Library.

New York *Shipping and Commercial List, and New York Price Current,* February 1832, 1840, 1850. Historical Society of Pennsylvania, Philadelphia.

Philadelphia *Commercial List and Philadelphia Price Current,* 1832, 1840, 1850. Historical Society of Pennsylvania, Philadelphia.

Philadelphia *Poulson's American Daily Advertiser,* January 1–7, February 1–8, April 20, October 23, 1825; January 1, February 1, October 18, 1830; January 5, February 2–8, October 12, 1835. Historical Society of Pennsylvania, Philadelphia.

Philadelphia *Public Ledger,* 1836. New York Public Library.

St. Charles (Missouri) *The Missourian,* June 24, 1820, to October 24, 1822. State Historical Society of Missouri, Columbia.

St. Louis Beacon, April 13, 1829, to December 6, 1832. State Historical Society of Missouri, Columbia.

St. Louis *The Farmers' and Mechanics Advocate,* 1834 to 1835. State Historical Society of Missouri, Columbia.

St. Louis *Free Press,* 1833. State Historical Society of Missouri, Columbia.

St. Louis *Missouri Argus,* 1835 to 1837. State Historical Society of Missouri, Columbia.

St. Louis *Missouri Gazette and Public Advertiser,* 1820 to 1822. State Historical Society of Missouri, Columbia.

St. Louis *Missouri Democrat,* 1855. State Historical Society of Missouri, Columbia.

St. Louis *Missouri Republican,* 1820 to 1828, State Historical Society of Missouri, Columbia; 1832, 1837, and 1839, Mercantile Library, St. Louis.

San Felipe da Austin (Texas) *Telegraph and Texas Register.* State Historical Society of Texas, Austin. (Now catalogued as in Newspaper Collection, University of Texas at Austin.)

Vandalia *Illinois Intelligencer,* October 12, December 7, 1822; April 6, 1826; April 7, 1827; April 5, 1828; January 3, February 14, April 18, 1829; January 2, April 3, May 1, 1830; and 1831. Mercantile Library, St. Louis.

GOVERNMENT DOCUMENTS

U.S., Bureau of the Census. *Compendium of the Enumeration of the Inhabitants and Statistics of the United States, 6th Census.* Washington, D.C., Government Printing Office, 1841.

U.S., Congress, House of Representatives. "Report of Committee on Claims," 30th Cong., 1st sess., H. Rept. 458, pp. 1-2.

U.S., War Department, Quartermaster General's Division. Copies of Contracts, Subsistence Department, Fiscal Years 1825–26 to 1828–29; 1829–33; 1833–35; 1836–42. Old Records Division, Washington, D.C.

———. Post Records of Fort Leavenworth. Old Records Division, Washington, D.C.

———. Office of Commissioner General of Subsistence, Quartermaster General's Division, Letter Book No. 10, August 1833–February 1835; Letter Book No. 11, February 1835–January 1836; Letter Book No. 12, 1836. Old Records Division, Washington, D.C.

BOOKS, ARTICLES, AND DISSERTATIONS

Andreas, A. T. *History of Chicago from the earliest period to the present time.* Chicago, A. T. Andreas, 1884. 3 vols.

Annual Review, History of St. Louis, Commercial Statistics, Improvements of the Year, and Account of Leading Manufactories, etc., from the Missouri Republican, January 10, 1854. St. Louis, Chambers and Knapp, 1854.

Atherton, Lewis E. "James and Robert Aull—A Frontier Missouri Mercantile Firm." *Missouri Historical Review*, 30 (1935), 3-27.

———. "Disorganizing Effects of the Mexican War on the Santa Fe Trade." *Kansas Historical Quarterly*, 6 (1937), 115-23.

———. "The Services of the Frontier Merchant." *Mississippi Valley Historical Review*, 24 (1937), 153-70.

———. "Auctions as a Threat to American Business in the Eighteen Twenties and Thirties." *Bulletin of the Business Historical Society*, 11 (1937), 104-7.

———. "The Cataloging and Use of Western Mercantile Records." *The Library Quarterly*, 8 (1938), 189-99.

———. "The Merchant Sutler in the Pre-Civil War Period." *Southwestern Social Science Quarterly*, 19 (1938), 1-12.

———. "Early Western Mercantile Advertising." *Bulletin of the Business Historical Society*, 12 (1938), 52-57.

———. "Western Foodstuffs in the Army Provisions Trade." *Agricultural History*, 14 (1940), 161-69.

————. "John McDonogh and the Mississippi River Trade." *The Louisiana Historical Quarterly*, 26 (1943), 1-8.

————. "The Problem of Credit Rating in the Ante-Bellum South." *The Journal of Southern History*, 12 (1946), 534-56.

Biographical Encyclopedia of Kentucky of the Dead and Living Men of the Nineteenth Century. Cincinnati, J. M. Armstrong and Company, 1878.

Buck, Solon J. *Illinois in 1818*. Springfield, Illinois Centennial Commission, 1917.

Catterall, Ralph C. H. *The Second Bank of the United States*. Chicago, The University of Chicago Press, 1903.

Chicago Board of Trade and Commerce. *Third Annual Statement of the Trade and Commerce of Chicago, for the Year Ending December 31, 1860*, Seth Carlin, Secretary. Chicago, Tribune Steam Printing Establishment, 1861.

Clark, Victor S. *History of Manufactures in the United States 1607–1860*. Washington, Carnegie Institution of Washington, 1915.

Cole, Arthur C. *The Era of the Civil War 1848–70*. Springfield, Illinois Centennial Commission, 1919.

Collier, L. T. "Livingston County Pioneer Settlers and Subsequent Events." *Missouri Historical Review*, 6 (1912), 201-6.

Converse, Paul C. *Marketing Methods and Policies*. New York, Prentice-Hall, 1921.

Dorrance, Ward A. *The Survival of French in the Old District of Sainte Genevieve*. Columbia, University of Missouri Studies, 10:2 (1935).

Edwards, Ninian W. *History of Illinois, from 1778 to 1833, and life and times of Ninian Edwards. By his son, Ninian W. Edwards*. Springfield, Illinois State Journal Company, 1870.

Eighty Years Progress of the United States, Thomas P. Kettell, ed. Hartford, Ct., L. Stebbins, 1867.

Encyclopedia of the History of Missouri, a compendium of history and biography for ready reference, Howard L. Conard, ed. New York, Haldeman, Conard and Company, 1901. 6 vols.

Foster, B. F. *A Practical Summary of the Law and Usage of Bills of Exchange and Promissory Notes; together with a series of tables, showing when bills, notes and drafts, drawn or accepted, at any date, will fall due. To which are added rates of commission and storage; equation of payments; and general information connected with the business of the Counting House*. Boston, Perkins and Marvin, 1837.

————. *The Merchants Manual, Comprising the principles of Trade, Commerce and Banking; with Mercantile Accounts; inland and foreign bills; par of exchange; equation of payments, etc.* Boston, Perkins and Marvin, 1838.

Graves, W. W. "In the Land of the Osages—Harmony Mission." *Missouri School Journal*, 1 (1924), 62-71.

Hansen, Marcus L. *Old Fort Snelling 1819–1858.* Iowa City, State Historical Society of Iowa, 1918.

Holcombe, James P. *The Merchants' Book of Reference for Debtor and Creditor in the United States and Canada.* Philadelphia, D. Appleton and Company, 1848.

Houck, Louis. *A History of Missouri from the Earliest Explorations and Settlements until the Admission of the State into the Union.* Chicago, R. B. Donnelly and Sons, 1908. 3 vols.

Hughes, John T. *Doniphan's expedition and the conquest of New Mexico and California,* William E. Connelly, ed. Topeka, Kansas, published by the editor, 1907.

Jenkins, John S. *The New Clerk's Assistant or Book of Practical Forms containing numerous precedents and forms for ordinary transactions, with references to the various statutes, and latest judicial decisions; designed for the use of county and town officers, merchants, mechanics, farmers, and professional men. To which is added an Appendix, containing the new Constitution of the State of New York.* Auburn, N.Y., Derby and Miller, 1850.

Johnson, Allen, ed. *Dictionary of American Biography.* New York, Charles Scribner's Sons, 1928–1936. 20 vols.

Johnson, Emory R., and others. *History of Domestic and Foreign Commerce of the United States.* Washington, Carnegie Institution of Washington, 1915. 2 vols.

McCurdy, Frances Lea. *Stump, Bar, and Pulpit: Speechmaking on the Missouri Frontier.* Columbia, University of Missouri Press, 1969.

MacGill, Caroline E., and others. *History of Transportation in the United States before 1860.* Washington, Carnegie Institution of Washington, 1917.

Mahan, Bruce E. *Old Fort Crawford and the Frontier.* Iowa City, State Historical Society of Iowa, 1926.

Mering, John V. *The Whig Party in Missouri.* Columbia, University of Missouri Press, 1967.

Napton, William Barclay. *Past and Present of Saline County Missouri.* Chicago, B. F. Bowen and Company, 1910.

Nystrom, Paul H. *Economics of Retailing.* New York, Ronald Press, 1930. 2 vols.

Paltists, Victor H. "Business Records of Brown Brothers and Company, New York—1825–1880." *Bulletin of the New York Public Library*, 40 (1936), 495-99.

Paullin, William Theodore. "Money and Credit in Western Trade 1816–1836." Doctoral thesis, University of Wisconsin, 1935.

Pease, Theodore C. *The Frontier State 1818–48*. Springfield, Illinois Centennial Commission, 1919.

Phillips, Ulrich B. *Life and Labor in the Old South*. Boston, Little, Brown and Company, 1929.

Portrait and Biographical Record of Marion, Ralls, and Pike Counties (State of Missouri). Chicago, G. C. Owen, 1895.

Review of the Trade and Commerce of St. Louis, for the Year 1849, as compiled for and published in the Missouri Republican. St. Louis, Chambers and Knapp, 1850.

Richman, Irving B. *Ioway to Iowa, The Genesis of a Corn and Bible Commonwealth*. Iowa City, State Historical Society of Iowa, 1931.

Ritter, Abraham. *Philadelphia and her Merchants, as Constituted Fifty to Seventy Years Ago, illustrated by Diagrams of the River Front, and Portraits of some of its Prominent Occupants, together with Sketches of Character and incidents and anecdotes of the day*. Philadelphia, printed by the author, 1860.

Robinson, Solon I. *Solon Robinson, Pioneer and Agriculturist, Selected Writings*, Herbert A. Kellar, ed. Indianapolis, Indiana Historical Collections, 1936.

Rourke, Constance. *Audubon*. Harcourt, Brace & Company, New York, 1936.

St. Louis Chamber of Commerce. *Annual Statement of the Trade and Commerce of St. Louis, for the year, 1856*, W. B. Baker, Secretary. St. Louis, George Knapp, 1856.

————. *Fourth Annual Report of the St. Louis Chamber of Commerce, for 1859*, W. B. Baker, Secretary. St. Louis, Baker and Hammond, 1860.

————. *Fifth Annual Report of the St. Louis Chamber of Commerce, for 1860*, W. B. Baker, Secretary, St. Louis, Merchants Exchange Reporter, 1861.

Salter, William. *Iowa, the First Free State in the Louisiana Purchase From its Discovery to the Admission of the State into the Union 1673–1846*. Chicago, A. C. McClurg and Company, 1905.

Scharf, J. Thomas. *History of St. Louis City and County*. Philadelphia, Everts and Company, 1883.

Scoville, John B. [Walter Barrett]. *The Old Merchants of New York City*. New York, Carleton, 1864. 4 vols.

Semple, Ellen C., and Clarence F. Jones. *American History and its Geographic Conditions*. Boston, Houghton Mifflin Company, 1933.

Stephens, F. F. "Missouri and the Santa Fe Trade." *Missouri Historical Review*, 10 (1916), 233-62; 11 (1917), 289-313.

United States biographical directory and portrait gallery of eminent and self-made men. Illinois volume, 1883; Iowa volume, 1878; Missouri volume, 1878; Wisconsin volume, 1877. Chicago and New York, American Biographical Publishing Company.

Viles, Jonas. "Missouri in 1820." *Missouri Historical Review*, 15 (1920), 36-52.

————. "Old Franklin: A Frontier Town of the Twenties." *Mississippi Valley Historical Review*, 9 (1923), 269-82.

Webb, James J. *Adventures in the Santa Fe Trade, 1844–1847*, Ralph P. Bieber, ed. Glendale, Calif., Arthur H. Clark Co., 1931.

Winslow, Stephen N. *Biographies of Successful Philadelphia Merchants*. Philadelphia, James K. Simon, 1864.

INDEX